MY STORY
(AND I'M STICKING TO IT)

MY STORY
(AND I'M STICKING TO IT)

By Alex Hawkins

——

Introduction by Dan Jenkins
Cautionary Preface by Don Shula

Algonquin Books of Chapel Hill

1990

To Elizabeth, my daughter and my heart strings;
my son, Steele, an unfortunate clone and my best friend;
my wife, Libby, for allowing me to be Alex Hawkins
... whoever that happened to be that day

Published by

Algonquin Books of Chapel Hill

Post Office Box 2225

Chapel Hill, North Carolina 27515-2225

a division of

Workman Publishing Company, Inc.

708 Broadway

New York, New York 10003

Printed in the United States of America.

Library of Congress Cataloging-in-Publication Data

Hawkins, Alex, 1937–

My story : (and I'm sticking to it) / by Alex Hawkins;

introduction by Dan Jenkins ; cautionary preface by Don Shula.

p.   cm.

ISBN 0-945575-54-8

1. Hawkins, Alex, 1937–   . 2. Football players—United States—
Biography.   3. Baltimore Colts (Football team).   I. Title.

GV939.H336A3   1989

796.332′092—dc20   89-35406

[B]   CIP

First Paperback Edition

10 9 8 7 6 5 4 3 2 1

INTRODUCTION

I t's about time Alex Hawkins wrote his own book—he's certainly helped fill up enough of mine. He's helped fill them up with what some people might call barroom humor but I would call your basic wisdom and philosophy.

I'm sure it was Alex who told me the difference between a slut and a bitch. A slut will make out with anybody. A bitch will make out with anybody but *you.*

Sorry to talk like Billy Clyde Puckett there for a minute.

Like Alex, that sumbitch just keeps creeping into my language.

About Alex's book. It's merely the funniest damn book that ever got wrote by an ex-athlete his ownself. He wrote it with his own hand and ear and paper and all that, and there wasn't a single sorry citizen who helped him with it.

In other words, Alex's book ain't one of them "as told to" phonies, the kind where the ex-athlete tries to remember what yesterday was like, and a mechanic comes in and makes him sound like he learned something in college besides "23 Lead" or "All hook," on two.

The first time I ever saw Alex was when he came down to Austin, Texas, in 1957, and tore the Longhorns' asses up in a game South Carolina won, 27–21, in Darrell Royal's first season at Texas. It was the first time I'd ever heard of Alex Hawkins, or a Gamecock.

"Who was that Hawkins?" I asked Darrell after the game.

"Hell, I don't know," said Royal. "We ain't tackled him enough times to find out."

Alex, of course, went on to a great career in the pros, though not as a running back. He couldn't have been a running back because he had the misfortune to get born both white and slow.

"Seems unfair," he always said.

What Alex's best position was has never been determined, owing largely to the fact that he was frequently hungover and lining up in the wrong places.

Me and Alex became good friends after he retired from the pros and introduced me to several Bible study groups in Atlanta as well as some after-hours drugstores where they had great milkshakes.

I did discover, however, that he read books and newspapers and liked to discuss interesting issues, unlike most athletes, who get lost if the subject strays too far away from money and mammaries.

I think Alex has found what he does best. He's a hell of a writer, is what he is—so just settle back and get ready to laugh and pretend he's telling you all this in a convivial saloon.

CAUTIONARY PREFACE

by Don Shula

Now that Alex Hawkins has written a book about his life and his years in the National Football League, I think it's only right that those of us who knew him back then should warn potential readers of the book about this man and the way he does things.

As a coach my philosophy has always been to expect maximum effort from the players in practices and during games, and otherwise—within reasonable limits—to let them live their own lives as they want. I admit, however, that the Hawk tested those limits severely. There were times when he showed up for practice looking as if he'd spent the previous several days and nights on the cattle-guard of the Orange Blossom Special. The imaginative explanations he offered for some of his off-duty exploits were way out, too. I'm not surprised that he's written a book.

Those years with the old Baltimore Colts were great years. There were joys and disappointments, setbacks and triumphs. They were a collection of rugged individualists who played the game of football *as* a team, and who enjoyed what they were doing. They loved being the Baltimore Colts, and the Colt fans loved them for being their team. The Hawk was an integral part of the Colt scene. It's impossible to think back on those times without thinking of Alex.

There was and is only one Hawk. Read his book and you'll find out why. He could always come up with a tall story. Just don't believe *everything* he tells you.

1

I woke up to the sound of a vacuum cleaner screaming in my ear, somewhere close by.

"Get that damn thing away from me," I mumbled.

"It's where it's supposed to be. You ain't," came the answer. Roland, the floor sweeper, cut off the machine, and I propped myself up against the foot rail of the bar. He handed me the sports section of the *Sun*.

"You're all over the paper today," he said, "and you didn't even get arrested."

I pulled myself up to my feet, and took a seat at the bar, and looked at the sports page to see what Larry Harris of the *Baltimore Sun* had written:

> July 2, 1969. . . . Yesterday the strangest crew since Morgan the Pirate sailed the Seven Seas, gathered to celebrate Alex Hawkins retiring from pro football. In attendance were Rocky, the bartender; Father Jordan, the hoodlum priest; Hymie the Mink; Uptown Bell and Black Bart; John Steadman, Fingers, and Gussie Downbeat, the bookie; Dick Syzmanski and Bobby Boyd of the Colts; Bob Ferry of the Baltimore Bullets; Peggy, the hooker; Yosh, the hitman; and Don Shula just to make sure it was true.

The article went on and on, just as the party had. I read for a few more paragraphs, then laid the paper down.

I had flown up from Atlanta the day before. The luncheon had started promptly at noon and had gone on until midnight, when

Bobby Boyd, co-owner of the Golden Arm Restaurant with John Unitas, came up to the bar and fixed those steely blue eyes on me.

"Hawk," he said finally, "you aren't going to unretire, are you?"

"No, Bobby," I replied, "you don't quit this game but once."

"All right," said Bobby, "then you're going to go out in style. Rocky, get me my bottle of vodka and get him his bourbon. We're going to drink straight shots till someone drops."

That someone had obviously been me.

Roland came up with some coffee. "What were you doing on the floor, Hawk?" he asked.

"Bobby must have told me to wait for him here," I answered sheepishly. Bobby Boyd had been right again. I had gone out in style. I checked my money. It seemed to be all there. That was strange. I'd never known Bobby to leave anyone with money in his pocket. Maybe he was mellowing, getting soft. But I knew better than that. The softest thing about Bobby Boyd was his front teeth.

Through the door came Rocky Thornton, the daytime bartender and sometime manager of the Golden Arm. He and Bobby had first met while he was working with the Coca-Cola Company in Baltimore. Rocky had worked with Coke in the sales department for twelve years. He had quit because he lost respect for them. As he put it, "I got no respect for a company that size that couldn't catch me stealing from them in all that time."

Rocky and I had met in 1963 and had become close friends. He was heaven-sent, although it may be stretching it a bit to mention Rocky and heaven in the same breath. He had a vast array of friends, characters from all walks of life. Through them I had learned to appreciate the city of Baltimore.

Rocky was 5'6", 233 pounds, and to tell the truth, looked something like a seal. His sleeve length was twenty-two inches, and his inseam was about the same. Rocky was not exactly healthy. He was diabetic, and his cholesterol count was the highest ever recorded in a Baltimore hospital—a hospital built in 1886. This prompted his friends to nickname him "Mudblood."

I had asked Rocky to take me to the airport in the morning, after my good-bye party, because I had learned years ago that if you walk away fast you can forget real quick. Rocky had agreed to drive me on the condition that we go through the city instead of taking the expressway, because, he said, he knew the city policemen better than the highway patrol. He turned to the sweeper and barked, "Clean this slaughterhouse up." Rocky loves authority.

Bobby had outsmarted me again, he explained to me on the way to the car. I had been drinking bourbon and Bobby was drinking water. Bobby always kept a vodka bottle filled with water for such occasions.

"Whitey," Rocky said, "I thought you knew that by now. He's been doing it to you for a couple of years." Admittedly I am a slow learner.

We got into the car and started down York Road toward the city. Each block we passed brought back memories of my ten-year residence. So many thoughts flew past as we drove by the Holiday Inn on Loch Raven, where the team stayed the night before home games, and the Bel Loch Diner where we had so many late night breakfasts after nights out on the town, which for me was nearly every night.

The Gridiron Club, on the left, which I had owned maybe a dozen times and fortunately had lost back gambling the evening after I won it. Gino's Restaurant, started in the sixties by Gino Marchetti and Alan Ameche, and which would make them millionaires. Past Kusen's, where the team snacked every day after practice. Thirty-third Street to the left, where the stadium, appropriately named the largest outdoor insane asylum in the country, was located. Brooks Robinson's bar and restaurant, owned by the only Oriole player of that era that anyone cared to know.

Hooper's, where Bert Bell, Jr., and I had the same breakfast every morning. Sweeney's, Baltimore's most famous bar, which was the Colts' hangout and was off limits to the wives. Over one block to Abel Avenue, where Bert and I had lived together, and which was home for the players' Wednesday night poker games.

On down through Little Italy, where we frequently took our wives for dinner. The Mariner Bar down on the docks, where Steadman, Laveck, Yosh, and I drank before they modernized it.

Then to the famous Block, where you had to take anyone visiting from out of town to show them Blaze Starr and her sisters. Rocky was making it tough on me. On toward Washington to the airport. Rocky wasn't saying anything, which was rare for him.

Driving down that expressway towards Washington reminded me of John Unitas. I always rode with him to the airport for our road games. He drove eighty miles an hour, right on the bumper of another car. It scared me to death, and when I asked him what he would do if the other car hit the brakes, he would always say, "Got no reason to brake, the road goes all the way to Washington."

About five minutes from the airport Rocky finally spoke. "Whitey, are you going to miss it?" he asked.

"Naw, Rocky," I lied. "It's time to go on to other things."

"Good thing," said Rocky, "because the last thing Bobby told you was you can't unretire, and you know how Bobby is."

As we pulled up to the terminal Rocky said, "Whitey, let me know when you're coming in, and I'll always have somebody pick you up. This driving scares me. I ain't had a license in nine years."

"I know, Rock," I said. We shook hands and hugged.

"I love you, Whitey."

"I love you too, Rocky." With that Rocky got back in the car and drove away. I think—I'd like to believe that I saw a tear in his eye. Rocky always was a pretty good actor.

I turned and walked into the terminal, checked in, and headed for the gate and the flight back to Atlanta. I passed by the other gates—Piedmont, Eastern, Allegheny, whatever—and heard the greetings from all the agents.

"Hi, Hawk!"

"Number twenty-five—my man!"

"Captain Who!"

"We'll miss you Hawk." And then one last refrain as I walked by: "Man, there goes one crazy son of a bitch!"

I got to the boarding gate and checked in. The agent upgraded me to first class, which was standard treatment for the Colts in those days. He gave me a window seat in the smoking section and said, "We'll never forget you, Hawk. Thanks for the memories."

I looked at him for about a five count, blinked, and boarded the plane without saying a word.

"Thanks for the memories." If anyone should be thankful for the memories, it was me. Here was a guy, and I didn't even know his name, who paid good money to see me play, and who paid my salary for a decade, and he was thanking me for the memories.

There is, if you are lucky, one moment in life, one frozen moment, one sweet spot in time, where everything is perfect. This was that moment for me. The completion of one life and the sheer excitement and adventure of entering into a new one. I had been so fortunate and privileged to have played in such a town, with such a team, in such a wonderful era of sports.

In football I was what is known as an over-achiever. I wasn't big, I wasn't fast. But for ten years I had managed to stay in the National Football League.

Hell, I would have played for nothing. More than that, I would have paid the Colts for allowing me to play. "Alex Hawkins," I thought, as I sat there, "you're the luckiest little boy in the entire world."

Yes, ma'am, I would be delighted to fasten my seat belt. No, ma'am, I do not mind anything. Yes, good person, I think I would like a cocktail if it's not too much trouble. Thank you, kind lady, for such lovely service. Everything is just marvelous and I can think of nothing else I need.

The plane was climbing to 32,000 feet when suddenly a question swept across my mind. Just exactly what are you going to do now, asshole?

All of your life has been one big game. All you have really done is put off growing up. Yes, you were successful at that, but what about from now on? It's time to grow up and face the real world. Football is a game, and games are played by children. You're thirty-two years old, and you have to go to work. That means you've got to get a job, just like everybody else.

It is about a two-hour flight to Atlanta, and then you'll *have* to grow up. You didn't have to take football seriously, but you sure as hell had better take life seriously or else it will stomp the hell out of you. No more fun and games, buddy. Get serious. Quit that laughing. You don't get fined fifty dollars for being late for meetings out here, you get fired. Got it? The coach doesn't make your decisions for you now. You have to do that all by yourself, and you had better damn well be right. The fun and the games are over, mister. This is for real.

Suddenly, I was terrified.

"Yes, ma'am, I believe I will have another drink."

Hadn't my math teacher in high school, Miss Childress, told me to prepare myself for the future? Do you suppose that growing up means I would have to be responsible, too? Surely not!

Didn't I remember my college coach, Warren Giese, warning me that I had to pay the price, and play by the rules that others played by? Unthinkable.

What was it that Carroll Rosenbloom, the Colt owner, said about getting established in business before it was too late? How late is "too late"? Didn't Commissioner Bert Bell, Sr., say that pro football should be a means to an end, rather than the end itself? Horrors, horrors, unspeakable horrors!

Wasn't it the old marine himself, Jim Martin, who always told his teammates, "Boys, play as long as you can, 'cause it's a cold world out there on the outside." I chose to think not. I did, however, wonder just where "out there" was located.

I would rather stick with my own motto, I told myself. "The secret of life is to catch on early and grow up late." Yes, I could live with that. There had to be life after football.

"Yes, ma'am. I would like another drink, fast . . . no, make that two, and be damn quick about it. I've got less than two hours to live." When she brought my drinks I think I was crying softly. There out the window, off to my right, was West Virginia. Thirty-two years ago, almost to the day, I was born down there, and I hadn't grown up yet.

2

Long before settlers arrived in what is now West Virginia, Indians used the region as a hunting ground. The Cherokee, Shawnee, and the Susquehanna tribes hunted there, but because of the brutal weather and rugged terrain they never really claimed the area as a permanent home.

When the first settlers arrived, they stated their intention to settle to the Indians. The Indians had no objection, as long as the settlers didn't cross the Ohio River. It is rumored that at least one Indian said to the settlers, "Do you idiots realize what you're getting yourself into? You'll freeze your tails off in the mountains, and damn near die of suffocation in the valleys. You'll break your backs digging in this ground, and for what? The land won't grow anything, and even if it did, you couldn't get it to market. If you find gas or oil, or even coal, some idiot will organize a labor union and strike and people will get killed, and who needs all that, anyway? Have at it, palefaces, it's all yours."

The state motto, "Mountaineers Are Always Free," reflects the spirit of the people who broke away from Virginia at the start of the Civil War to form a separate state. They were mostly immigrants from Germany, Great Britain, Hungary, Ireland, and Poland. They were hardy and robust, fiercely independent and proud.

"West By God" Virginians, as they refer to themselves, are the most cantankerous, obstinate, and downright hard-headed people you'll find anywhere. The surest way to get a hillbilly to do something is to tell him he can't do it. My God, are they bull-headed! Nevertheless, there is a certain beauty in their simple, honest stubbornness. They are taught to respect honesty. A handshake is as binding as a contract.

The state is rich in mineral deposits, but the old Indian was right when he noted the problems of getting it out of the ground and to the marketplace. Scratching out a living in the mountain area was tough, and making a good living in the cities was not much easier. One of the few who did was my Grandfather Hawkins.

Grandfather Hawkins was born in Charleston, West Virginia, shortly after the Civil War. He was very successful in the insurance business and in real estate. He also ran a fine amusement park, with a nickelodeon, bandstand, and shooting gallery, in the Edgewood area of Charleston. A mover and shaker he was, and a show biz person as well.

He was married twice and those marriages produced ten children. Three of those by his second marriage were boys. The eldest, Chilton Taylor, better known as Chick, went to school at Virginia Military Institute, where he was a member of the football team.

The middle boy was named Steele Alexander. He was a big man for that time, standing 6'4" and weighing 230 pounds. He was the best athlete in the family. He, too, went to VMI and played football. He loved sports, but he loved business as well. He amassed a fortune through investments in oil and gas wells around the country.

Then there was Catfish, my dad. Born Nathan Taylor Hawkins, he was the youngest, smallest, and happiest of the three. He was only 5'6", 165 pounds, and looked like Spencer Tracy. He was the happiest human being I've ever known. In addition to that, he made other people happy. He loved everything and everyone, and everyone loved him. Men, women, children, people of all ages and color, it didn't matter to Catfish. He loved people.

He had no passion for the military, sports, or business. After high school he enrolled at Augusta Military Academy near Staunton, Virginia, a preparatory school for VMI. Grandfather Hawkins felt like Catfish needed a little maturing before going into the fray of life. Lord, was he right! Catfish didn't "find himself" at AMA.

At VMI things were no better, but before they could dismiss him Grandfather Hawkins passed away and Catfish went home to take care of his mother.

Dad made his headquarters there in Charleston, but that was only his home base. He loved laughter and he loved people, and there just wasn't enough of either in Charleston. So he traveled. That was in the late 1920s, the era of the Big Bands. Paul Whiteman, Benny Goodman, Tommy Dorsey, Harry James, and that crowd were just getting started, and so was Catfish. He had inherited some money, but he had no real sense of responsibility, and a tremendous zest for life. So when a band he liked played in Charleston, and then left for another engagement, Catfish went with them. If he really liked the band, he would sometimes travel with them, staying gone a couple of weeks at a time.

This went on for years. He danced through three or four states, and through all of his money. Returning to Charleston from one of these trips, he wound up in the unlikely town of Bradshaw, deep in the heart of the coalfields.

He was now thirty-three years old. In Bradshaw he met a sixteen-year-old girl, 5'11", 155 pounds, named Lula Ann Payne. She was the star of the girls' basketball team at Yeager High School. Little did Catfish know, but his dancing days would soon be over.

He had a cousin who owned three drug stores in West Virginia, and one of them was right there in Bradshaw. It didn't take Catfish long to return to Charleston, get his belongings, convince cousin Bob that he needed help, and take over as manager of the Bradshaw Drug and Pharmaceutical. Why anyone would want to settle down in the coalfields of West Virginia is hard to figure, but love does strange things to people.

Men had only three choices in the coalfields: moonshine, coal mine, or move on down the line. Catfish chose to move on down the line. Once again he was moving in the opposite direction from everyone else. While everyone else was trying to get out of the coalfields, he was moving in. Even more astonishing was the fact that he was doing all this at the very height of the depression.

Although the stock market had crashed in 1929, the Great Depression did not reach its height until 1931–32. With 30 percent of our population out of work, Catfish had created himself a job.

Lula Ann Payne, known better as Big Lou, lived in Stringtown, a small community of coal miners, three miles south of Bradshaw, in McDowell County, which is in the extreme southwest corner of the state, less than ten miles from the Virginia border and not much farther from Kentucky. If there is a tougher part of the country to grow up in, I'd have to be shown it. Life was not easy in the sovereign state of McDowell County. My Grandfather Payne was Welsh and German. Grandmother Payne was English, Irish, and one-fourth Shawnee Indian. Lula Ann Payne was the oldest of five children. The youngest sister made her way to California, the youngest brother went to Wisconsin, and the third child prospered in St. Albans, West Virginia. The oldest boy, Berlin, would remain in the coalfields and die of natural causes at the age of forty-eight.

Flat land was at a premium in Stringtown. There was one road into and one road out of the valley. The mountains went straight up both sides at a ninety-degree angle. A small creek ran alongside the road. On the western side of the road there were small shacks and honky-tonks. The houses were built on the banks of the creeks, with the front doors opening onto the road. The backs of these shanties were supported by poles driven down into the creek bed. Just a few feet beyond the creek was the base of the mountain.

On the other side of the road there was a little more land, about two hundred feet or so, big enough to set a house, a small front yard, and enough room for a small garden and some farm animals in the rear before the mountains rose straight up again. This is where my Grandfather Payne lived, in a two-story house on about an acre-and-a-half plot of land, both easily the largest in town.

The first television in Stringtown was a seventeen-inch black-and-white that I gave my grandmother in 1960. Drinking water had to be carried in buckets from a spring well about four hundred yards away. Rain water was caught in large barrels at the four corners of the house, for washing clothes and bathing. This is the way it had been in the early 1900s, and this is the way it was in 1972 when I was last there.

Saturday nights we would sit on the upstairs porch and watch and listen to the miners in the honky-tonks across the road taking out their frustrations on each other. Fights and shootings were routine on paydays. Law, if enforced at all, was by whim. By Monday, after the bills were paid and the whisky consumed, the miners were broke again. You didn't just die of old age in the coalfields, you simply wore out.

Almost everyone in Stringtown worked in the coal mines; the exception was my Grandfather Payne. He had been hurt in the mines, and thereafter stayed "outside" to cut pine timbers for the mines. He also farmed and grew corn for the moonshiners because they paid a higher price for his product. Life was cheap in McDowell County; it was the perfect place to learn one lesson: survival.

Catfish moved to Bradshaw in 1931, and in less than a year he had talked Big Lou into becoming his wife. He was thirty-three, she was sixteen. There would be one condition. Catfish would have to stop drinking and settle down.

The deal was struck, and within a year or so, my oldest brother, Skip, was born. Less than four years later, I arrived at Welch Memorial Hospital, on July 2, 1937, just in time to get in on the depression. Big Lou had been brought up to handle hard times, and it was she who ran the family. I doubt she ever realized how bad things were, because this was all she had ever known.

All was fine, until one Saturday night in 1938 some of the local miners started shooting up the town. Several of the stray bullets went through our house, and Big Lou stated flatly that this was no place to raise a family. In less than a month, Catfish had moved his family of four to South Charleston, 145 miles north.

3

We moved into a small house on Main Street in South Charleston. The house was all that was left of Catfish's inheritance; he had danced away the rest. There was a small living room, two bedrooms, a kitchen, a dining room, and a bathroom. The living room had a small gas fireplace that was supposed to heat the entire house. There were linoleum floors that stayed cold all the time. The house sat on a narrow lot, less than forty feet wide, but the backyard was deep enough to support athletic games of all kinds.

The Great Depression was still going on, but somehow Catfish got a job once again. This time it was with the Electric Company, as a meter reader. It didn't pay much, but Big Lou was a genius at handling money matters.

On September 1, 1939, Germany invaded Poland and the war in Europe was on. Catfish got a job as an electrician at the Naval Ordnance Plant, which was already manufacturing war materials for what soon would be our allies in World War II. Suddenly the depression was over and South Charleston was a boom town. Defense plants were springing up everywhere. To a two-year-old the war meant nothing. And when it ended, it didn't mean much more to me as an eight-year-old except that Catfish had steady work, and there would always be food on the table.

Catfish had, in fact, settled down. He had stopped drinking and traveling around. The only time I ever remember him drinking was once at Christmas time, when I was about eight. He always played Santa Claus for the people in our neighborhood. When he didn't return home in time, Big Lou sent Skip out to try to locate him. I was playing with my younger brother, Jimmy, in the front yard when I spotted Skip and Catfish coming down the street. Catfish was walking with one foot on the curb and one foot in the street, and crying his eyes out because he thought he was crippled.

His new hobbies were playing penny-ante poker and fishing. His poker games were truly beautiful. He always played head-to-head with one other person. He would play all afternoon, and I don't believe anyone ever lost more than fifty cents. According to him, he never lost.

His fishing trips were more infrequent, because he had neither a car nor a driver's license. The Kanawha Valley, where South Charleston was located, had become the chemical capital of the country. Union Carbide, WestVaco, DuPont, and several other major concerns had been polluting the rivers with chemicals for years. This had killed the gamefish population, and all that remained was an occasional carp or catfish. Coal was being washed in many of the other streams, and that also killed the gamefish. The really good fishing streams were miles away, so Catfish had to improvise.

First, Catfish would find a drunk—not just any drunk, but one that he liked, and who had nothing to do on Saturday, was broke, and had a car. He would buy a bottle of whisky. He would then load Skip and me into the car, long before the sun was up, and we would drive thirty or forty miles to whatever stream we were going to fish that day. Only after we had arrived at the designated spot would he give the driver the bottle of whisky. The driver would knock down the entire bottle and pass out, and we would have the entire day to fish and talk together in near-privacy. At day's end we would load up our gear in the semi-rented car, wake the sleeping driver, who by this time was stone sober, and drive back home. The plan never failed, and he pulled it off for years. I might mention, however, that in all those years we never caught a single fish.

Our backyard was the gathering place for the young people of our neighborhood. Every day when school was over, the kids would assemble there for games. We played football until the season ended, then basketball, then baseball, which we played right through the summer. In the forties baseball was big. TV had not yet invaded our lives, but we would listen to baseball on radio. Professional football and basketball were being played too, but nobody was paying much attention to them.

When we were not playing the three major sports, we were playing things like matchball or popsicle-stick baseball. A diamond match box or a popsicle stick was used in place of a baseball, and a cutoff broomstick was the bat. We didn't know it at the time, but we were developing great hand-to-eye coordination.

All of our games were unsupervised by adults. By supervising ourselves we learned a great deal. For one thing, it made us more self-assertive. We would stop playing the instant an adult would come on the scene. No one ever told me why, and in those days you didn't bother to ask. You simply did what the older boys told you to do.

Every neighborhood had an older boy who pretty much set the rules for the others to follow—not exactly a bully, more like, say, an enforcer. He was good in sports, popular with the girls, feared and respected by his peers. When I was very young, ours was Termite Hardin.

Termite initially gained his fame and recognition by the simple fact that he had the prettiest and best bicycle in town. In addition, he could ride down our alley with a boy on the back fender, one on the handle bars, and yet another on his shoulders! He was *wa-tosh-e-wa-ich-e-bon*—the number one guy.

When Termite got older he awarded his position to Terry Lilly, whose younger brother Wardie was my best friend. This entitled me to some extra benefits. Anybody who stepped out of line in those days simply got his rear end kicked. Punishment was swift and certain. Case closed. It was not considered fair, however, for a large kid to beat up a much smaller kid, so when anyone my size stepped out of line with Terry, he simply told me to whip him. It was always considered smart to do what Terry said, so I would do just that.

In just a matter of days, I had advanced to "Junior Enforcer." It was, I suppose, a position of honor, but what I never told anyone was the fact that I hated to fight. (I still do.) I did what I was told, but after the fight I would make some excuse to leave for a while, and go somewhere and cry. I just did not have the heart to fill the position of "Junior Enforcer."

In August of 1945, we were playing football in the backyard as usual when all hell broke loose. People started running up and down the street yelling and crying and laughing, shooting off guns and fireworks. The sirens were blaring, always an indication that something big was happening. We stopped our game for long enough to find out what was going on, just as Mom came running out of the house screaming that the war was finally over, the Japanese had surrendered, and the troops would be coming home. I allowed that was good, but could we get back to our game? She walked back into the house and we continued on, just as if nothing had happened. Here I was, only eight years old, and already football had taken hold of my life.

After the war ended the defense plants closed, and Dad had to look for work elsewhere. He soon joined a labor union and went to work as an electrician doing construction work. The depression was over, of course, but hard times returned to West Virginia. All of a sudden, jobs, which had been plentiful there in South Charleston, were hard to find. Catfish went back on the road, and this time he wasn't dancing, he was working. He worked for a while in Parkersburg, then Wheeling, then up to Steubenville, Ohio, back over to Weirton, and on up to Pittsburgh. Wherever the union could find him work, he'd go. Depending on how far away he was working, he would usually get back on weekends.

Mom stayed home as usual. She had a house to keep and three boys to raise, and a husband to miss and worry about. Catfish couldn't bring himself to worry—or if he did, nobody could tell it. Anything that we did was just fine. Anything that Mom did was perfect. He was too busy living life to worry about the small matters. He let Lou do that; she was better equipped for it. He never spanked any of us; that too was reserved for Big Lou. He didn't have the heart for disciplining boys. He couldn't stand to see people cry. He also couldn't stand to see people in trouble, or in pain. He was a sucker for a sad song. If a fellow union worker came through town needing help or money, he would look up Dad, tell him a sad story, and Dad's money changed hands. He rarely even remembered the names of those who borrowed from him. He'd give them all we had.

It's hard to explain, but we loved him for that. We did kid him about being such an easy mark, and he would defend his actions by proclaiming, "We'll get that money back when we need it the most." We never did. Although Big Lou didn't like it one bit, she never let on in front of us. Late at night he heard from Lou on the subject, but not in front of us boys. He was the man of the house, he was the provider, and what he said or did was law. That was the way it was back then.

My brother, Skip, was four years older than I was, so I usually emulated his actions. He was a straight-A student, so I became a straight-A student. He was fast becoming an outstanding athlete, so, naturally, I tried to follow suit.

Skip went to high school and began to make a name for himself in sports, but a horrible thing was happening to me. I was getting shorter. It wasn't that I was shrinking, but that everybody else except me was growing taller.

I first noticed this in the fifth grade, when I was eleven. Initially I wasn't very upset. Mom explained that some people just matured earlier than others. By the middle of the sixth grade, however, I was growing increasingly impatient. As I entered the seventh grade, my impatience turned into alarm, and by the eighth grade it was outright panic. I was only five feet tall, and weighed in at 105 pounds. I blamed Catfish for my inferior genes. He only laughed and assured me I would grow.

I even made him take me to the doctor, who was of no help. He looked at Catfish, standing only 5'6", and volunteered the information that some people were just shorter than others. I hated the doctor. Why hadn't he said "taller than others"? My male friends were all four to five inches taller than I was, and outweighed me by thirty pounds.

By the summer of my fifteenth year, there was no change. There was no question about it; the jury was in. I was a dwarf. Skip was six feet tall, 175 pounds, and the star of the football and baseball teams. He would be going to college on a football scholarship. As for me, I would be entering high school and meeting new girls who were two inches taller than myself.

I was just about to give up any hopes of happiness, when suddenly it happened. First I got warts. Dozens of warts, all over my hands and arms. Nobody would touch a ball that I had touched. It was all over. God, how life loves a cruel joke. The onetime "Junior Enforcer" had been reduced to a wimp, with warts!

I informed Big Lou that I would not enroll in high school. In turn, she informed me that I would. I did. When I went out for the football team, they didn't have anything small enough to fit me, so I taped my pants up to keep the knee pads from touching my black high-top shoes. My first helmet was made of leather, and to make matters worse, it was orange-colored. It really didn't matter how well or poorly I practiced, I was too funny-looking for the coach even to consider putting me in a game.

Bill Weber, our coach, was tough, but a good man. He not only allowed me to continue on in practice, but even encouraged me. He told me to hang in there and keep plugging. All I needed was confidence, he said, and that would come. He was a small man himself, and I suppose he admired my determination.

My sophomore year was not much better, but I did manage to grow a couple of inches and put on a few pounds, so there was a small ray of hope. Then, just when I thought things might be turning around for me, I lost one of my front teeth. There wasn't enough money for a false tooth, so I had to go over a year without one.

Can anyone have any idea how I felt? Confidence would come, my ass! Confidence came from knowing and feeling, not hoping or wishing. There is nothing mysterious about confidence—it comes with success—and I had been having damn little of it. I had nightmares of opening our football program and reading this:

Alex Hawkins
3rd team H.B.
5'3"

16 years old
115 lbs.
No front tooth
No pubic hair
Plenty of warts
No reason for confidence

Whenever I laughed or smiled I would cover my mouth with my hands and expose my warts. When I showered I wore a towel to cover that baldness. It was a very bad year.

Finally, during the spring and summer of 1953 everything began falling into place. I shot up seven inches in height, gained fifty pounds, my warts disappeared, and I now had a forest of pubic hair. Catfish had found a steady job in Charleston, and not only did I get a false tooth, but caps were made for all my teeth in front. The caps did not come easily; I had to sit in a dental chair for two days, without novocaine, while the dentist drilled my four front teeth down to the size of match sticks. In West Virginia nothing came easy.

I felt sure that athletics would be my vehicle to success. Football would be my transportation out of the state, and the route to excitement, adventure, and riches. At last I was big enough to compete, and I promised myself that I would not only excel, I would dominate. My confidence was building. I had paid my dues, and my time had finally arrived. I was not only going to be a starter, but a star.

Three games into the 1953 season, the Black Eagles were 0–3. I was the starting quarterback and things were not going as well as I had planned. Jerome Ruby, our new coach, had installed a new offense, the T-formation. I could claim that it takes time to adjust to a new system but that was not quite the truth. The truth was that we played a lot better once Jerry Chandler replaced me as quarterback. After I moved to the halfback spot, we finished the season with a 5–5 record.

The star of the team was Ron Steele, a little boy from down the block who had replaced me as "Junior Enforcer." He weighed only 150 pounds, but he was fast and tough, and his timing was incredible. When he tackled or blocked, he would uncoil like a spring, exploding at the precise moment of impact. I studied his every move and worked hard to learn to develop his technique.

Strange things were happening. Life was getting easier for me. I noticed a direct relationship between athletic prowess and peer acceptance. The better I performed on the playing field, the less work I had to do in the classrooms. I found that my friends and classmates were more than willing to help me with my school work, and this applied to my teachers as well. They began expecting less of me in the classroom, and I didn't disappoint them. While I had been an A and B student up till then, I now was a B and C student, and nobody seemed to mind. Girls in my class would gladly help me write my term paper, or better still, even write it for me. When we had a test they would allow me to copy their papers. I was frequently invited to their homes at night to study, but we almost never got around to the studying. I was taking college preparatory courses and it didn't seem to matter what kind of work I turned in, I always made a B or C, which was good enough to make me eligible for sports. Local merchants were offering me discounts, or even giving me things. In short, I was turning into a jock, and I loved it.

By the fall of my senior year, I was 6'0", weighed 175 pounds, and was devoting all my time to sports. I made third team All-State in football, but once again I was overshadowed by Ron Steele, who made the first team. It seemed that stardom would always elude me; I always ended up being second or third best.

I remember vividly a football game against Charleston Catholic High School. A small school and perennially the weakest team on our schedule, Charleston Catholic had a *black* player on its team. This was before the public school system was integrated, so it stood out in my mind. Charleston, West Virginia, was a melting pot of nationalities who were uneducated in racial bigotry. There were very few blacks in West Virginia, and none in South Charleston. A small community of blacks did live under a bridge south of the city limits, and another group under a bridge north of town. I grew up thinking that blacks were people who lived under bridges.

Ron Steele and I were linebackers on defense, and he came to me early in the game and announced that one of the two of us was going to hit the black guy on every play. Between Ron and myself, we made his day pretty miserable. So here were two boys who had no history of racial bias, taking it out on one unsuspecting black kid just because he was a different color. It may be a strange study in human nature, but that's how it was in the fifties. What makes it ironic was that Ron Steele ended up accepting a football scholarship at West Virginia State College, as the only white player in an otherwise all-black school.

I wound up making All-State in basketball and baseball, and I also found time to win my letter in track, thereby becoming the first athlete in South Charleston High history to letter in four sports. By the close of my senior year I was being heavily recruited by several colleges. I had twenty-three basketball and three football scholarship offers. Deep down I knew that my future would be better served as a football player but my basketball coach, Buck Jamieson, was being considered for the head coach's job at Marshall University, and I promised him that if he got the job, I would go with him. He would not know whether he got the job until June, so I could not commit myself.

The football coach at West Virginia University was Pappy Lewis, and he pretty much got his way in the state. If he wanted you to attend WVU, you did. He was a great guy, but he was big and gruff, and he intimidated other coaches by refusing to allow them to recruit in the state. He had a network of spies that kept him informed of any possible tampering with *his* players. If they tried to meddle with any of his prospects, he would simply offer to fight them. Only the year before, the best football player in the state had signed with South Carolina, and Pappy did not intend to let that happen again.

It was late June when Buck Jamieson was notified that he did not get the head job at Marshall. I felt sorry for him, but that released me from my obligation. I was invited to play in the All-Star football game in Charleston in late July, along with Ron Steele. We were quartered in the Daniel Boone Hotel in Charleston. Assistant coaches from all of the state colleges visited practices daily, but Pappy Lewis didn't mind, because he knew that they would get only the players that he didn't want.

One afternoon during our practices, there was a knock on the door of my hotel room, and when I opened it a stocky little man literally jumped into the room and quickly closed the door behind him. He introduced himself as Ernie Lawhorn, from the University of South Carolina. He had registered under an alias, and had rented the room directly over mine. Pappy Lewis was a man he did not want to meet, he admitted, but he had been sent up there to sign the best halfback he could find. South Carolina had already signed the best halfback in the nation, a boy named King Dixon, he told me, and since both the starting halfbacks at USC would be graduating the following June he was pretty sure that the two of us would be starters for the next three years. (Back then freshmen could not play varsity sports.) Ernie was honest and direct and I liked him immediately. I promised him that I would not sign with any other school without first visiting USC. We talked for only a short time, and then he left, taking the stairs rather than the elevator up to his room.

The All-Star game was played, we won, and I was voted the most outstanding player, even ahead of Ron Steele. Finally I was the number one guy! The University of Kentucky and Indiana University both offered me scholarships to play either basketball or football. A Kentucky contact man even offered me a farm if I would sign with them. He was too smart to give the location or size of the farm, and I was too dumb to ask.

Meanwhile two assistant coaches from West Virginia camped at my door back in South Charleston, and would not leave until I agreed to visit the campus and meet Pappy Lewis in person. I was packing to go with them when Catfish told me that Ernie Lawhorn was outside behind the house and wanted to talk with me.

I went out the back door, got into his car, and we drove around for a little while. He had seen the two coaches on the front porch and had elected not to confront them directly, he explained. A representative from South Carolina would be up the following week to take me to Columbia for a visit. Ernie promised that he would work out any problems I might have. Then he drove me back to the back door of the house and reminded me of my promise not to sign with anyone until after visiting USC. I liked the cloak-and-dagger game and I liked the man I was playing it with; he had a gleam in his eye and mischief on his face.

I went back inside, picked up my gear, and headed for Morgantown with the two assistants. I was not enchanted with Morgantown, but Pappy Lewis was a most impressive man, positive, relaxed, down to earth. He offered me a full scholarship, which consisted of room, board, books, tuition, and fifteen dollars a month for laundry. I liked Pappy, but I told him that I would not be able to let him know for another week. I went home still unsure. I never was good at decision-making; it all seemed so final.

It was August of 1955. I sought the counsel of a neighbor, who had gone to West Virginia and had been a football player. He offered this advice: "Get the hell out of here, Alex. There's nothing for you in this state. The future lies in the South. Everybody is moving to the South, so go down there and start your life. You don't want to work at Union Carbide for the rest of your life. You go on down south, and I'll drive Catfish down for some of the ball games in the fall."

A representative from South Carolina flew up to escort me to Columbia. On the flight down he laid out a proposal. If I signed up, I would receive a full scholarship, with room, board, books, tuition, and $15 a month for laundry—plus $1,500 a semester, new clothes twice a year, three paid flights home, and a new car in my sophomore year. He could not put it in writing, he said, but I could trust him to see that I got it. He was not going to do this himself, but he had a sponsor lined up for me who would take care of it.

Early the next morning I took an entrance exam. Afterward they took me to a small lake just outside of town to go water-skiing. The home I was staying in was beautiful by comparison to any I'd ever been in. The sunshine was brilliant, the sky was clear, the lake was unpolluted, and the girl who taught me to water-ski was beautiful. She was charming and spoke with a cute Southern accent. She could slalom and do acrobatics. I felt like I had died and gone to heaven. Right then and there I signed. They asked me if I might like to spend another day, and I screamed an affirmative.

By the time I got back to South Charleston the news of my signing had hit the sports pages. My leaving the state bordered on treason. People passing by in cars would roll down their windows and curse me. How could I do such a thing? Who did I think I was, anyway? Wasn't West Virginia good enough for me? Huh? Overnight, friends and fans of mine had turned violently against me.

I was hurt and disillusioned that friends would change their attitudes so quickly.

At home Big Lou was noncommittal, but Catfish was certain

that I had done the right thing. Everything would work out fine, he said. But then, he always said that about everything that came along. After a couple of days of this, I had had enough. I packed my belongings, said my good-byes, and left for the University of South Carolina. I wasn't quite sure what a Gamecock was, but I was ready to become one.

6

South Carolina is a difficult state to describe or to understand. Compared to, say, Texas, it is like the dark side of the moon. A Texan is proud of his state, and he is loud and verbal about it. South Carolinians are every bit as proud of South Carolina, but they are quiet and not boastful. They simply ignore anybody who doesn't like or doesn't understand their way of life. They never take the time to defend or explain their life-style. One thing is certain: they are not about to change it.

Being in South Carolina during the 1950s was especially pleasing. There was virtually no crime, so there was no reason to lock anything. There were no drug users, with the possible exception of the drummers in dance bands from the West Coast. There was no social disorder, and everyone appeared to be happy with their situations. Shag music dominated the beach front, then swept inland through the Carolinas. Men wore Bass Weejun loafers, madras shorts, and alligator shirts. Life was so good for most of the people of South Carolina that they chose to freeze it right where it was. Someone must have said, "Life just can't get no better than this," and everyone agreed, so they stopped things right there and never even bothered to enter the 1960s.

The University of South Carolina was not known for its academic excellence. No one ever referred to it as the Harvard of the South. Nor was it famous for its football teams. In the sixty-three years the Gamecocks had been playing college football, they had produced not a single All-American. Perhaps even worse was the fact that in the same period of time the Gamecocks had made only one bowl appearance, the Gator Bowl in 1946. They had lost that—to Wake Forest. Since the University could not lure better athletes from other states with promises of bowl appearances or making All-American, they had to take pretty much what they could get. It might be more accurate to say that they got the players that the other schools didn't want.

Rex Enright was the head coach, and a nicer, kinder gentleman will never be met anywhere. Coach Enright lost more games than he won, but no one ever mentioned firing him, because somehow he always managed to beat the archrival Clemson Tigers. At one point, he went six years without losing to them. For the Carolina alumni that was quite good enough.

Because of the harassment back home I reported a week early. The varsity was already practicing for its opening game, but the rest of the student body would not report for almost three weeks, so Columbia was a pretty lonely place for me.

The football team lived in Preston Dormitory, directly across the street from the practice field. The varsity squad occupied the first floor of the dorm, the freshmen lived on the second floor, and there was a stairway at the south end of the dorm so that no one had to disturb the privacy of the varsity players. A good many of them were older men, Korean War veterans, some of them twenty-four or twenty-five years old, while I was a mere eighteen-year-old boy.

West Virginians are not outgoing people to begin with, so it was natural for me to be standoffish. Having reported early, I was alone on the second floor of Preston dorm. During this time of isolation I was adjusting to a totally new environment. The biggest change was the food. I had grown up eating meat and potatoes; now it was grits, rice, and boiled okra. No wonder these locals were small. I attributed it to their diets, and more or less likened them to the Chinese.

The August heat was oppressive, but the air was still clean and the sky still blue. But where was the beautiful girl who had taught me water-skiing?

The week dragged by, until Friday came and the freshman team finally began arriving. There were fifty-five members on our freshman squad on scholarships, from all over the East Coast. In all my life I had never heard so many accents. In fact I had never heard *any* other accent before, because I had never been out of the state of West Virginia, and everybody in West Virginia talked the same.

Where was King Dixon? He was the one I wanted to meet. I wondered what the best halfback in the country looked like. One day a brand new red 1955 Chevrolet convertible pulled up and parked outside the dormitory. Several of the players rushed over to greet the driver, and I knew it must be King Dixon. He was shaking hands and exchanging pleasantries, fully in control of the entire scene.

As I watched him, I wondered how much money he was making, and how he came to get a new car in his first year. I resented him instantly, and the resentment boiled in me for almost the full minute it took him to search me out and speak. He was short, stocky, bowlegged, and his hair was cut short in a military fashion. He was positively charming, and the minute we shook hands I liked him.

King Dixon was what every father wants his son to be. As a player, a person, and a student, he was a coach's dream. The very name, King Dixon, didn't hurt. It was perfect in print. He could run, he could pass, and he could catch a football. He could block and tackle, and he had speed as a broken-field runner. He was thrilling and exciting, a crowd pleaser who could go the distance. He could not, however, leap tall buildings in a single bound, as had been reported in the *Columbia Record*.

King was the first person at breakfast and the first out of the shower. His room was organized and meticulous. After classes and practice he would go to the library with his girlfriend, Augusta Mason—not a bad name itself—whom he would later marry. She then became Augusta Mason Dixon, which did not hurt him in South Carolina a few years later when he ran for public office. He was, of course, a dean's list student and the obvious captain of our team, not to mention a respected squad leader in the ROTC.

As for me, well, I was less inclined to get up early. I rarely made breakfast, and if I did I went on to my nine o'clock class. There

I would position myself in the rear of the classroom next to several of the better students and close enough to be able to duplicate their answers on exams in the likely event that their answers were better than mine. I chose to be a C student because I did not consider it fair to cheat and make A's. I was, however, a perfectly well-mannered student, and never spoke up or volunteered to take part in classroom discussions. Why let new information clutter my mind?

My first major was in Business Administration. One day I made a big mistake in Economics class. I was sitting there, daydreaming as usual, when suddenly, for no reason at all, I began to listen to the professor. He was one of those Harvard guys, or maybe a Yalie. He was talking about deficit spending, and he was saying that it was perfectly all right and that, frankly, he was in favor of spending more than you made. Well, Catfish had been doing that for years, and I knew it didn't work. So I raised my hand and made this known to the professor. He started talking about outputs and GNP and guns and butter, and, all in all, he was not making much sense to me. So I closed my mind to his argument. I knew it wouldn't work. Every time we were asked to explain the theory of deficit spending on exams, my answer was the same, "It doesn't work." I failed that course three times, before I finally changed my major to avoid economics. I never let logic or fact encumber my thinking. In no time at all I was also drummed out of the ROTC. I could not see that there was any point in shining my shoes until they glistened, then going straight outside and marching on a dusty field.

After football practice I would go to a movie, play cards, or shoot some pool. My roommate and I agreed that the beds should be made and the sheets changed at least once each semester. All in all, as a student, a person, and a player I was a coach's nightmare. . . . except on game days. Alex Hawkins was what every father wants his stillborn son to be like.

We had players on the freshman team from Alabama, Georgia, New York, New Jersey, Ohio, Pennsylvania, Massachusetts, Virginia, and North Carolina. Nearly everyone from out of state was being paid something by someone. The Northern players were naturally referred to as "Yankees," and went around together. The Southern boys mixed a little better, while privately resenting the intrusion of these Yankees. Being from West Virginia I was caught in between the two factions, neither fish nor fowl. I didn't really fit in with either side.

My Southern teammates had little or no trouble adjusting to their situation. They were right at home, playing by the rules they had been brought up to play by. Most of them already had a host of friends, both male and female. Their major adjustment was getting to understand and accept their Northern teammates. The Yankees, on the other hand, were having every bit as much trouble as I was adjusting to this new way of life. Only on the football field were they truly comfortable. They stayed pretty much to themselves. They couldn't figure out how anybody could live on grits and rice, and it was also puzzling to them why everyone was called "Bubba" or "Bo."

When the 3,600 nonfootball students reported for classes, I had been anxious to see what they would be like. It didn't take me long to realize that being accepted by them was going to be an uphill struggle. They were a little skeptical of the jocks. We were perceived as a novelty item, to be viewed from a distance but not allowed to get too close.

It seemed to me that there were not many pretty girls in school at USC. Most of the nice, pretty girls went to girl's schools, like Winthrop, Converse, or Columbia College. I soon learned that a "nice girl" *never* dated two types of men: soldiers from nearby Fort Jackson, or Yankees. To be seen in the company of either was enough to ruin a reputation.

Weems Baskin, the freshman team coach, knew we were good, and would good-naturedly tease the varsity coaches about us beating them. We knew we were good, too, and never doubted it for a minute. Our freshman team lost only to a powerful Georgia Tech team, by one point. King Dixon was the star, and nobody resented it. I was known only as the "other" halfback, but that was all right with me for the time being. I had seen my competition, and was very comfortable with it.

As for the varsity football team, it won three games out of ten that year, and one of the losses was to Clemson. By spring practice Rex Enright moved over to athletic director, and Warren Giese was made the new head football coach. He had been an assistant coach at Maryland under Jim Tatum, and Tatum had won a national championship at Maryland, so we were all excited.

Giese was a good-looking, well-built man, young, clean-cut, and well-organized. He called each of the players in to his office to meet him, and showed us the football that Tatum had given him as a souvenir of the national championship. Giese informed me that he was keeping Dixon and me together, no matter what. We would stay with each other, whether on the first team or the second team, as a tandem. What this meant, of course, was that for either of us to make the first team, both would have to clearly beat out our competition for the starting lineup.

Next he called a team meeting, and informed us that the paying of athletes at South Carolina was over. All promises made would be honored through the spring, he said, but that was that. If we didn't like it, he told us, we could make a list of any three schools that we would like to attend, and he would personally call these schools and recommend us to them.

I thought about the $3,000 and the free trips back home, and about the new clothes twice a year. Mostly, however, I thought about the new car that I was supposed to receive in the fall. It didn't seem fair. It shouldn't be happening to me. To make matters worse, I had never been able to find the beautiful girl who taught me to water-ski. I had looked for her everywhere, but she had just vanished.

So just before the spring term ended, I went to Coach Giese's office with a sheet of paper. On it were the names of three schools: Texas, Oklahoma, and Kentucky.

7

That summer I went back to South Charleston and got a job with the City Maintenance Department. The job paid $1.10 an hour, and I was happy to get it. I soon found I was the only worker who was actually getting paid. The others were winos working off their fines. I spent the summer hauling garbage, painting curbs and parking spaces, and blasting rock from a quarry. After we dynamited the rock loose, we took nine-pound sledge hammers and turned big rocks into little ones, then hand-loaded them onto trucks for road repair. Imagine how much fun that was, handling dynamite with a bunch of winos.

I had to be at work at the city garage at 8:00 A.M. each day. The garage was two and one-half miles from our house, down the railroad tracks. I carried my lunch in a brown "paper poke," and ran those tracks to and from work each day. By the end of the summer I was in superb condition.

While I had been away at college, Catfish had found a buyer for our little house on Main Street, and he had bought Big Lou a two-story house directly across the alley from the old place. It had only two bedrooms, but there were two window-unit air-conditioners, a basement, and wall-to-wall carpeting. With the money Big Lou saved by not having to feed me and my older brother, who was now in the naval air service, she bought her first TV set. God, we were proud of our new home! I had never invited a girl into the house on Main Street, because I was so ashamed of it.

I was now dating a girl named Betsy Day, who was home for the summer. We had started dating during my senior year in high school. She was a classy lady, and in the beauty queen section in the Duke University yearbook. All that past year, we had been writing one another and I had visited her one weekend in Durham in the spring.

The Duke University campus was the most beautiful place I had ever been, but I somehow resented the elegance and beauty. All of Betsy's friends at Duke were so well-dressed and polished, and seemed so comfortable with themselves. Everybody had been nice and pleasant, but I found the entire experience intimidating. I was definitely out of my element.

For no apparent reason, I developed a dislike for Duke University. I remembered, back during the previous fall, I was going down the stairs of Preston Dorm before the opening varsity game, which was against Duke. South Carolina had not beaten Duke in twenty-five years. Some of the varsity players had been laughing about how badly Duke was going to beat them. I was appalled. My contempt for the Carolina varsity players grew in direct proportion to my dislike of Duke University. To hell with beating Clemson; it was Duke that I was gearing myself for. I would personally do something about the Blue Devils.

But how was I going to do that if I didn't go back to South Carolina? Throughout the summer I was waiting for word from Texas, Oklahoma, or Kentucky. The phone did not ring. Finally I called Coach Giese to get an update on my status. He stated that he had written all three schools and had given me splendid recommendations. He couldn't imagine why I had not been contacted, he said. I was not to worry about it, he told me; he would look into it personally. He also reassured me that if I changed my mind about leaving I could always return to South Carolina on a regular scholarship. I hung up the telephone thinking it would only be a matter of time until one of the three schools would contact me.

Sometime in or about the first week of August I was in Al Wells's pool room, when I ran into Jake Bodkin. Jake had been the 170-pound center on our high school football team. After graduating he had joined the army and had become a paratrooper. I hadn't seen him in over two years. In those years, he had matured physically and had grown to about 220 pounds. He was as strong, and as stubborn, as a U.S. Army mule. If he could play football at 170 pounds, I thought to myself, what would he be like now that he was 50 pounds heavier? If I were going into battle, Jake was the kind of guy I would want in my foxhole.

Suddenly I got a great idea. "Jake," I asked, "what are you going to do now that you're out of the service?"

"Don't know," he replied. "You got any ideas?"

"I just may have a hell of an idea," I told him.

It was getting late in the summer and I still had not heard from anyone. It was time to get this matter settled once and for all, I decided. One thing was certain: I was not going to stay in South Charleston and break rock for the rest of my life.

I walked to my house and called long distance to South Carolina. "Coach Giese, this is Alex. Have you heard from any of the schools I asked you to contact?"

"Gee, Alex," he said, "no, I haven't. That is strange, I would have thought at least one of them would have contacted you by now."

I was angry. If those schools didn't want me, I sure as hell didn't want them. It never dawned on me that Giese might not have contacted any of the schools. All I knew was that I hated Texas, Oklahoma, and Kentucky for not wanting my services.

"Coach," I said, "I'm going to be up front with you. I don't think it's fair not getting the money, clothes, or trips home that I was promised."

"Alex," he said, "I thought I made it very clear to every member of our team that those days are over. From now on everybody will be treated equally and fairly. Actually, Alex, fifty-two other players were receiving extras, and you are the only person who has resented having to conform to NCAA rules."

"Okay then," I said, "how about the new car, Coach? I can't even date without borrowing Dixon's car."

"I'm sorry, Alex," Giese said, "but those are the rules, and you must learn to live with them. Will you be coming back to school this fall?"

Well, what were my options?

"Coach, I'll be there this fall, but I'm going to bring a friend of mine with me, and he needs a scholarship. I figure it's only fair that if I don't get my money, you can give my friend a scholarship. And he can play." At least I guessed he could.

"Well, Alex," he answered, "this is a most unusual request. First he'll have to pass our entrance exam, and then we'll have to see him work out."

"He is not dumb, and he can play," I insisted.

"Well, Alex, we'll have Coach Bartos fly up there and look at your friend next week. It's kind of funny that you called. We were talking about you and Bobby Barrett"—a teammate at South Carolina—"just yesterday. We were wondering what kind of shape you all were in. Well, gee, Alex, it was sure nice hearing from you, and we're looking forward to seeing you in a couple of weeks. We're going to have a real fine team this year."

I hung up the phone and started back to the pool room. When I got there, I took Jake Bodkin aside.

"Do you want a football scholarship at South Carolina, Jake?" I asked.

"Why not?" said Jake. "I can't dance."

"You can't shoot pool either." We had other war veterans on our football team who were on the GI Bill, and I knew that they were receiving $115 a month from the government towards their education. I figured that I could hustle Jake out of at least sixty bucks a month shooting pool, so all was not lost.

Jake passed the entrance exam and was awarded a full scholarship. My pride had been pacified, and for the time being my differences with Warren Giese were over.

8

Our freshman team was composed of players of assorted backgrounds and reputations. I had not gotten around to meeting many of the varsity players the year before. As already noted, South Carolina had not always been able to attract the most desirable athletes in the country. All in all, Preston Hall resembled the casting set for *Frankenstein*. The dormitory was a nut house.

Tom Stewart was a lumberjack from Macon, Georgia, who had just returned from either the Canadian or Alaskan wilderness, he was not sure which. At any other position than quarterback Tom could have been All-World. They put him at linebacker and he was great. They played him at center and he was easily the best we had. They tried him at tight end and he was fantastic. The trouble was that he refused to play anywhere but quarterback, and he was a lousy quarterback. The dilemma must have caused him great mental strain. One morning I was going to breakfast about 7:00 A.M. when I looked up at a tree and spotted Tom crouched on a limb overhanging the sidewalk, about twenty feet up in the air.

"What are you doing up there?" I inquired.

"Waiting for someone to jump on, you stupid bastard," he hissed. "What do you think I'm doing?"

We had a nose tackle named Vince Gargano, who did play-by-play announcing on every play he was in. It went something like this:

"Gargano sits up on the head of the center." As the ball was snapped he would continue, "Ball is snapped, Gargano beats the block by the center, pursues to his left, and brings down the ball carrier for a loss of two. Great play by Gargano." He would then go back to the huddle.

Then there was Ralph Forsano from Brooklyn, who would sit on his windowsill with a .22 rifle and shoot pigeons off the gymnasium roof. When the authorities confiscated his rifle, he got himself a bow and arrow and went right back to work. It was not uncommon to see a passing car with an arrow sticking out of its hood.

Prentice Peabody was a banker's son from Augusta, Georgia, who could play a little, but never really took football seriously. Prentice was the only player on our team with a bank account. On one occasion Giese called him in to admonish him for his lack of dedication to the game. "Prentice," he said, "you have got to learn to pay the price for success."

Prentice reached into his pocket, pulled out his checkbook, and inquired, "How much is it, Coach?"

Then there was a guard from Virginia named Jack Ashton, who got impatient waiting for a student to get off the telephone in our dorm. After a few minutes he walked over, yanked the phone from his hand, knocked him cold with the receiver, hung the phone up, and then made his call.

But of all the people who stayed in Preston Hall, the topper was Corky Gaines, from Fayetteville, North Carolina. Corky had just returned from Marine Corps service, where he had been a heavyweight boxer. He had boxed Floyd Patterson, and was the first person ever to knock Patterson off his feet. He was about 5'11", and weighed 235 pounds, with a twenty-nine-inch waist and a fifty-four-inch chest. He had a nineteen-inch neck, a chipped tooth in the front, and not one but two cauliflowered ears. Corky had the disposition of a cottonmouth moccasin. Everyone said that he was very sensitive about his ears. Sensitive? Corky was paranoid. If anybody laughed around Corky, he had better have something Corky could laugh at, too. He knocked five people off the pavilion porch at Pawley's Island one night without asking any questions, just because they were laughing. He was the undisputed cock-of-the-roost at South Carolina.

There are two things in this world that have always worried me most. One is old age, which I can do nothing about; the other is boredom, which was never a problem in Preston Hall. You entered Preston Hall at your own risk. A nonathlete, who will be referred to from this point on as a *civilian,* never dared to go inside, whether invited or otherwise. Even if you lived in Preston Hall, you never opened the door and walked out into the hall without first peeking out to see what might be going on. You could get run over by a motorcycle or gunned down by a shotgun blast. Once I opened the door to the bathroom and was greeted by a live five-foot alligator. Nobody bothered locking doors, because if someone wanted to get in, he would just knock the door down. Torching doors and mattresses was common as well.

Jesse Berry, an assistant coach, was the trouble shooter for the athletic department, so he was the dormitory supervisor. God love his heart, Jesse, his wife, and their newborn daughter had to live in a suite in Preston Hall. I do hope that the child turned out normal. Consideration for others is not something that jocks take very seriously.

We had three weeks to get ready for our opening game against Wofford, which meant that I had three weeks to earn a starting halfback job. Dixon was winning out over his competition, but true to his word, Giese was going to keep Dixon and me together, no matter what. So we were still playing on the second team.

Back then we played two-platoon football, but what that meant was that we played both offense and defense. The first team would play the first eight minutes, and then the second team would come on for the remaining seven minutes of that quarter. Insofar as playing time was concerned it really wasn't so very important to be a starter, but the pride of winning the starting assignment was what counted. One week before the first game my competition went down with a broken leg, so Dixon and Hawkins were awarded the starting halfback assignments.

At practice the previous spring, Coach Giese had installed the new system he had learned from Jim Tatum at Maryland. There was absolutely no reason to question the system, because at Maryland Tatum's teams had gone undefeated three times and played in four postseason games. It didn't take long to learn the system, which was designed perfectly for my mentality. Technically it was called the split-T offense. It consisted of eight offensive plays, and our defense was a 5–4. That, in its entirety, was the "system."

I had no reason to question its simplicity, because what did I know about football? Although Gus Dorais had caught the first forward pass for Notre Dame way back in 1913, Warren Giese figured it was a bad idea. The only time he wanted to see the football in the air was on extra points, after we had scored. Our only pass play, the halfback option pass, could be thrown right or left. We decided that was plenty, because we beat Wofford easily enough in our opener and the following week we upset Duke 7–0, defeating them for the first time in twenty-five years.

Columbia went wild and the University of South Carolina did, too. The authorities immediately awarded Warren Giese a lifetime contract which he quickly accepted, and he held them to it when they tried to fire him following the 1960 season, after he went 3–6–1. He still has an office at the university today. It was never made clear to me why Giese could collect his money, but could not allow me to collect mine. I've been suspicious of coaches ever since.

We had fifteen sophomores on the two starting units, and the future looked bright for the Gamecocks. If there was enough money available, the best players in the country could be recruited, even if they were undesirables. We went on to a 7–3 season, which equaled the best record Carolina had chalked up since the season of 1925. Before that record was improved on, another twenty-eight years would elapse.

Together Dixon and I accounted for 1,422 yards in our first varsity season. Warren Giese and I had gotten along splendidly. I was sure that he must be a genius, and I never questioned anything he said or did. Dixon set the example, and I followed in blind faith.

9

Towards the end of the football season an alumnus, Bright Stevenson, invited me to dinner at his restaurant. During the course of the evening, Bright told me that he had seen me play and that he liked my reckless style. He went on to tell me that he thought I needed to join a fraternity, Pi Kappa Alpha. He would take care of the details and the expenses if I would join. He did, I did, and I was thereby integrated into the fraternity system.

I spent that spring socializing with the Greeks. Making good my promise to myself, I was mixing with the civilians. It gave me the chance to try to understand what the "real" collegiate world was about. It came as a surprise, but I liked it. It was not at all like the physical world of Preston Hall. These people, for the most part, were civilized. They had their fun, but kept it in perspective.

Everything was turning up roses for me. It was working out just as it had done in high school. The better I played football, the more things opened up and the easier life became. People were offering to do things for me, and I loved having them do it. Girls who hadn't spoken to me the year before were smiling and flirting with me. I was dating here and there, and I was happier than I had ever been. I was starting to feel like part of the scene. I had failed Economics again and dropped Spanish, but I could make it up in the spring or, if that wasn't enough, go to summer school. I changed my major to psychology.

Warren Giese and I were the best of friends, and in spring drills I was gung-ho. Everybody was certain we would be undefeated in the fall, and none more sure of it than I. No longer was I "the other halfback." It was Dixon and Hawkins now.

Just when I thought things could get no better, they did. That spring a fraternity brother said he had a friend who wanted to go out with me. The girl was little Libby Bagnal, of Manning, South Carolina, easily the finest lady on the campus. At first I couldn't believe it. Libby was a girl that I had tried desperately to date in my freshman year. At the time she was a freshman, too, and a little unsure of herself, if that could be possible. She was five feet tall, weighed ninety-two pounds, with a perfect body and a dynamite smile. She was a living doll; Mattel must have made her clothes. I had been trying for a year and a half to get her to notice me, but nothing had worked. She would always speak, but would never let me catch her eye. Besides, she was always holding hands with her high school boyfriend. He wasn't much bigger than she was, and he wore black and white saddle oxfords. He wasn't big enough for the volleyball team, and we didn't have one anyway. There was no way he deserved her. What a mismatch, I thought, and I hated him.

For over a year Libby had ignored me. The more she ignored me, the more determined and desperate I became. One day Corky Gaines and I chased Miss Libby and her pint-sized boyfriend down the street. We were gaining on them when they bolted into a parked car and locked the doors. They were shaking, and we were laughing, having no idea what to do. Corky and I exchanged glances, smiled, and started pretending that we were going to turn the car over. We were growling and snarling and shaking the car. Finally we got so tickled that we stopped and walked away. I wondered how she could have forgotten all that.

Libby and I dated for the first time, then we kept dating for the rest of the spring until she went home to Manning for the summer. I went to summer school and worked as a cashier in a car wash. There were always a dozen or so jocks who had to attend summer school to be eligible for football in the fall. The ones who attended summer school, it goes without saying, were always the most undisciplined and usually the most fun.

In general, if you describe athletes, the adjectives high on the list will be self-centered, excessive, irresponsible, selfish, pampered, childish, rude, crude, naive, daring, and, finally, dangerous. I like irresponsible, dangerous people, because they are exciting. The excitement starts when they enter a room. You know where they are, but you are never really sure what they will do or say. Has anyone ever noticed the trouble that athletes get into in the off-season? No matter what sport you're talking about, the off-season is a dangerous time for an athlete. They are easily bored. It's like George Patton without a war, or Norm Van Brocklin without an enemy.

I failed both courses that summer, but at the eleventh hour met a girl in the Registrar's office who changed my F's to C's. She even suggested it was just as easy to write in an A as an F, but I felt that was going too far and declined to be greedy.

After classes were over I went back home to spend a few days with Big Lou and Catfish. The second day home I ran into Jake Bodkin. He couldn't wait to show me his new car, a red and black 1927 Reo. He had bought the car for a hundred dollars and offered to let me buy in as a partner for fifty dollars. Surprisingly enough, the 1927 Reo was in near-perfect condition. The car still had the original paint, with "Reo Joe" lettered in white on both doors. The windshield rolled out in the front, and there was six feet of space between the back and the front seats. There were four windows in back, all of them with shades that rolled up and down. It had spoke tires and a hand-carved wooden steering wheel that was almost as big as the tires. The only drawback was that it had to be hand cranked to get it started. Jake insisted on being the driver, so I was the cranker. This, however, entitled me to sit in the back seat.

It was a pretty sight: two lunatics driving down the road in a 1927 Reo, one in the front, the other in back smoking a cigar. We didn't have a worry in the world, or if we did we were too dumb to realize it.

Along about this time, Jake started doing some very strange things. It seems Jake had seen a Hindu or someone like that walk on hot coals and stick pins through various parts of his body. Jake refused to be outdone. He reasoned that if they could do it, he could.

First he began extinguishing cigarettes on the bottoms of his feet and in his palms. Thereafter he moved up to cigars. He learned to chew up and swallow light bulbs and then drinking glasses. He jammed ladies' hat pins through his lips, shoulders, and legs. I understand there is an art to this, but Jake didn't know it; he just did it. We quickly turned this into a fairly profitable enterprise. When the novelty finally wore off Jake outdid himself by biting the head off a live chicken. Thereafter we could get no bets.

When school started Jake and I were rooming together and having our fun in Reo Joe. Neither of us had ever owned a car before. Although Jake was usually the driver, a couple of times while he was cranking the car, the crank stuck. He explained that if the ignition were not turned off the crank would tear up the radiator. He showed me how to get the crank out by using his foot. Jake wasn't much on detail, so he didn't bother to explain to me that the heel of my shoe was supposed to catch the crank on the upswing. The whole thing looked simple enough to me.

Right after lunch on the Wednesday before our opening game with Duke, Libby and I were at the fraternity house in Reo Joe. I cranked the car, and the crank stuck. I shouted for her to turn off the ignition, but she couldn't hear me. To avoid tearing up the radiator, I stuck my foot in the crank. The crank hit my foot and knocked me fifteen feet across the lawn. Libby drove me to the Athletic Department, and the trainer informed me I had broken a toe. The toe had already swollen to about three times its normal size.

I walked down to Coach Giese's office. "Coach," I said, "I just broke me toe." He looked down at my foot and asked me to explain how I had broken my toe. I told him. He listened thoughtfully and said: "Alex, I'm going to tell you two things. Number one is that you *are* going to play against Duke. Secondly, you are never, ever to do anything like Jake does again, because Jake is just not like other people." He went back into his office and closed the door.

By Saturday the swelling had gone down until the toe was only twice its normal size. The trainer shot the toe full of novocaine and it deadened the pain, but I still couldn't get my foot in my shoe. So they cut the toe out of my shoe, and I played.

In the ninth game of the season, we were playing at home against North Carolina State. They were undefeated in the Atlantic Coast Conference, and their star halfback, Dick Christy, was being touted as an All-American. If I were ever going to be a star, I thought, this was the perfect opportunity.

With only one minute and nine seconds remaining in the game, I threw a touchdown pass and then kicked the extra point, to tie the score at 26–26. On the last play of the game State tried a desperation pass which I intercepted at our twenty-yard line. I had already played fifty-six minutes of the finest football I had ever played in my life. Now with no time left on the clock, I streaked down the left sideline. At midfield I picked up some blockers and cut back to my right. The end zone was just twenty yards away, and I was reaching down inside myself, searching for that extra something that only champions and thoroughbreds are supposed to have, at which point I was run down from behind by the entire N.C. State team.

The gun had sounded the game's end, but there had been a penalty called against us, giving N.C. State one last play. Christy then kicked a forty-six-yard field goal, the first and only field goal he ever tried, to win 29–26. Christy had scored all twenty-nine points for State, and of course was the hero. He was voted the ACC Player of the Year, while I made second-team All-ACC. So it was second place again for me.

We finished the 1956–57 season with a 5–5 record. I viewed a .500 season then as I do today: as bad news. I knew that if I was going to be a star, I would have to improve my running speed.

I also knew that we had too much talent on that team to settle for a five and five record. My faith in Warren Giese was waning. His system didn't seem to be working any more. Knowing that we almost never put the ball in the air, every team we went against had used an eight-man line on us. The only football that I knew was what I had been taught by Giese, but I also knew that without the forward pass we would be seeing many more eight-man fronts in the future.

10

That spring I was elected one of the tri-captains for the coming fall. Giese initiated a spring workout program; we were supposed to play handball at the YMCA three days a week. For a few weeks I complied good-naturedly, but I became bored once I realized I could beat everybody. Giese called me in to lecture me about obedience and discipline. It would be a bad example for the rest of the team, he contended, if one of the captains did not participate with the rest of the squad. My argument was that I probably got more exercise running around a pool table than they got playing handball. He countered with, "It doesn't look good if you set yourself apart."

The next month Giese held back my fifteen-dollar-a-month laundry check for not attending these workouts. Shortly thereafter I borrowed his car and had an accident that cost him considerably more than the fifteen dollars to repair. I think he believed that I had done it intentionally. The cold war between Giese and me was heating up.

I no longer believed in Warren Giese or his system. Like a child I found myself bending every rule that he would mandate, and like a child, when he refused to punish me, I lost respect for him. I was already a maverick, but now I was becoming a renegade.

Some people can handle success better than others. I did not handle it well at all. Libby was the only rudder in my life, my one link with sanity. She had won the hearts of all my friends, teammates, and fraternity brothers. We were not going steady, but she was definitely my No. 1 girlfriend.

She was a tough act to follow. She did nothing wrong, always knew the right things to say and do, and didn't smoke, drink, or swear. She was the best driver I've ever been with. We got her a chauffeur's outfit and she was the official driver for Reo Joe. She was perfect.

Someone like Libby can put a lot of pressure on my sort. Being an overachiever in athletics was one thing, but trying to be good enough for Libby was something else entirely. By late spring it seemed all too clear to all that Libby Bagnal was just too good for me. I suggested that she date Jimmy Leventis instead, the president of the student body and the best-looking guy on campus. She must have agreed, because she did.

That spring Jesse Berry, trouble shooter and assistant coach, was summoned to Giese's office. Giese had learned that I was not attending classes regularly, and that it was becoming questionable whether I would be eligible to play football the following fall. Poor Jesse was assigned the responsibility of seeing to it that I went to classes. Giese made it clear to Jesse that if I wasn't there in the fall, he wouldn't be, either.

Jesse Berry was one of the most dedicated men I've ever known. He was in my room every morning, waking me, dressing me, and going over classwork with me as he walked me to class. He knew more about my courses than the professors. To get me out of bed he developed more gimmicks than an Armenian rug salesman. Jesse always seemed to know my moods, and he would go from threatening violence—"Alex, you son of a bitch, stand up and fight like a man"—to pleading with tears in his eyes—"Alex, think of my wife and child. If I lose this job, it's all over for them."

It seemed cruel for a grown man to be subjected to this, but more often than not I felt he enjoyed it. It was as if he had secret acting ambitions; every pose he struck was convincing. This madness lasted until my eligibility was assured, after which Jesse was relieved of his acting duties.

Even though my right to play football in the fall was secure now, Jake and I still had to attend summer school, along with a dozen of my teammates. Giese made it mandatory for everyone in summer school to sign up for a physical education course being given at seven o'clock each morning. That 7:00 A.M. came mighty early to anyone who kept my hours. Sometimes we had to sleep fast, and other times we got no sleep at all.

Our instructor was Frankie DeMars. He was an old boxer, and tough as a pine knot. He made it quite clear that he would not hesitate to knock us on our butts if we stepped out of line, and there was no doubt in our minds that he could and would. He was about sixty-five years old, but he still had that look in his eyes that boxers have. His hands were still lightning fast, and we knew somehow that he still wanted to mix it up.

I had developed an interest in boxing back in high school. One of my friends had some Joe Louis fights on film, and we would watch them in slow motion, with a classical music background. I marveled at the grace and rhythm of the great heavyweight champion, and I looked forward to learning the sport.

Frankie announced that he was going to put us in boxing condition in time for football season. I didn't know what boxing condition meant, but I soon found out. He challenged us right off by informing us that only one A would be given in his course. I looked at Jake, and he looked at me, and the challenge was on for the entire summer. I was going to get that A.

At seven o'clock sharp, we would jump rope for five minutes. We then did sit-ups, push-ups, and chin-ups for five minutes each. Grades were determined by how many of these you could do in the time allotted. Next we climbed a forty-foot rope up to the ceiling by arm power alone, without the use of our legs. After that we sparred with the heavy bag for one minute and then punched it with both hands for one full minute. Anyone who thinks that this doesn't sound difficult should try it sometime.

We then paired off and boxed for three separate three-minute rounds, supposedly changing opponents after each round. Jake and I didn't; we banged away at each other for three rounds. We finished up the day's workout with a one-mile run that had to be completed in less than six minutes. Try to envision me doing this five days a week, throughout the summer, with the previous night's stale draft beer still on my stomach.

We boxed with sixteen-ounce gloves so that no one would get

hurt. The idea of boxing was to condition us and improve our footwork. We were not supposed to throw a right hand punch, but to jab and move. Jake and I ignored this; we stood toe-to-toe and swatted each other with rights and lefts for the full nine minutes. Anyone who didn't know better would have thought we hated one another. Jake was always coming up with something new, such as his version of an uppercut, or bolo, punch. Three times that summer I had to visit the infirmary for stitches to close cuts on my mouth and eyes.

It was on one such occasion, when I was waiting outside the infirmary, that Libby Bagnal came driving by. She saw me sitting there bleeding, and it must have brought out her maternal instincts. Her little warrior was injured and bloody, and she couldn't stand it. So she stopped the car, and we talked things out. After that, for whatever reason she might have had, we began dating again.

11

We opened the season my senior year with an 8–0 win over Duke. Our second game was against Army at West Point. It was Army's opening game of the season, and we had no films of their games to study. It was generally conceded that Army had a fine team, led by All-American halfback Bob Anderson. Here was a dream come true for me. The opportunity to beat Army at Michie Stadium before the New York press corps was as much as I could ask for. It would be the perfect showcase for the relatively unknown Alex Hawkins.

When we reached Bear Mountain I was surprised to find headlines reading "Hawkins versus Dawkins." I had never heard of this other halfback, Pete Dawkins. I was also not familiar with Red Blaik, who was entering his twenty-fifth season as coach of the Cadets.

One of the first things a military man learns is the importance of the element of surprise. Red Blaik had learned it well.

The first suspicion that we might be in for a long afternoon came as we walked across the field to meet Army's captain, Pete Dawkins. I looked down to my left at King Dixon, 5'8", 165 pounds. I then looked across at the approaching Pete Dawkins, at 6'2", 215 pounds of magnificent manhood. I whispered to Dixon, "Look at them and look at us. We're in trouble." It had taken me four years and 800 miles, but I was finally looking at the best halfback in the country.

Army beat us 45–8 in one of the biggest fiascos ever witnessed. Red Blaik had decided to open the season with the lonesome-end formation. The lonesome end was Bill Carpenter. He never entered the huddle; they signaled him the plays.

Keeping track of Bill Carpenter was just the start of our problems. Pete Dawkins was the finest college player I have ever seen. The much-advertised duel between Hawkins and Dawkins never developed. Army went undefeated that year, and Pete Dawkins won the Heisman Trophy. The biggest mismatch, however, was Warren Giese vs. Red Blaik. Vince Lombardi, who had coached under Blaik, called him the greatest coach he had ever worked with, and I have no reason to doubt it. The lonesome-end was a professional football formation that the colleges hadn't tried yet. Our 5–4 defense couldn't possibly contain this offense, but it was all that we had. Red Blaik had made history—at my expense.

Two weeks later we lost to North Carolina, 6–0. All I saw in that game was an eight-man line. We had to punt the ball thirteen times.

About that time, I made a crucial mistake. I started thinking. I was not a student of the game, but I knew that we were doing things the hard way. For the past three years, we had shown only one offense. The ball was always snapped on the count of two. Every day in practice we ran 225 live plays. Since we only had 8 different plays, this meant we had run every play twenty-eight times every day for the past three years. If I knew our offense backwards and forwards, then so did our opponents.

It finally occurred to me what my problem was. Giese and his system were boring me to death. This caused me to make an even bigger mistake; I started taking myself seriously. I decided that since I was captain of the team, I would have a talk with Giese about his oversimplified system. So I went to Giese's office for a conference. My first suggestion was that we pass the ball more. When he refused that suggestion, I requested that he change quarterbacks in favor of one with a little more imagination. When this idea was coldly rejected, I stormed out of his office, but not before I had slammed his national championship souvenir football from Jim Tatum down on his desk and resigned as team captain. This caused both of us some confusion, because neither of us knew what it meant.

Giese summoned the other two captains to his office to discuss the situation. First he informed them of my rather unusual behavior and then went on to speculate that there might be something seriously wrong with one of the team's tri-captains. Since I was the only captain not present, Dixon and Keith were able to figure out that he had me in mind. Giese got more explicit by suggesting that I might be undergoing a nervous breakdown. He even went so far as to predict that I would either end up in a straitjacket or become a millionaire, a forecast that was as baffling to them at the time as it is to me today. Dixon and Keith were totally confused. To put an end to the rather bizarre conversation, they suggested that everyone involved should forget the events of the day, and that probably I would, too. The meeting was then adjourned.

After I had slammed Giese's trophy ball on his desk and stalked out of the room, I too was questioning my somewhat erratic behavior. All Giese was trying to do was run his football team, while all I was trying to do was run his football team for him. He was clearly in the right, and I was clearly in the wrong, so why shouldn't I admit it? I was aware that I was overreacting. There was absolutely no reason for such excessive, compulsive, and exaggerated behavior on my part. I was definitely wrong. I therefore took the only course open to someone of my mental and emotional maturity. I stopped talking to Giese.

We were scheduled to play Clemson that week in a "Big-Thursday" match-up at the State Fair. Because I was not from South Carolina, this game was never a big thing to me. In the three years I had been there we hadn't beaten Clemson. As a matter of fact, we hadn't even scored against them.

This time, a really strange thing happened in that game. We were trailing 6–0, with just over three minutes to play in the first half. All of a sudden our quarterback took the snap from center, dropped straight back, and threw a forward pass to a wide receiver a good thirty yards behind their secondary. We scored and went in to the locker room at halftime tied at 6–6.

It had taken nearly three full years, but, as God is my witness, we had finally discovered the forward pass. The play must have blown Tiger coach Frank Howard's mind. Not only did we have a forward pass play, we had actually completed one! This death-defying maneuver opened up our running game and we destroyed Clemson, 26–6. We did not have to use our "trick" play again.

My worst suspicions had been realized. We were every bit as good a football team as I had thought. With the aid of a passing offense, we could have beaten every team we had played against for the past three years, with the probable exception of Army.

My resentment of Warren Giese was intensified. Someone had to be held responsible for this gross misappropriation of talent. I took it upon myself to act as both judge and jury.

It had been well over a week since I had spoken to Giese when Ernie Lawhorn took me aside. "Why are you not talking to Giese?" he asked.

"I don't like him," I answered.

"Alex, Warren asked me to find out why you weren't speaking to him. I can't go back and tell him that."

"Yes, you can," I argued. "You just tell him that I'm not going to talk to him because I don't like him."

After practice that day, Warren called Ernie in. "Did you find out what's wrong with Alex, why he's not speaking to me?"

"He just told me that he wasn't speaking to you because he doesn't like you," Ernie answered.

"That's very strange," said Giese, "very strange indeed."

Life is too short to hold grudges, so twenty-six years later I finally starting speaking to Warren Giese again.

A loss to Maryland the following week kept us out of the Orange Bowl. To atone for this loss I quit going to classes. We won the remaining four games to finish with a 7–3 record. In the last game I bowed out by throwing three touchdown passes. When I returned to my dorm the following Monday, I found my bags were already packed and waiting outside. The housing director had been notified by the administration that due to excessive absences I was no longer a student at the University of South Carolina.

12

I moved in with a fraternity brother who lived just off campus and waited for the pro football college draft, which back then was held the last week in November. I had been selected Player of the Year in the Atlantic Coast Conference, so it was generally understood I would go high in the draft. All that fall I had been receiving mail from the Los Angeles Rams and Detroit Lions. Pete Dawkins was the only player I had seen who was better than I was, and as far as I was concerned, making it in pro ball would present no problem.

At the time I couldn't have named five pro football players. I knew that movie star Jane Russell was married to Rams quarterback Bob Waterfield. I liked the Rams' helmets, and the idea of dating starlets in Hollywood was not altogether offensive to me, either. I was pretty sure the Rams would draft me.

In those days there was nothing sophisticated about the college draft. The various teams would send out forms, which you would personally fill out and return, concerning your height, weight, and speed. I couldn't wait to be notified that the Rams had selected me in the first round.

When the call came through, it wasn't from Los Angeles, but from Green Bay, Wisconsin. I was sick at my stomach. The Green Bay Packers. Good God! The worst team in pro football! Last year they had won only one game. People didn't get drafted by the Packers, they were exiled there.

I didn't even know where Wisconsin was. Before I returned their call I rushed out to look at a map. After throwing up a couple of times, I called Jack Vainisi, their administrative assistant, who congratulated me on having been the first person drafted in the second round. Since there were only twelve teams in the NFL, this made me the thirteenth best player in the country. If I was that good, why did I have to go to Green Bay?

Jack told me he would fly down to Columbia the next day to talk over my contract. When he arrived I met him in his hotel room, and if I'd ever seen a man in distress, it was Jack Vainisi. He was nervous and sweating, clearly beside himself. He explained that his child was seriously ill, and he needed to get back to Green Bay as soon as possible. He offered me a contract for $11,000, and agreed to advance me $1,000 of that contract if I would sign immediately.

What did I know about contract negotiating? The average salary in the NFL was $9,500, he said, but he was willing to go higher, because their number one pick, Randy Duncan, had signed with the Canadian League, which was the only option a player enjoyed at that time. Just the day before, Clemson's coach, Frank Howard, had called me to say that he could get me a $15,000 contract from Montreal of the Canadian League. When I told this to Vainisi he warned me that if I went to Canada I would never be heard of again, and that I might even end up losing my American citizenship. I didn't want to lose my citizenship, and the thought of never being heard of again was even worse. So on December 18, 1958, the Green Bay Packers announced the signing of a fast, powerful running back from South Carolina named Hawkins.

I cashed the Packers' check, asked for 500 one-dollar bills, put them in the trunk of Libby's car, and drove around town paying off my debts to local merchants and friends. I would open the trunk, count out the cash, then close the trunk, and go on my way. Libby didn't say anything, but she looked at me suspiciously. I think she already knew I was not altogether a well person.

The day after Christmas I went to Mobile, Alabama, to play in the Senior Bowl game. On a scale of one to ten, my confidence was now at a solid ten. I had been the best player in the state of West Virginia in high school, the best player in four states in college. I was now prepared to become the best football player in the world.

The North team was coached by Joe Kuharich, of the Washington Redskins, and our Southern team was coached by a little man named Paul Brown, of the Cleveland Browns. At our first meeting, this Paul Brown addressed the team as follows: "The winning team gets five hundred dollars. The losing team gets three hundred dollars. You can start spending your five hundred, because I can beat Joe Kuharich with a team of trained monkeys."

I didn't know a thing about pro football, or about this meticulously dressed little man named Brown, but I did admire his confidence. When we studied under Paul Brown, we did just that. He was brilliant. This was the first classroom that I ever paid attention in. There were no plays handed out. We took notes at every position, offense and defense. His meeting room was his classroom, and Paul Brown was the professor of football.

We had only twenty-five players on each team, so everyone was expected to learn every play from every position. I was scheduled to start at defensive cornerback, but I was told I would also play offensive halfback.

One day Paul Brown was going over the offensive guards' assignments when he noticed I wasn't making notes. "Why aren't you taking this down?" he inquired.

"Because I don't play offensive guard," I shot back. "If I have to play offensive guard, we might as well forfeit," I said.

Brown studied me solemnly for a moment, then softly he said, "Hawkins, you're a dog, and you'll never make it in the NFL." I've admired him ever since for being the first person to realize that. Still, he played me on defense in the Senior Bowl, and of course we beat Joe Kuharich and the North team, inasmuch as Brown had already willed it to be so.

My experience with Paul Brown had not been pleasant, but there was something remarkable about this man, even though I felt certain that I could never play for him. He was about as much fun as a traffic jam, but I had to admit that he commanded respect. He had a definite quality about him.

Still, I could not forgive him for calling me a dog. The very idea of his telling me that I'd never make it in the pros—what did he know about it? Who did he think he was, and just exactly what had he ever done?

Later I found out that I had played for a football genius, the dean of football coaches. Paul Brown was a legend in his own time. He had started as a coach at Massilon High School in Ohio, and, while there, he had won 89 percent of his games before going to Ohio State, where he won the national championship in just his second year. From there, he went to Cleveland to coach a team in the new All-America Conference. The Browns, named after him, went to the championship games eleven times in twelve years in both the AAC and then the NFL.

An innovator, Paul Brown was the first coach to call plays for his quarterback. Virtually every new play that came into the league was Paul Brown's conception. He was the first to use year-round coaches, the first to design face bars for helmets, the first to use psychological testing on his players, and the first coach of the modern era to employ black athletes in the pros. For well over a decade he supplied the rest of professional football with quality players who could not live up to his own high standards on and off the field.

To list a few of the coaches who learned their football directly under the tutelage of Paul Brown, there were Chuck Noll, Don Shula, Bud Grant, Weeb Ewbank, and Bill Walsh. Imagine how foolish I felt when I found out all this.

While there in Mobile I sat in the hotel lobby watching a football game on a television set. The Baltimore Colts and the New York Giants were in overtime, playing for the championship of the NFL. I watched the Colts' quarterback, John Unitas, take his team down the field. He certainly wasn't graceful, and his passes were wobbly, but somehow they found their way into the hands of an equally awkward-looking receiver named Raymond Berry.

Then I watched a lumbering fullback named Alan Ameche make his way up the middle of the field for big yardage on a draw play. Then, although within easy field-goal range, Unitas risked an interception and completed a pass to Jim Mutscheller, who went out of bounds at the one-yard line. I couldn't believe it. On the next-to-last play of the game, Ameche, the plodding one, stumbled over the right side of the line and fell into the end zone with the winning touchdown. The Baltimore Colts were World Champions.

The fans and the announcers were going crazy, and it was exciting, but I was far from impressed. If these people I had just watched were going to be my competition, then I had nothing to worry about. Such was the arrogance and ignorance of a twenty-year-old know-it-all.

13

The University of South Carolina honored my scholarship, so I enrolled for the spring term. However, I wasn't any more serious about my studies than before, so by the middle of March I had dropped out of school again.

With the aid of my new bankroll I discovered Columbia, South Carolina's night life. South Carolina was dry, but I could get mixed drinks at the private clubs scattered throughout the city. Each of these clubs had a nightly poker game. During the war years, professional gamblers had come to Columbia from all over the country to gamble with the soldiers at Fort Jackson. The poker games were honest; they didn't have to be dishonest. These were expert card players, professional gamblers, who were there working. I was just there playing, having fun.

No one drank at these games except Bright Stevenson and myself. We seemed to be more aggressive than the other players. We stayed later, drank more whisky, told more stories, played more hands, had more fun, and lost more money than the rest of the players. We figured we were more competitive. The other gamblers must have really liked us, because it got to where they wouldn't even start the games until Bright and I arrived. We stayed up most of the night and slept the next day.

The routine that I had established for myself was beginning to tell on me. For one thing, I was putting on weight. That didn't worry me, because I had to be big to play in the pros, anyway. What did worry me was that Libby was concerned. This reversal of my nights and days couldn't be good, she said. She told me that it just wasn't natural for a man to live the life of a dog. Oh, oh! That made twice in a year that I had been referred to as a dog, and both times by people whom I respected.

Then suddenly Catfish passed away. I had never shown him the love and attention he deserved, and now he was gone. This hurt me more than I liked to admit. Catfish had worked very hard for all those years just to provide for us. He had never asked for a thing for himself; everything he had ever done was for others. In my book that made him a pretty big man.

It was time to take a good long hard look at myself. I did not like what I saw. I had been a giant pain in the rear end to anyone in a position of authority. I had dropped out of school in both the fall and spring terms. I had failed English and Spanish, and both in the same semester. I didn't even have a language I could speak well except "deal." I had dissipated my body and finances. All in all, I could see, I had turned into a selfish, no-good, sorry bum who was headed nowhere. I was paying a high price for low living.

I confronted Libby with these descriptions of myself, and she admitted that she could not disagree with my assessment. Then she bowled me over by suggesting that we get married.

Marriage was the last thing on my mind. I was not responsible for myself, and I certainly didn't want additional responsibility. Being married to Libby would be a no-win situation, I thought. If I were as worthless as we both agreed that I was, how could I live with a saint? Libby Bagnal did nothing wrong whatsoever; she lived an orderly, Christian life. It was plain that we had nothing in common.

As a stalling tactic, I asked her why she was willing to marry me. "Number one," she responded, "I will be graduating soon, and I do not want to go back to Manning and teach school for thirty-six hundred dollars a year."

"Number two," she continued, "I love you."

"Number three," she stated matter-of-factly, "I honestly do not think you can look after yourself."

I had already learned that when we disagreed on anything, Libby was usually right. It would be so easy for her to settle down; the only thing she would have to change was me. And moreover, I didn't think I could look after myself, either. So we were married. And we still are.

The Green Bay Packers had located a furnished house for us,

not far from Lambeau Stadium. I reported to St. Norbert's College, just outside of Green Bay where the Packers trained. No one ever brought their wives to town until preseason was over and the rosters were set for the year. The veterans wouldn't violate this code, and for a rookie to do so was unpardonable. This breach of etiquette did not endear me to anybody.

There were only twelve teams in the NFL in 1959, as compared to the twenty-eight teams today. There are nearly 1,400 pro jobs today, as compared to 432 back then. With so few positions open, the competition was very intense. There was really only a slight difference between the players who stayed and the ones who were sent back home. A man not only had to be good to be kept on those 36-man rosters, but compatible as well. Problem players were not tolerated.

In our first meeting Vince Lombardi, who had just taken over as coach, set the record straight. "Welcome to the Green Bay Packers," he said. "From this day forward, I want you to concern yourself with only three things and they are in this order: your God, your family, and the Green Bay Packers."

Vince explained what he expected, or rather, demanded of us. He talked of love, family, pride, character, and winning. He spoke of sacrifice, singleness of purpose, mental toughness, and the importance of ignoring pain and playing with injuries. He went on for quite some time about what was required of us if we were to become Green Bay Packers. If I understood him correctly, what he was looking for was a combination of Gary Cooper and Red Adair.

It was obvious that he believed what he said, but he was fanatical about it. He was consumed with an almost superhuman desire to excel. He appeared to be frantic to get started. Lombardi was a great communicator of human emotions; his facial expressions conveyed his every feeling. He was simple and direct, fundamental and elemental; I could see in his eyes that a fire burned inside the man.

There is no one else I've ever known who was quite like him. When a man can hold you numb with a look, strum your heart with a smile, make your day with a pat, or ruin your life with a frown, you will know you have just met the reincarnation of Vincent T. Lombardi.

I looked around that meeting room and what I saw was fear, respect, and resolve. I felt the same way. But how was one man going to accomplish his lofty goals with this bunch of losers? Last season this was not only the worst team in the league, but the worst team in the entire history of the Green Bay Packers. There was no doubt that Vince was a strong-willed and powerful person, but to attain the goals he had mentioned, he would have to be even better than Paul Brown. If that were the case, it scared me to think of how much fun I was going to miss, playing for this man.

The Packers practiced in Green Bay, about fifteen miles from St. Norbert's. I knew Libby would be there for our first practice, and I couldn't wait to tell her about this strange person. Bobby Jackson was a rookie from Ole Miss whom I had played with in the Senior Bowl. We sat together on the bus ride into town. Bobby was as taken aback as I was about Lombardi. Bobby was wide-eyed as he whispered, "Does that man scare you like he scares me?" I was too numb to say anything except the obvious: "He sure does." Looking around the bus, I could tell that we were not alone in our fear.

We dressed at Lambeau Field, where the Packers play their games. Practices were held on an adjoining field, just across the street. Lombardi was walking just ahead of Bobby and me. On the way he spotted two linemen making their way to practice. "Both of you are fat and out of shape," he told them. "Neither of you looks like a Packer. Turn in those uniforms, you are dismissed."

Neither of them argued or objected. They turned right around and did as Vince told them. Whoever they were, they were the first two Packers to be cut by Vince Lombardi at Green Bay.

That summer, it was unusually hot in Green Bay, with the temperature soaring well into the nineties. Lombardi must have loved this, because we were about to learn about mental as well as physical toughness. Practices were only about an hour and a half long, but we must have spent half of that time doing grass drills. We would run in place, drop to the ground when signaled, then bounce back up, and run in place again. This seemed to go on forever, but nobody ever quit. The only thing I liked about these grass drills was that as long as I was running in place, nobody could tell how slow I was.

As he walked among us, Lombardi would call out, "I know you're tired and I know it hurts, but this is what it takes to be a Green Bay Packer." He was trying to make us feel special about being a Packer. What was so special about a 1–10–1 team?

I was just about to drop when Lombardi finally halted these drills. I felt sure they were done only to get our attention on the first day of practice. I was mistaken; they went on for as long as Lombardi coached at Green Bay.

That first day we put in only two plays. We ran them over and over. The following day we added two more. This went on for a week or so, until Lombardi announced that the offense was complete. I couldn't believe it. Paul Brown had used more plays than that in the Senior Bowl.

I had nothing to compare the Packer personnel with, but it was obvious that these guys were good. I concerned myself with the running backs, and in no time I became very concerned. Lombardi had moved the former Heisman-Trophy-winner Paul Hornung from quarterback to halfback. Jim Taylor was young, but determined and powerful. Veterans like Don McElhaney, Hal Carmichael, and Howie Furgeson were pressing for their jobs. Rookies like Tim Brown, Don Smith, and George Dixon were all running ahead of me. Lew Carpenter seemed to play every position on the offensive team. We knew that only four runners would make the team. I didn't like my chances.

The offensive line had Jim Ringo at center, Jerry Kramer and Fuzzy Thurston at guards, and Forrest Gregg and Bob Skoronski at tackles. The tight end was Ron Kramer, and the wideouts were Max McGee and Boyd Dowler. The quarterback would soon be Bart Starr. The Packers were loaded with talent, and just waiting for a man like Vince Lombardi to come in and take them over.

The only time I ever saw Libby was for a couple of minutes after each practice. I was miserable with worry. What a humiliation it would be, to be cut by the last-place Packers. Who would consider picking me up? Maybe I could catch on with a Canadian team. I knew I could not get back into school, and certainly I did not want to go to work. The *only* thing I wanted to do was play football, and I wasn't good enough. The harder I tried, the worse I got. I was not a person to be pressured, and I was pressuring myself, and Vince Lombardi was helping. Somehow I had to make Vince understand that you don't have to motivate an overachiever.

In that first meeting he had told us to pay no attention to anything he said to us on the field when he was angry. He assured us that he wouldn't even remember it himself, once practice was over. He apologized for being overly emotional, but he also made it clear that he could not change.

I had never had people scream or even raise their voices at me—not until Lombardi. That man was driving me crazy. He would stand toe-to-toe with us and scream at the top of his lungs. Spit would fly out of his mouth, along with the most unflattering remarks concerning our IQ, parentage, and place of origin. As soon as he finished, he would forget it, just as he had said. But I couldn't. I wanted to crawl up on my mother's lap, put my head on her bosom, and sob. If this was real life, it was entirely too cruel for me.

It was not that Vince was singling me out. It was just that I was a little boy trying to play a man's game. Everybody was scared except Paul Hornung, Max McGee, and Emlen Tunnell. Somehow what Lombardi said and did never seemed to bother them. They let it roll off their backs.

I was trying to cover up my fears by acting flip and cocky. I don't think I fooled anyone, but I did manage to upset the veteran players. Back then, you were considered a rookie until *after* the first game of your second season. Rookies were made to sing for their supper. At the evening meals, first-year players were asked to stand up and sing their college alma mater. I honestly didn't know we had one, so I declined to oblige. Rookies never drank beer with the veteran players after practice. I did, without giving it so much as a thought. Rookies were never invited to play in the poker or boraye games. I invited myself, and ignored their harassment. And after a while they even came to accept me. Well, to be quite truthful, they never actually accepted me; they allowed me to play because I was the worst boraye player in camp.

It was at one of these poker games that I realized who the team leader was going to be. Jim Ringo was the team captain, but on a team like that, being captain meant next to nothing, because everybody was so afraid of Vince Lombardi. One evening, Paul Hornung walked into a room where a poker game was in progress. He produced no money, but laughed, made room for himself, and went light on the ante. There were no objections, and he continued to play. No one ever questioned Paul, or doubted his word. All knew that he would make good on his debt. Ringo was their captain, but Paul was their leader.

This was a losing Packer team; make no mistake about it. They were scared and unsure, and they talked like losers and thought like losers. On August 14, 1959, we were watching the world champion Baltimore Colts play the college All-Stars in Chicago. Fuzzy Thurston, who had just been traded over from the Colts, remarked, "You just can't run against those Colts, nobody can. Who's going to block Big Daddy Lipscomb?" Jerry Kramer chimed in that he was certain he could not block Art Donovan, not even once. Hank Gremmiger admitted that he could not sleep on the night before he played against Lenny Moore. Jesse Whittenton marveled at the way John Unitas looked right and threw left to Raymond Berry without so much as a glance.

To a man, the Packers were singing the praises of the Baltimore Colts. I was disgusted with the whole bunch of them. I went back to my room and scratched my hives. I hadn't slept well in a couple of weeks. Lombardi's tirades were getting the best of me.

14

We played our first preseason game in Milwaukee. There was nothing for me to get excited about. I knew my number would not be called. With Lombardi we had to earn the right to play in a game, and I had definitely not done so yet.

After that first preseason game, we practiced only once a day. Half of those dreaded grass drills were behind me. I thought that half of Lombardi's screaming was behind me, too, but that was not so. I screwed up twice as much. What I did not know at the time was that most pressure is self-imposed.

We broke camp after that week of training. I said good-bye to St. Norbert's College. In those days, when the Packers went on the road for preseason they stayed wherever they played. I was not getting to see Libby much, anyway, and while she had not said so, she doubted that I would be staying with Green Bay. She said she thought she might go home for a while and visit her family. We had driven her car up here, but her parents had sent her an airplane ticket home. I should point out that her parents had not been overjoyed at having me as a son-in-law. Getting their daughter back was worth forfeiting her car, they must have decided. It was a deal. It would help out with our finances too, because at that time players didn't get paid for their time in training camp. The only pay was fifty dollars per preseason game, and we had only played one game.

Libby must have been lonely, because only a couple of the players lived year-round in Green Bay. She had met and become friendly with Marie Lombardi, and Marie had offered to have Libby come and live with her while we were on the road. I had never met Marie Lombardi, but I figured if she was anything like Vince, Libby would end up getting screamed at, so I had advised her against it.

We were going to San Francisco to play the 49ers, and since I had never liked discipline, regimentation, or confinement, the break in routine was welcome. I found that the West Coast agreed with me. My limbs were looser, and my sad look turned into a smile.

What impressed me about the game was how old the 49ers' quarterback, Y. A. Tittle, looked. He was bald. Hugh McElhany and Joe Perry looked old, too, and they were stars. If someone could play this game at their age, then maybe I was making more out of it than was there. My spirits were lifted.

Next it was on to Portland, Oregon, just to play the Philadelphia Eagles. Pro football was starting to be fun. Now that I was relaxing, my play was showing signs of improvement. I loved being on the road. The days, which had previously dragged at St. Norbert's, were now speeding by. The great Northwest was beautiful country. The trees and sky seemed so much bigger out there. Was it possible? Everything looked so clean, lush, and fresh. I had come a long way from South Charleston, West Virginia.

One afternoon I stepped into a bar and spotted Emlen Tunnell sitting alone, having a beer. Emlen was the oldest member of the Packers, in his middle thirties. He had come into the league in 1948, and had moved to the Packers from the Giants along with Lombardi. He was what Vince referred to as a great clubhouse information man.

Em was the communication link between Lombardi and his players. After eleven great years with the Giants as a defensive safety and punt returner, he was nearing the end of his career. He was "street smart" and he loved Vince Lombardi. He also loved pro football and New York City. In 1967 Emlen Tunnell would be the first black player inducted into the pro football Hall of Fame.

Emlen was a black man at the time when pro football was a white man's game. The year before Lombardi came to the Packers, Nate Borden had been their only black player. I don't think any

NFL team had more than five blacks on its roster, and most teams had fewer. The Washington Redskins had none. The word around the league was that any team with more than three blacks on its roster was asking for trouble. In those days, that was the prevailing thought.

As we talked, I realized that this was the first black man with whom I had ever had a conversation. I had talked with blacks before but had never had a real sit-down session. Emlen said pro football had been good for him, that he had made more money than the average guy and had seen more places than he ever thought he would. The first three years were the toughest, he told me. If I could hang on for three years, I could probably play for ten. And where else could I make this kind of money doing something I loved?

He loved New York because, as he put it, "Nobody cares if you're black, white, or green. All they want to know is who are you, who needs you, and what's your road game?"

Vince Lombardi had been a head coach at St. Cecilia's High School in New Jersey for six years while he was attending law school at Fordham. While there Vince had won thirty-six straight games and six state titles. After that he had been an assistant coach at West Point under Red Blaik, before joining Jim Lee Howell with the Giants.

"You've got to understand," said Emlen, "This guy has waited a long time for a head coaching job, and he knows what he wants to do. Vince wants a lot and he's got a lot he wants to do and say. I'm here to help him. He's a hell of a man." From then on, I looked at Lombardi very differently.

We moved on to Bangor, Maine, to play the New York Giants. How many twenty-one-year-olds get to see so much of the country? Emlen Tunnell was right, pro football was a great game, once you learned to relax and enjoy it.

When we came on the field that night, I saw Charlie Conerly holding snaps for the Giants' place kicker, Pat Summerall. His hair was gray, and his face looked like it had worn out three bodies. I was shocked at how old he looked. How could anybody bring himself to hit an old man like that? Little did I know at the time, but Charlie was as tough as a two-dollar steak.

The next-to-last preseason game was in Winston-Salem, North Carolina. Week by week the squad had been gradually reduced, and it was getting close to the cutting edge. We were down to forty-two players, and Vince felt it was time to see whether I deserved to be one of the thirty-six who would make the squad.

That night I was the starting halfback. The way Vince worked things was that anyone who started the game played the entire first half. If for any reason Vince replaced a player before the half ended, the man replaced could pretty well bet that he would be on the waiver list the following Monday. In those days it was rare for more than three rookies to make the team, and we still had half a dozen or so. This was my chance.

Just before the game somebody gave me an amphetamine capsule and told me it would help me. It was a big black capsule that was referred to as an "L.A. Turnaround," a term meaning that a truck driver could take one in New York and drive to Los Angeles and back without going to sleep.

I was in the starting backfield with Paul Hornung, Jim Taylor, and Bart Starr, all three of whom would later be enshrined in the Hall of Fame in Canton, Ohio. The first play was a reverse, with me carrying the ball and Max McGee having to make the key block. The key to any reverse is speed, of which I had precious little, while McGee was not known for his blocking. When we broke the huddle Max said, "Good luck."

I was dropped for an eight-yard loss, and things went downhill from there on. Before the first quarter ended Lombardi took both Bart Starr and me out of the lineup. I was sitting on the bench trying to collect my thoughts, which by now were somewhere around Kansas City. The pill had worked. I heard this sniffling and crying, and when I looked to see where it was coming from I saw Bart Starr sitting down from me sobbing. "He took me out," he said. "He took me out of the game."

Well, he had taken me out of the game, too, and I knew my fate. It was late in the preseason; who was going to pick up a rookie who couldn't even make the Packers team?

I looked at Bart sitting there crying, and remembered what Vince had said about quarterbacks: "Of all the people on your ball club—and you are involved with them all—there is no other with whom you spend as much time as you do with your quarterback. This is a game through which you find self-expression, and if it isn't, you don't belong in it. Then the quarterback is the primary extension of yourself and he is your greatest challenge." If Vince Lombardi wanted a great challenge, he had one sitting right there beside me, crying.

We headed back to Milwaukee, where we were to train for the final preseason game. We were having breakfast on Monday morning when coach Bill Austin, known as the Turk, tapped Babe Parilli on the shoulder, told him that Coach Lombardi wanted to see him in his office, and to bring his play book. This was the gentle way of saying you are no longer with this club. No further explanation was necessary.

When this happens, the room gets deathly quiet. Minutes later the Turk put his hand on my shoulder. In all of football there is no feeling like it. You are not needed, not necessary, not wanted.

I went to my room, got my playbook, and entered Lombardi's office. "I guess you know why you are here," he spoke. "I'm trying to find you a job with another team. Pittsburgh has shown some interest and I'm checking with the Canadian League, but it's late. Good luck to you and I mean that."

I had to have the last word, of course, so I said, "I'll be seeing you around." I didn't really think I would, but I had to say something.

I was in my room when Babe Parilli came in and offered me a ride back to Green Bay. His wife was driving down to pick him up. We wanted to clear out at once. Nobody cares to be around a player that has just been released. It's as if he has a disease that may be contagious.

In all those weeks of training Babe and I had not been close but from our ride back, nobody would ever have imagined it. We bought a case of beer—making sure first that it was not a Wisconsin brand—and sat in the back seat sprint-drinking for the hour-and-a-half ride. We consoled each other with how unfair it was. What a stupid mistake Lombardi was making. By the time we reached my house, Parilli had me believing I was an All-Pro, and I had him convinced that he was All-World. Misery loves company. I went right on drinking at home. I didn't try any of the bars in Green Bay, because nobody would want to befriend a recently released Packer.

It was late morning when I finally answered the telephone, which was ringing away. It was Babe Parilli. "You lucky dog," he said. "Haven't you heard? You've been traded to the Baltimore Colts!" I was speechless. From a last-place to a first-place team, and I had nothing whatever to do with it. "Call the Packers' office and they'll tell you about it." Parilli said. "You lucky son of a gun."

Before I could get my head clear the phone rang again. This time it was Don Kellett, general manager of the Colts. "When can you get here?" he asked. I explained that I had to do something with the house, and that I would be driving, but I could be there on Thursday. He told me to go straight to practice at the stadium when I arrived.

On the day I was cut I hadn't even talked to Libby; I didn't know what to say. Now I picked up the phone and called her to tell her the good news. She told me to go ahead and load up the car with our belongings, which consisted of a seventeen-inch television set, some summer clothes, a few dishes, and pots and pans, and she would be in Green Bay by 6:00 P.M.

The plane was late, and she didn't arrive until midnight. She got off the plane, climbed into the car, and we headed off into the night. I was driving, and after a while I fell asleep at the wheel. Then Libby took over, until just outside of Milwaukee she too ran off the road. After that we decided to check into a motel. She had not slept the night before for worrying about me, while I was hungover and tired from being up late. The pattern was to follow us for years to come.

I called Don Kellett the next morning to tell him about the delay. I couldn't imagine why he seemed so upset with me. "Listen to me," he said. "Either you get here today or don't bother to come at all. We want to see you work out before we leave for Louisville on Friday. It's your only chance to make the team. There are still three more cuts to be made. Take the next flight you can get for Baltimore, and your wife can join you later. Work it out on your own, but you better get here today. Call my secretary and tell her what flight you're on, and someone will meet you at the airport." He hung up.

The last and only flight for Baltimore left from Chicago, sixty miles away, at 1:30 P.M., and it would be close, but if we hurried I could make it. We got in the car and headed for Chicago's Midway Airport. When we arrived at the airport I had only ten minutes to make the flight. I opened the trunk of the car, got out my suitcase, threw some dirty clothes in it, slammed the trunk on a shirt, and started my dash for the terminal.

"What to do? Where to go?" Libby was screaming as I headed for the terminal on a dead run.

"I'll call you," I yelled to her.

"Where are you going to call me?" she asked.

"Go to my mother's in West Virginia!" I yelled back as I entered the door.

I looked back at Libby, standing there with tears running down her face, waving good-bye. When I got to the plane the door was closing. As we taxied to the runway I looked out of the window, and there was Libby, still waving good-bye. She had only met my mother once. Here was this sweet little thing, left alone in Chicago with twenty dollars in her purse. I had fifteen dollars, but a chance at a job.

On my plane ride to Maryland I had a chance to think. Who and what was with this Don Kellett? What kind of talk was that, "Get here today or don't come at all. Work it out on your own"? I had never worked anything out on my own, so why should I start now? What kind of people was I dealing with, anyway? First there was the pompous Paul Brown. Then the tyrannical Vince Lombardi. Now it was this dictatorial Don Kellett. Was pro football a game for madmen, and if I stayed around, would I become one, too? Maybe old Emlen Tunnell was right. Pro football was like New York City. "Who are you? Who needs you? What's your road game?"

15

By the time the plane was fully aloft, my confidence level, which at one time had been a solid ten, was now down to around four. No, ma'am, I would not care for one thing. I don't want to be any bother. As you can see, my seat belt is fastened and my seat is in the upright position. Here in my pocket are cigarettes that I normally smoke, but I would not dream of lighting up, for fear of offending someone. I know I should stop smoking, and I shall as soon as I find time to be hypnotized. Yes, I know you can tell by my nose that I've played football, but that was a long time ago and it was a very unpleasant experience. No, sir, I am not unfriendly, it's just that I don't have anything to say that you would find interesting. Besides, my breath is offensive and I'm wearing yesterday's socks.

What had these football people done to me? I felt I had just completed a correctional course for overdeveloped smart alecks. It was as though I had compensated for a slice so much that I had turned it into a duck hook. I had been run out of West Virginia, South Carolina, and now Wisconsin. I felt like a boll weevil; I was just a-looking for a home, but nobody wanted me around.

As we circled over Baltimore, Maryland, to land, I looked down at the city below me. It was old, grim, tired, and run down. Ye gods, déjà vu, it was West Virginia all over again.

At the gate a shabby little man met me and drove me to the Lord Baltimore Hotel. He was the assistant equipment manager. He dropped me off and told me that the head coach, Weeb Ewbank, would be coming to see me after dinner. He handed me a Colt playbook and told me to study it until Weeb got there. He instructed me to sign for anything that I wanted; it was all on the Colts.

The hotel was old but comfortable. I propped myself up in the king-sized bed and began to examine the book. The offensive plays looked just like the ones I had studied at the Senior Bowl. Now this was pro football, not at all like that rinky-dink offense of the Packers. Hell, this playbook was four times as thick as theirs.

There was a knock at the door, and when I opened it there stood a small man with a warm smile and kind, gentle eyes. This was Weeb Ewbank. We talked for a while, and he asked me about the Packers. I had heard that sometimes a team would pick up a player for a rival team, pump him for information, and then release him. I was too smart for that. I told him I knew everything about the Packers, but that it would take too long to tell him now.

Weeb gave me a puzzled look and asked whether I had any questions. I made mention that the offense looked like the one I had learned in Mobile at the Senior Bowl. He admitted as much, and told me he had coached under Paul Brown at Cleveland. He had just spoken to Paul about me that day, he said. That got my attention. When I asked him what Paul had said, he smiled. "Paul said you were a fine football player but needed to do some growing up," he told me.

Weeb then said his good-byes and asked me to report to practice the next morning at eleven. We would leave straight from practice for a game with St. Louis, in Louisville, Kentucky. He marked a dozen or so plays, told me to concentrate on them, and said that I would see action against the Cardinals.

When I arrived at Memorial Stadium the next morning, I saw a statue of Babe Ruth outside it. I was impressed. Green Bay had nothing like this. I went inside the stadium like a little boy going to school for the first time. I asked the equipment man if he had a spare pair of size 11 shoes. In those days you had to furnish your own shoes. I had left Milwaukee in a hurry, I explained, and had forgotten mine. He gave me a knowing smile and promised to find me a pair. He did, but they were a center's shoes. A center puts so much pressure and weight on the outside of his feet when he is snapping the ball the leather on the outside of his shoes soon becomes as soft and as yielding as cloth. So if you put on a pair of his shoes, your feet will literally slide off the outside of the soles. Few people realize that, and I didn't either, until after I had stumbled and fallen down throughout the short practice. The sports writers stood around, shaking their heads and whispering to one another. After practice I told Weeb about the shoes and he was relieved, although not totally convinced. I borrowed a different pair of shoes.

There was a player among the Colts whom I had known from college. On the plane to Louisville I sat beside him and we discussed our experiences in pro ball. Three more players would be released on Monday to round out the squad, but he felt very comfortable. That was strange; why didn't I?

My first roommate with the Colts was No. 44, Bert Rechichar. Why they had paired the two of us was a mystery to me. I came into the hotel room, and offered my name and handshake. He shook my hand and answered in a growling voice, "I'm 44. Listen, I'm going out for a while. I'm going to run the water in the tub in the bathroom. Don't open the bathroom door. If the coaches come by, you tell them I'm taking a bath. I'll see you tomorrow." And for the night No. 44 was gone.

The next morning No. 44 came back into the room. "Anybody come by?" growled 44.

"No," I answered.

"Then turn off the damn water, you jackass." I had let the water run all night long, without so much as opening the bathroom door. I had learned my lesson in Green Bay, and I was going to do exactly what I was told.

It turned out that I didn't play in the game against the Cardinals after all. Weeb Ewbank had apparently made up his mind one way or the other about me. I had to wait until Monday to find out that I was a member of the team. I called Libby at my mother's home in West Virginia and nonchalantly informed her that she could come on up to Baltimore, because I was a member of the World Champion Colts.

In Green Bay, Vince Lombardi had been lord and master of the Packers, serving both as coach and general manager. They had no individual owner, since they are owned by the city. The Colts, on the other hand, were coached by Weeb Ewbank, but owned and controlled by Carroll Rosenbloom. The Packers had been the worst team in football in 1958; the Colts were the world champions. The Colts had John Unitas as quarterback and a host of stars of similar magnitude. The fear, tension, and doubt of the Packers had been replaced by the class and confidence of the Colt organization.

When I had time to study my Colt teammates, I didn't know what to think. Nearly every Packer had been young and athletic in appearance. The Colts were older and, to put it kindly, less Spartan-looking. Compared to the Packers, they resembled a circus troop.

Gino Marchetti looked the part of a player, but he reminded me of L'il Abner. Raymond Berry looked like an undernourished bond salesman. Artie Donovan was wrinkled and old, with hair like a wet possum and a stomach that marched before him by six-tenths of a mile. Alan Ameche was built like a diamond matchbox. Lenny Moore had legs like a great blue heron, and I wondered why they didn't break when he just walked on them. Jim Parker was huge and overweight; he didn't eat, he fed.

As for John Unitas, here was a total mystery. He was from Pennsylvania, but he looked so much like a Mississippi farm hand that I looked around for a mule. He had stooped shoulders, a chicken breast, thin bowed legs, and long dangling arms with crooked, mangled fingers fastened to a pair of very large hands.

The craziest part of it all was that these seven men were All-Pros, and six would later become Hall-of-Famers. When they put uniforms on these naked bodies and practice started, I knew exactly why. There was a light, businesslike air about practices. These were older men going about their business. Six hundred thirty-eight NFL players had served in World War II, and twenty-one of them were killed. Some of these players had been in that war. They had killed, and had seen men die. A game of football was nothing to them. They looked at football as a career. All of them knew it would end one day, but nobody discussed it. These men were hardened professionals.

Weeb was organized but low-keyed. Rarely did he raise his voice. He left most of the actual coaching to his assistants. Unitas ran the offense himself and made most of the corrections. He was a general. The real work began after practice. The receivers would stay on the field and time the pass patterns. Raymond Berry was always the last to leave. He and John would stay on the field for hours. I wondered why John's arm didn't fall off from throwing so much. I never knew him when he didn't have a sore arm.

I was still staying at the hotel until I could find a place for Libby and me to live. She had the car, so I was hitching rides and taking cabs. Carroll Rosenbloom, the owner, offered to drive me downtown, saying that he wanted to talk to me. None of the players had asked me about the Packers. They were more concerned with the Bears and the Rams. I had scarcely closed the car door when Carroll asked, "What kind of a man is Lombardi and what kind of team are the Packers?" I told him that Lombardi was nothing like Weeb. His offense was simple and basic, one that anyone could learn in a day or two. He was a good coach, I supposed, but I hated all that screaming. As for the Packers, there were some damn good athletes on the team. They had a lot of young talent. If they found a quarterback, they could be tough.

Libby and I found a place to live on York Road, near the stadium. The trolley cars shook us awake in the mornings, but it was a place to put our heads down. There were very few apartments available in Baltimore at that time, and we were happy to have one.

Training camp was where you really got to know your teammates, and since I hadn't been with the Colts then, I stayed mostly to myself. There was a lot to learn about the offense, and it was keeping me busy. The veterans were friendly enough during practice, and they didn't harass the rookies, but I was aware of the fact that I was not really a part of the team. They had their own bars, where they gathered for beers after practice. They weren't rude about it, but it was clear that rookies were not invited. They had been World Champions the previous year without me, and I knew that to be a part of the team I would have to prove myself. At Green Bay I had learned that it was better not to assert myself.

This was a great football team. All dreams of becoming a star were discarded. I only wanted to be one of the thirty-six best Colts in the world.

We opened the season at home against Detroit. I was a left halfback, playing behind L. G. DuPre. L. G. was not a gifted athlete, but he was a competitor, and Weeb and the rest of the team had faith in him. I was playing on the special teams, which at that time were not taken very seriously. The defense had stopped the Lions on their first possession and I was on the punt-return team.

When I went out on to the field I was approached by a linebacker named Bill Pellington. Bill was the meanest, dirtiest, most vicious player on our team, if not the entire league. He was not very friendly in the locker room, and there was something about a football field that made him even more hostile. He was on the most-wanted list of every team in football. There is a difference between being mean and being dirty. Bill Pellington was both.

My assignment was to keep their end from getting downfield on the punt coverage. Bill had hands that looked like claws. He had brilliant blue eyes that sat deep in his head, a menacing hawk-like nose, and a cut on his forehead. Blood ran down his face. He looked like a hangman. "Don't you fuck up, rookie," was all he said as he glared at me.

"No, sir, Mr. Pellington, I won't." I was horrified. I would surrender my life before I fucked up.

When the ball was snapped I threw my body at their end, knocking him off his feet. I knew that was not good enough for Pellington, so I held onto his legs to keep him from getting to his feet. Anyone would have thought I had just raped his sister. He scrambled to his feet like a maniac, thunderous blows crossed my head and back, and he was kicking me in the ribs. Then he headed downfield. I got up and followed him until the play was signaled dead. He started back after me like a madman, screaming wildly, "You rookie son-of-a-bitch, if you ever hold me again I will kick your lungs out."

"No, sir," I replied. "No sir, I will never hold you again, I promise."

From then on I had no idea what to do. I was afraid of this nameless opponent, but even more terrified of Bill Pellington. These were crazy people. I hadn't a friend on either team. I wished I was back in my mother's lap again.

We were 4–1, with Green Bay coming to town. On Wednesday of that week L. G. DuPre was lost for the season, which meant that I would be the starting halfback. The Colts activated Mike Sommer, who had been released by the Redskins, as a backup to me. It was a humbling experience to be in the same backfield with Alan Ameche, Lenny Moore, and John Unitas. I felt like an intruder.

I was having a so-so game, until in the third quarter I injured my knee. The injury would sideline me for the next five weeks. After my injury, I could contribute nothing to the team's success. I was on the team, but not a part of it. I felt useless, and I *was* useless. I did have the good sense to stay clear of the veterans. Nobody likes an injured rookie. I went to the training room for treatment, stayed around for a while through the meetings, and left when practice started, so as not to be in the way. I was not even missed, and that upset me, too.

The nighttime hangout bar for the Colts was Sweeney's. For years it had been the most popular bar in Baltimore. It was strictly off limits to the wives. I needed desperately to compete, and my knee would not allow me to do it. I took all my frustrations out on the pinball machine in Sweeney's. I played it for hours at a time. I cursed it and kicked it and pounded on it. I hated that machine.

I got so obsessed with beating that machine that one night I got four hundred nickels and I made the owner lock me inside for the night. I played that machine until ten the next morning.

Libby was getting concerned over my behavior once again, so to bolster my rapidly depleting feelings of self-worth, I told her to buy herself a new coat. It was getting cold about that time, and all the other wives had new raincoats with raccoon collars. She was so excited and looked everywhere for one, but no store had one small enough to fit her. Finally she found one at Robert Hall's for $19.95. She cut the labels out of it and wore it the next five years.

We alternated days driving the car. When she had the car I would call her to come and pick me up. Since wives were not allowed inside Sweeney's, if I was not waiting outside for her when she arrived, she would wait for me across the street at the White Coffee Pot. Once she said that if I didn't quit playing the pinball machine so much she was going to get a job as a waitress there. I looked into it, but she was too short to reach across the counter.

The next week Jim Brown scored five touchdowns against us as Paul Brown handed us our second loss. The very next weekend we lost to the Redskins. With only a twelve-game schedule, four losses would generally eliminate a team from the chance to win a divisional title. We knew we had to win five straight games.

Weeb was so frustrated that he wept in the meeting on Tuesday. "You guys are pissing it away," he cried. "You're too good to just piss it away." As we were leaving the meeting I heard Alan Ameche remark, "What in the hell is Weeb crying about? Let's just win the last five." That kind of confidence inspires leadership. We won the next three games, then headed for the West Coast for two weeks, where we were to play the 49ers and Rams.

We were staying at the Cliff Hotel in downtown San Francisco. The hotel was being repaired, and there was scaffolding on the outside of it. We knew we had to win both games out there, so the pressure was on. That night I went out and had a few beers, but made it back for the 11:00 P.M. bed check.

I was rooming with a rookie from Houston named Hal Lewis. Earlier that evening I had decided to sneak out after bed check. I devised the perfect escape route. The scaffolding only went up as high as the ninth floor. The Cliff Hotel was small with only one elevator and a small lobby. I was on the fourteenth floor, and didn't dare risk using the elevator. The plan was to take the back stairway to the second floor, crawl out a window, and drop from the scaffolding into a pile of sand on the sidewalk at the back side of the hotel. It was a foolproof plan.

I waited for bed check, then dressed again and shot down the hall to the back stairs. When I got to the ninth floor, the stairway was blocked, impassable. No plan is without a hitch, so I improvised. I went out onto the scaffolding on the ninth floor and started climbing down.

There I was, climbing nine floors down the outside of a hotel in downtown San Francisco, and thinking that I wouldn't be seen. When I got to the second floor, the scaffolding ended. No problem; I would drop into the sand. Any fool should have known that they cover sand with boards at night. Until then I hadn't bothered to look down. When I did, a crowd of about fifty people had gathered and was cheering me on. In that crowd were several sports writers from Baltimore. I waved to the crowd, dropped to the sidewalk, and went on my way.

When I returned to the hotel about 4:00 A.M., the Colts had a security officer posted at the elevator. To go up I would have to sign my name and produce my room key. I was caught, and I knew it. I signed my name boldly and searched for my room key. When I opened the door to my room the lights were on. Hal had waited up for me. There are people who enjoy being the bearer of bad tidings and Hal was one of them. "You're caught," he said. "Weeb came up here himself. I tried to cover for you and put a pillow in your bed." On the desk was a note instructing me to come to Weeb's room in the morning.

The next morning I went to Weeb's room. This mild-mannered man had turned into a raving maniac. "I don't know where you were last night or who you were with, but I do know you weren't in your bed. Ordinarily I would kick you off the team right now and let you find your own way home. I can't do that to this team because we don't have another halfback if Sommer gets hurt. I'm trying to find one right now and if I do, you're finished. You have your choice of being fined five hundred dollars or phoning your pretty little wife and explaining to her where you were." Five hundred dollars was more than my weekly take-home pay, so I played that game for nothing.

We won both games on the West Coast and went home to Baltimore to play the New York Giants for the championship.

Pat Summerall had kicked three field goals, and the Giants were ahead, 9–7, in the fourth quarter. They were controlling the game, and had moved the ball into field-goal range once again.

It was fourth-and-one on our twenty-eight-yard line. Rather than settling for the possible three points, they chose to send

Alex Webster, their big fullback, off the right side for the first
down. He was stopped short by Gino Marchetti and Artie Donovan. Had Webster been successful in getting that one yard, there
is no doubt in my mind that the Giants would have been champions. Instead Unitas drove the Colts seventy-two yards for the
score and an eventual 31–16 victory. For the second consecutive
season the Colts were world champions.

Although I had had no intention of ever living in Baltimore, I
had nevertheless fallen in love with the city. True, it was tired,
old, and run down, but the people who lived there more than made
up for that. The people were great, and their love for the Colts
was even greater. It would take me years before I fully understood
how deep and real this love affair was.

Baltimore was the eighth largest city in the United States. A
blue-collar town lined with row houses and neighborhood bars, it
was completely devoid of pretense. Its people had no illusions, pri-
marily because Baltimore was surrounded by Washington, Philadelphia, and New York. Washington has the federal government,
Philadelphia has the history, and New York has New York.

Baltimore was viewed as a redheaded stepchild by these other
cities. At worst, it was looked down upon as inferior. At best it was
ignored. The Colts changed a lot of that. From a ragtag bunch who
moved in from Dallas in 1953 they had risen as champions. They
took on the Redskins, Eagles, and Giants and beat them all. The
Colts became the city's claim to national pride. To Baltimoreans
the Colts were living proof that their city was a better city than
any of these power centers.

From the time the Colts won their first championship in 1958
onward, the people of Baltimore could no longer be scorned or ignored. When an outsider started singing the praises of his city,
the Baltimoreans could and would steer the conversation over to
the Colts, to victory and success. The Colts gave the city a feeling
of achievement and importance, and the city gave the Colts its
love and loyalty. The Colts loved the city and the city loved the
Colts with a passion that scarcely exists in sports any more. It

was a neighborhood affair that will probably never be experienced again in big-time athletics.

From the moment that Alan Ameche scored in overtime against the Giants in 1958, the city of Baltimore belonged to the Colts. Now, with the second consecutive championship under our belts, you cannot imagine what it was like to be a member of the Baltimore Colts.

16

That spring Libby and I spent the off-season with her parents in Manning, South Carolina, a sleepy little community of 3,800 people, sixty-three miles southeast of Columbia. Soon I settled into the routine of everyday life in a small Southern town. Libby's parents had finally learned to accept me, though tolerate might be a better way to put it. After a week during which I slept through most of the day, Mr. Bagnal, my father-in-law, suggested that I learn to fish. There wasn't much else to do in Manning except to fish, hunt, and play bridge. My fall had been pretty much a vacation as it was, so I chose to extend it through the spring.

I could not get back into school, and I was too proud to ask for a job. Now that I was rich, my thoughts turned to becoming an entrepreneur. The winners' share for the '59 championship was $4,674, and Carroll Rosenbloom had matched that amount out of his own pocket, so with almost $13,000 in my bank account I contemplated an investment in real estate.

Just off the coast of South Carolina there was an island that Libby had raved about for years. Her description of the island, with its marsh tackeys, wild monkeys, and beautiful live oak trees, had me entranced. Land on this exotic island could be purchased for $200 to $500 an acre. Although I had never actually seen the island, I had read somewhere in a magazine that ocean-front property was supposed to be a good investment.

I figured that we could drive down, take the ferry over to the island, and pick up twenty-five acres for no more than $300 an acre. That would come to a $7,500 investment, leaving me plenty to live on until next year's championship. I arrived at the figure of twenty-five acres because that was my jersey number with the Colts. I would just go down there, act dumb, and hope that the landowners hadn't read the same magazine I had about the value of ocean-front property.

That night at the dinner table I told my father-in-law my plans. Mr. Bagnal was a farmer, and who knows more about land than a farmer? I was too late, he informed me. Just the year before, a causeway had been built over to the island, and the land was now selling for $1,000 an acre. Some of the beach-front property was going for as much as $2,000 an acre, he said, and I wasn't fool enough to pay that much for island property. I was not about to pay $2,000 an acre for land on Hilton Head Island. (Nowadays the going price for an acre there is $1,000,000 and up.) Every day for over a month, I hunted and fished until I got a call from the C.W. Haynes Company in Columbia, a well-respected, established real estate company, to come to work with them. My Hilton Head venture had opened my eyes to the prospects of real estate, so in March we moved to Columbia.

Somehow I circumvented getting a real estate license, and reported for work. At that time about the only people moving in and out of Columbia were military personnel, and most of our listings were around Fort Jackson. Fort Jackson was located in the sandhill, scrub-oak section of the county, and the houses were moderately priced homes ranging from $7,000 to $11,000. I would be working strictly on a commission basis. For several weeks I rode around with other salesmen, familiarizing myself with their listings. Finally I started showing houses on my own. I got a signed contract on one for $9,600, but the buyer didn't qualify for the loan. I went back to work, and I got yet another contract. Again the buyer failed to qualify. This was disappointing, but I kept at it.

One afternoon I was showing a house to a soldier and his wife who were emphatic about security for their three-year-old son. I had the perfect little one-owner home, with a waist-high cyclone fence in the backyard. It was well within their price range, and I could taste blood. The third time around was the lucky one, I told myself.

We were standing in the backyard and I was extolling the graces of this magnificent estate, when a large black dog belonging to the next-door neighbor leaped over the fence into our yard. The mother quickly scooped up the small child and started for the car. As the dog approached, I tried nonchalantly to detain her by telling her what a fine dog it would be for her son to play with. In a matter of seconds the dog had bitten into the back of my leg, removing my pants from the knee down. The husband was just closing the car door as I dropkicked the fine, friendly canine halfway across the yard. So much for the real estate business.

I couldn't wait to get back to training camp. Pro football was really a very civil way of making a living. As for real estate, it was obviously not my calling, and besides, it was boring.

Needing some action, I returned to the poker games at night. On one particular evening I played until 8:00 A.M. When I got home I opened the door and there stood Libby. She had been waiting up for me and was not at all happy with me. "Where have you been all night?" she demanded.

"Actually, I got home about eleven-thirty last night," I began. "I didn't see any lights on, so I figured you had gone on to sleep. I decided to lie down in the hammock. Libby, the moon was full and every star in the heavens was out last night. It was the most beautiful thing I've ever seen. I guess I fell asleep and just woke up."

"That's all well and good," she said, "but I took the hammock down last week."

I replied, quickly and adamantly, "Well, that's my story and I'm sticking to it."

Libby just stared at me for a few seconds, shook her head, and went to the kitchen and poured me a cup of coffee.

Every athlete dreams of one day playing on a world championship team. I had stumbled into that in my very first year. I should have been satisfied, but somehow I was missing the feelings that should go with this accomplishment. Why did I never wear my championship ring? Was I just a miserable person? I thought about it a lot that spring. It had all happened so fast. It had all been too easy. To have worried so much and worked so hard and still be cut from the Packers, and then to turn around, do nothing, and find myself on a world championship team.

What had really been tearing at me was the fact that I had not contributed one thing to that success. There was a terrible, empty feeling about just being along for the ride. I wanted desperately to be a part of the Baltimore Colts. They were champions two years in a row, but I was not. The deep burn of determination was igniting inside me. Damn it to hell, I would be a part of the next championship season.

17

T he Colts trained at Westminster College, about thirty
miles west of Baltimore. It was not like the Packers'
training camp, where everyone had been so scared and
tense. Here I did not feel like a nameless cog in the wheel of a
Lombardi machine. In the Colt camp there were no signs of pressure, fear, or desperation. The Colts were world champions two
years running, and there was a positive, relaxed, optimistic air
that surrounded the team. We were only thirty miles from Baltimore, and two or three hundred people would attend almost every
practice. "Colt mania" had permeated the area.

Instead of grass drills there were loosening-up exercises. The
emphasis was not on mental toughness or conditioning as much
as on limiting injuries and staying healthy. The Colts were a veteran team with proven players. There was no rush or panic about
getting in shape. The focus was on getting ready for another championship season. The season did not begin until the last week in
September; there would be seven exhibition games preceding our
opener. Only Raymond Berry came to camp physically ready to
play a game.

The year 1960 was the year that the Dallas Cowboys entered
the National Football League. L. G. DuPre had been sent to Dallas
in the player-allocation draft. I thought that would leave the halfback spot open to either Mike Sommer or myself. At our first
practice, I found that I was playing defensive cornerback. I had
always been better as a defensive player, so it didn't upset me at
all.

Playing defensive cornerback against the Colts' offensive team
was not exactly a sinecure. I was trying to cover Raymond Berry,

and it was downright comical. Nobody on our team could cover Raymond. But then, nobody in the league could, either, so I didn't feel bad about it.

Weeb Ewbank delegated most of the coaching responsibilities to his assistant coaches. He might make some corrections, but they were always in a quiet, positive fashion. Practices were organized and relaxed. In short, football was not a life-or-death situation.

There was no dread of training camp with the Colts. Many of the players reported early. It was astounding to me how this grizzled bunch of veterans, who were so terribly serious when we were making our stretch run last fall, had been transformed into giggling little boys romping around like summer campers.

Weeb was nowhere near as dynamic as Lombardi, nor did he command the respect of Paul Brown, but in his own modest way he was very effective. He could recognize talent better than any football coach I have ever seen. Where he had found these people and what he had seen in them were questions that only Weeb Ewbank could answer. Almost half of the Colt players had been free agents or castoffs from other teams. Modest as most of their beginnings were, twelve of these ragtags became All-Pros, and six of these players would be elected into the Hall of Fame.

Being a second-year player on a team like this was akin to being in purgatory. You weren't a rookie, but until the first game had been played you weren't a veteran, either. John Unitas solved my problem. Early in camp he invited me to join him for a beer. When you went anywhere with Unitas, you were automatically accepted. Every man on that team knew the value of John Unitas. With Unitas healthy, they were a championship team. Without John, it was too horrible even to consider. So important was Unitas that for two years, 1959 and 1960, he didn't even have a backup quarterback.

John Unitas was *the* quarterback. No one ever knew or cared what John's salary called for. On his arm rested the hopes of the team. The one cardinal rule on the team was to keep Unitas healthy. To allow John to be hit was a sure one-way ticket home. Without John and his leadership the season was over. It is impossible to exaggerate the blind, unquestioning faith this team had

On one of our family fishing trips. Catfish, shirtless, and the driver are on the front row, with my brother, Jimmy, between them. The driver's wife is at top center, and I'm at top left.

Captain of the All-State Basketball Team, at South Charleston, West Virginia, 1955.

End run, high school football. I'm carrying the ball, and Ron Steele (1) is leading the way.

Jake Bodkin, myself, and our 1927 Reo auto.

King Dixon and myself with a young Gamecock fan.

As University of South
Carolina Gamecock, 1958.
Notice that the Confidence
Level is about a 10.

Atlantic Coast Conference Player of the Year, 1958. Libby Bagnal is making the presentation.

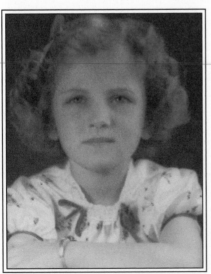 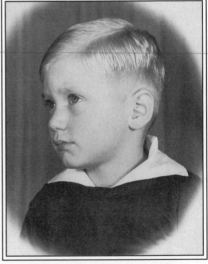

Libby and I were four years old when these photographs were made. Now how in the world was *he* going to look after *her*?

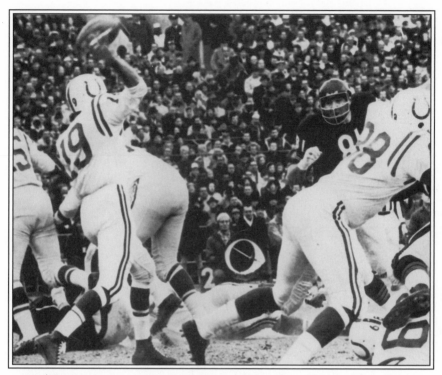

John Unitas in action. Here's the man and the arm that guided the Baltimore Colts to a second NFL Championship the year I joined them. Jerry Hill (45) and John Mackey (88) are providing the protection, and the Chicago Bears' Doug Atkins is trying to get to him.

Weeb Ewbank pictured in friendly discussion with an official.—*Courtesy Weeb Ewbank*

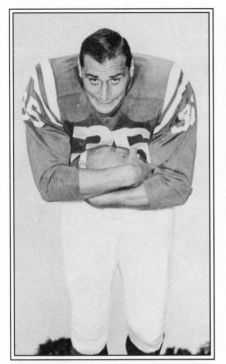

Four Colts. Clockwise, from top left: Alan Ameche, Jim Parker, Bobby Boyd, and Joe Don Looney.

Running the ball with Wendell Harris.

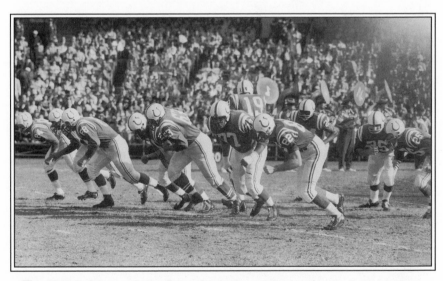

The 1960 Baltimore Colt offense. In the line, left to right: Jim Mutscheller, George Preas, Alex Sandusky, Buzz Nutter, Art Spinney, Jim Parker, and Raymond Berry. Backfield: John Unitas, Lenny Moore, Alan Ameche, and myself.

Colt backfield, 1960. Left to right: myself, Alan Ameche, John Unitas, and Lenny Moore.—*Courtesy* Atlanta Journal-Constitution

At Artie Donovan's retirement ceremony. Gino Marchetti (89), Artie, Bill Pellington, and Lou Grasmick.—*Courtesy John Steadman*

in that man. Greatness can sometimes be measured more accurately not by what one man can do, but rather by what one man can inspire others to do. When John was on the field anything was possible. The Colts didn't just think that; they *knew* it.

Big plays are usually made by big players, and we had plenty of those. Any nine or ten players on that team could and had come up with crucial plays when they were needed. They had both confidence in and respect for each other. Winning does that to a team. Nothing breeds success like success.

The thing that impressed me most of all was their love of the game. They had such a deep respect for the game of professional football that it bordered on reverence. Not one of them played the game for money alone. Not one of them felt the game owed them anything. They were there because they loved what they were doing. In a sense, it was a continuation of childhood, a way to keep from growing up and having to act maturely. This was not a business to them, it was a way of life. These were proud people, and they were proud of the game they played. Every one of these players put more into the game than he took out of it. It was a privilege to play and be associated with these men.

The men who played professional football in the 1950s made very little money, and enjoyed almost no job security. Each player knew that he was expendable. Teams and leagues had folded, or had changed residences like the early Colts. It is a matter of record that in a span of five years the Colts had been located in four cities. In various disguises, the Colts had gone defunct in Baltimore, Boston, New York, and Dallas, before settling back in Baltimore. Three men were responsible for the Colts' success: Carroll Rosenbloom, Weeb Ewbank, and John Unitas. The players were used to playing offense and defense. Nearly everyone played more than one position. What Weeb said time and time again made sense: "The more things you can do, the better chance you have of making the team."

I hadn't been in camp the previous year, so this was all new and exciting to me. You can learn only so much about people during practice and meetings. It is when you drink with them or sit down to a poker game that you can get to someone's core. Stories tend to get stretched a little after a few beers, but I was convinced that the game was a lot more demanding in the 1930s, 1940s, and 1950s than later on. There was something about the 1950s, and the stories that the older Colts told about those times, that was romantic to me. It didn't seem to matter who was telling the story, one man's name always cropped up: Bobby Layne. He seemed to be everybody's hero. Unitas was colorful and flamboyant on the field, but Bobby Layne was colorful both on the field and off. He was the Errol Flynn of football.

No doubt it has been like this since the beginning of time. Things were always a little better, or a little more glamorous, a few years ago. I must admit I enjoyed their stories, but by the same token, life couldn't have been sweeter for me than it was right then. The days flew by. There just wasn't enough time to do everything I wanted.

Ameche was the organizer of the card games, and Donovan held court at the taverns. I didn't join the beer drinkers unless John invited me. Through John I learned the remora-fish theory. A remora is a small fish who attaches himself to a large fish and travels with him on his back. It is a safe, easy, effortless, efficient way to travel. The remora expends no energy and takes no risk, but arrives at his destination at the same time as the large fish. I traveled that way with John whenever I could.

We started the exhibition season with an intrasquad game in Baltimore, with the proceeds of this game going to the Police Boys Clubs of Baltimore. To give an idea of what kind of promoters the Colts were, 50,000 people attended this scrimmage. This game and similar promotions cemented relationships between the Colts and the Baltimore Police Department, which was something that would come in handy, for me in particular, for years to come.

It was after this intrasquad game that I approached Weeb about moving me back to offensive halfback. I was clearly no match for Raymond Berry, or anybody else for that matter. The next week we played the College All-Stars in Chicago. Mike Sommer, our starting halfback, was injured, so I got the starting assignment. Just before the game I went to John Unitas and told him I might be confused with some of my assignments. He said, "Whitey, if there is ever any doubt about what you should do, just stay close to me." It was a lesson that would prove invaluable to me for the next few years. Seeing to the protection of John Unitas was worth a few missed assignments.

The injury to Mike Sommer turned out to be more severe than originally thought, so the job was mine for as long as I could hold it. With only a thirty-six-man roster and thirteen teams, you not only had to be good, you also had to be durable.

The Baltimore Colts were not only a great football team, but a great organization. They not only had top player personnel, but a quality front office as well. From the top to the bottom, the Colts were the class of the NFL. Not every team traveled first class in those days, but the Colts always did. Coats and ties were required as travel dress. We stayed in the finest hotels, and dined in the best restaurants. When we visited a city, the press and media came out to greet us in numbers. When we visited the West Coast, movie stars such as Clark Gable and Mitzi Gaynor were there to have pictures taken with Unitas, Marchetti, and Ameche. The Colts were most definitely America's team.

Carroll Rosenbloom was the owner that every NFL player wanted to work for. He was a knowledgeable football man, having played halfback at the University of Pennsylvania. In fact, the league commissioner, Bert Bell, had coached him in college. It was Bert who had almost forced the franchise on him. Rosenbloom was wealthy, bright, and charming. His business interests were many and varied. They ranged from electronics to railroads, from textiles to motion pictures. He was slick, Rosie was. He could hand-peel a porcupine without getting pricked. He knew how to build an organization, and he knew how to win.

Every person in the Colts' organization was hand-picked by Rosenbloom. When Rosie entered the NFL, he didn't plan to participate; his plans were to dominate. When he couldn't hire Paul Brown or Blanton Collier, he chose Weeb Ewbank, who had worked and studied under Brown for five years. Three of the assistant coaches had also studied under Brown. When he hired Weeb in 1954, he gave him five years in which to win a championship. Five years and eight minutes later, the Colts beat the Giants in overtime for their first world championship.

Down through the ranks of his organization, from trainers and player personnel to equipment managers, everyone was qualified. Perhaps Rosenbloom's greatest acquisition was vice-president and general manager Don Kellett. Like Rosenbloom, Don had played halfback at the University of Pennsylvania. To his credentials were also added professional baseball, college coaching in basketball and football, sportscasting, and television executive chores. Don was a top-flight speaker and particularly gifted in public relations. He was the best general manager I have ever come across.

When I went to Kellett's office to talk contract that year, he handed me a blank contract and told me to sign it. I told him that I couldn't sign a contract if I didn't know how much I was playing for. He just looked up and said, "Sign it, you can trust me." I signed the blank contract.

Today the average salary for a professional football player is $250,000, but in 1960 it was less than $10,000. A couple of days later, I received my copy of the contract, and it called for $11,500. That was a $500 raise over the previous year, and I hadn't even played. I felt like I was taking money under false pretenses.

The Colts were poised and ready to win their third consecutive NFL championship, something that had never been done before. I was more than ready to be a part of that whole history-making process.

18

We were expecting our first child in October, so Libby decided it was wise to stay home and have the baby in Manning. She wasn't sure I had gotten over my pinball madness.

I lived with Jim Colvin, a rookie defensive tackle from Houston. We found a furnished apartment on Charles Street that normally catered to older people and that required a full, one-year lease. We were Colt players, however, so naturally this was waived.

We rented an efficiency apartment with one double Murphy bed and a small couch which made into a single bed. Since Jim was a Texan, we flipped a coin daily for use of the double bed. He had driven to Baltimore in an old beat-up reddish-orange Studebaker that had faded under the Texas sun. His wardrobe consisted of three white T-shirts, three pairs of faded jeans and a five-hundred-dollar pair of alligator boots, which he had purchased with the bonus he received for signing with the Colts.

Colvin was a typical Texan, with a quick temper and an equally quick laugh. While in college he had been married for a short time, but it didn't take. His first try at marriage had soured him on women. He didn't exactly dislike them, he'd talk to them, but he refused to listen to them talk.

Jim had spent a great deal of his youth across the line in the border towns of Mexico. The most dangerous thing I did each day was to wake Jim from his sleep. The instant I touched him, he'd swing at me with his right hand and reach for his wallet with his left. I have no idea how many times he had been rolled. A devout bachelor again, he was full of fun and raring to go. He had enough nervous energy for six people, so that together we had enough for twelve.

We ran the streets pretty hard that year. I couldn't let him go out by himself, and I didn't like being alone. Jim's preference for a specific kind of woman often took us to the Block. The Block had made Baltimore famous. Until the Colts came to town it was all anyone ever knew about the city. Among the local gentry it wasn't considered the place to be seen, but friends visiting from out of town insisted on being taken there.

The Block consisted of a group of sleazy strip joints that lined Baltimore Street. Supposedly it was off limits to Colt players, but that was strictly unenforced. Nearly everyone viewed it as sanctioned sin. It happens in the best of cities. Blaze Starr had the best bar on the strip, and she was far and away the best-known stripper of her time. Candy Barr may have been more exotic to some, but in my book Blaze Starr was the classiest dancer of her time, and maybe ever. She reminded me of Miss Kitty of Gunsmoke; she was a lady and a great student of human nature. Without being vulgar or ostentatious, she knew what aroused the fever in men. Blaze had that rare talent of making every man in a crowded bar think she was dancing for him alone. She was an artist.

She was also a responsible person, and looked after her two younger sisters who also danced there. The younger of the two was named Debbie, and, while not as talented a dancer, she was perhaps more beautiful. The other sister, Faye, was not so attractive. She was overweight, unkempt, with a drinking problem. Blaze made Faye do her number in a bathtub full of bubble bath. This accomplished two goals: you could see only her arms and face, and she could get as drunk as she wanted and still not fall off the bar.

As is often the case, some of the dancers were hookers, while others were just dancers working for tips and a percentage of the drinks that men bought them. We were Colt players, so everything was on the house. Some of these girls were working their way through school, and others were just working. The working girls were usually more interesting than the students.

The expression, "heart of a whore," has been misinterpreted

and greatly misunderstood. Some of these dancers were quite educated and very intelligent. I soon discovered how little I knew
about women, and how much women knew about men.

One theory as to where the term *hooker* came from is that Joe
Hooker, a general in the Union forces during the Civil War, traveled with prostitutes in his entourage. Although a relatively me-
diocre general, having been beaten badly at Chancellorsville by
Stonewall Jackson, Hooker was popular with his troops and his
forces were known for their high morale. The girls were called
hookers in the general's honor.

The Colts won their first two NFL games by scoring sixty-two
points and allowing only seven. Our third game was in Green Bay.
When I had left there the previous year, Jim Taylor couldn't remember his plays. Jerry Kramer and Fuzzy Thurston both had
agreed that nobody could run on the Colts. Hank Gremminger
couldn't sleep the night before he faced Lenny Moore. Jess Whittenton had vowed that nobody could cover Raymond Berry.

That afternoon Unitas was intercepted four times. Gremminger
had two of those interceptions, and Whittenton a third. Kramer
and Thurston must have blocked somebody, because Jim Taylor
rushed for three touchdowns and the Packers whipped us 35–12.
What in the world was going on up there in Wisconsin? Who was
this Henry Jordan and where had this Willie Davis come from?
What had gotten into Bart Starr? We reeled a bit from the defeat,
but we reasoned that no team had ever gone unbeaten before, so
there was no need to panic. These Colts were pressure players
and when it came right down to it, they could win when they had
to do it. A winning team is comprised of people with great respect
for each other. I had not yet earned their respect.

We were 6–2, with a two-game lead, when we went to play the
Bears in Chicago. There was something special about the week
of the Bear game. It was not just this Bear game, but any Bear
game. The Chicago Bears were not only the Colts' rivals; they
were archrivals with every team in the National Football League.

The Bears were owned and coached by George Halas. Ever since he founded this team back in the 1920s, he had been a believer in playing tough, physical football. His team was known as the monsters of the Midway. When we played the Bears in Chicago, we knew we were going to be beaten physically, on the scoreboard, or both. They had some of the best and toughest defensive players of that era. Men like Doug Atkins, Bill George, Larry Morris, and Joe Fortunato were moving around on defense similar to the way the Bears do today. Bill George was the defensive captain, and Clark Shaughnessy was their defensive coach. They switched locations so much that it was rumored that only three people actually knew the Bear defense: Clark Shaughnessy, Bill George, and God.

Weeb Ewbank got "Bear fever" every time we played Chicago. It would always start on Tuesday before the Sunday game. He would become hyperactive and run around nervously sweating, muttering things that were unintelligible. He would get forgetful and scream out for people who were no longer on the Colts. He had tried to send L. G. DuPre into our first game with the Bears. The difficulty was that L. G. had gone to the Dallas Cowboys the year before.

Meetings and practices were always longer. Special security guards were hired to keep George Halas out of our practices. Halas, of course, was in Chicago coaching the Bears. This went on all week long. Weeb looked for bugging devices in our own dressing rooms. As game day approached, he quit talking in the meetings and instead wrote things out on the chalkboard, for fear someone was listening in.

It was an unusual rivalry we shared with the Bears. While it was always physical, it was also friendly. As we were getting off the bus to enter the stadium, Bill George and Doug Atkins sauntered up to Unitas and me. Both George and Atkins had great respect for John, but they knew that he was the man that had to be controlled if they were to win. In an effort to ignite Doug, George kiddingly spoke, "Doug, this is John Unitas. I want you to know what he looks like, because this is as close as you're going to get to him today."

No one upset Weeb like Doug Atkins. Every time he'd pass Jim

Parker he'd snap, "Doug Atkins don't put no chill in me, Jim."
After about the eighth time he said it, Jim would respond, "Doug
Atkins don't put no chill in you, Weeb, because you don't have to
play against that big son of a bitch." Atkins was big, and there
wasn't an ounce of fat on him. He was 6'9", 280 pounds of mighty
mountain muscle. He had never lifted a weight in his life, and ste-
roids had not yet been invented. He was just big, strong, and talented. With the lone exception of Gino Marchetti, he was the best
defensive end in professional football. Doug had gone to school at
Tennessee on a basketball scholarship, and he could high-jump
nearly seven feet. He was the only player who was a threat or challenge to Jim Parker, the best offensive lineman who ever lived.
Few people who knew them will even argue the fact. The matchups
between these two were always classics.

The Bears played their games at Wrigley Field, and everything
about the experience was intimidating. The visiting team dressed
in a room that could accommodate a dozen people perfectly. The
problem was that there were thirty-six of us, plus coaches and
staff. We had to take turns dressing, the offense first and then the
defense.

To get to the field, we had to walk down a flight of steps and
across a gangway to the dugout. We were actually right there in
the crowd, with nothing but a layer of chicken wire separating us
from the fans. The Chicago fans would throw things at us, growl,
curse, and hang on to the wire like they were fighting to get at
us. Once we made it to the field, we were loudly booed by a crowd
that was dressed almost entirely in black. Images of Al Capone
rushed through my head.

At one end of the field there was a brick wall over eight feet
high, situated two inches behind the back of the end zone. More
than one receiver had hit that wall, running full tilt going after a
pass in the end zone. A brick wall doesn't give much.

Halas was one of the founders of the National Football League,
and he was both feared and respected by the officials. We could
not look for a close call to go in our favor. It may just have been
my imagination, but I could almost swear that Halas kept a dog

on the sideline, which would just happen to trot out onto the field when the Bears needed a time out late in the game. It was always the same little white dog, and it never appeared when we needed the time out, only when Chicago did.

Out of ten years of pro football, our game with the Bears in 1960 is the one that I most remember. It is probably the one that the players on both teams remember best, because neither team recovered from the physical beating handed out that day. This particular game was the most savage contest I have ever witnessed in sports. It didn't resemble a football game so much as a dog fight. The Colts were not considered an especially physical team, but this day was different.

From the first snap of the ball until the last, it was the most bitter and brutal struggle I've ever seen. Injured players on both teams were moving onto and off the field all afternoon, getting themselves repaired, and then returning for more. Neither team would back off. At one point late in the game I looked around and every player I could see was bleeding from somewhere or other. Since I was conspicuously clean, I found myself brushing up against players, trying to get some blood on my jersey.

The Bears were in front, 20–17, and the Colts had the ball inside the Chicago forty-yard line, with just seconds remaining in the game. On third down, Unitas called a deep pattern to Lenny Moore. He told me to stay in and block. The Bears were blitzing, and Bill George managed to get hold of one of John's legs. George held him long enough for Atkins to get free and finish him off. Finishing him off was just about what Doug did. There was nothing uncalled-for about the lick he gave John; it was just the fact that Doug was so powerful.

John was slow getting up; we knew he was hurt. The trainers and doctors were running onto the field as Doug stood towering over John's limp body. Doug just stared down at him for a second, and then he spoke: "Well, kid, that's about it for you today."

John propped himself up on one hand and replied, "Not just yet it ain't." When I saw John's face I almost threw up. His nose was slashed and mangled, and his face was covered with blood. It was as if he had been hit with an ax.

Have you every noticed how deathly quiet things get when a great player goes down? A hush settled over Wrigley Field as they took John to the sideline. It seemed to take a full ten minutes to clean him up and stop the bleeding. After packing his nose full of cotton, he trotted back on the field. When he reached the huddle his nose had already swollen to twice its normal size, and both eyes were almost swollen shut. On fourth down, with no time outs and only nineteen seconds left on the clock, John called the identical deep pattern to Moore. Lenny beat his defender as Unitas uncorked a perfect thirty-nine-yard scoring strike to win it, 24–20.

It was the most dramatic finish and the damnedest spectacle I had ever seen. Things like this don't just happen; they're caused. The man who caused this one, John Unitas, just walked off the field as if it were an everyday occurrence. No high fives, no dancing or celebrating, no fingers pointed upwards designating, "we're number one." Here was the greatest quarterback who ever played the game, walking casually off the field, having just finished a day of work. This was what he was paid to do. How often do you see that kind of dignity anywhere, anyplace?

Only injured players reported in on Mondays. The next Monday our training room was standing room only. I may well have been the only player who was there merely out of pure curiosity. I wanted to see what John must look like. Actually, for a guy trying to impersonate the Elephant Man, he didn't look all that bad. His entire head was swollen, and both of his eyes were black and blue. I didn't even recognize him at first. John told everybody there that he would be ready by Sunday, and that they had damn well better be ready, too. Unitas had to be ready; he was our only quarterback. I was starting to find out what pro football was all about.

The following week, the San Francisco 49ers beat us in the closing seconds of the game. We still had a one-game lead over the Packers, but the injury toll was mounting. The next week we were trailing the Detroit Lions 13–8, with just fourteen seconds remaining when once again Unitas responded with a perfect pass and Lenny Moore made an unbelievable catch to put us up 15–13.

But with just eight seconds left, Lion quarterback Earl Morrall completed a short pass to Jim Gibbons, who ran sixty-five yards for the winning touchdown. We were crushed.

It was not only a heartbreaking defeat, but a costly one as well. During that game Alan Ameche, a standout fullback and team leader, suffered what proved to be a career-ending injury. The loss of Ameche was devastating. We were now losing the games that championship teams have to win. We were tied with Green Bay for the divisional lead. It seems that their quarterback, Bart Starr, had developed a hot hand that I for one was certain would cool. After all, Starr was the same wimp who was sitting beside me that day in Winston-Salem, North Carolina, crying.

Both the Packers and the Colts finished up on the Coast with the Rams and 49ers. We were a crippled team when we arrived in L.A. There wasn't an offensive player who wasn't hobbled in some way or other. Still, the Colts were champions and were accustomed to winning the "must" games. The Packers, on the other hand, hadn't won a championship since 1943. What did they know about winning? How could they win with Bart Starr quarterbacking Lombardi's silly little twelve-play offense?

Yet somehow Vince Lombardi and the Packers won both of their games on the Coast, while we lost both of ours, and two weekends later I was back in Manning, South Carolina, watching the NFL championship game between the Philadelphia Eagles and the Green Bay Packers.

The game was anything but a classic. The Eagles were not really a top-drawer football team, but they had managed to win ten games and the Eastern Division crown. They were basically a two-man outfit. Norm Van Brocklin was their quarterback, and Chuck Bednarik was their defense.

With just seconds left on the clock, the Eagles were ahead 17–13, and Green Bay had a fourth-down situation on the Eagle ten-yard line. Jim Taylor got the call, but was stopped inches short of the first down by Bednarik as the clock wound down. It was the last game ever played by both Bednarik and Van Brocklin. It was also the last time a Lombardi team was ever beaten in a playoff game.

From there he went on to win nine straight, and Bart Starr went on to become one of the great quarterbacks of the game.

Naturally I had been pulling for the Eagles the entire game. I was certain that we would have beaten the Eagles, which would have made the Colts the only team ever to win three straight world titles. The Colts had fallen just short of immortality, and who doesn't want immortality? I would have been part of this one, too.

I hadn't performed especially well that season, but I had played every down. It began to dawn on me that I had just missed a once-in-a-lifetime opportunity. The Colts were not a young team, and injuries to older players do not heal as fast. The fact that the Packers were a young team was disconcerting. If this was the end of a dynasty for the Colts, it certainly had been a short one for me.

19

When I reported to training camp in the summer of 1961, I found out where I stood. I picked up the Colts' press guide and it read as follows:

The Colts head into training camp with no less than four positions in the wide-open category.

I read on:

The *general uncertainty* of the left halfback job has created this condition. *Tom Matte, Jerry Hill* and *Don Kern* are solid halfback prospects. If Matte makes it, he could give greater dimensions to the attack with his running pass.

There was no mention of me, not a word. Quickly I flipped to my picture to see my biographical sketch. It read only:

Obtained on waivers from Green Bay in '59.

Was that all? Was that it? Just the year before, they had labeled me a "swift breakaway threat." I quickly flipped to this Tom Matte person and it read, "A swift, strong runner, the Colts' *No. 1 draft choice* is pegged for left halfback duty." I fumbled through the pages to Jerry Hill. "A *third round pick,* this durable, heavy-duty runner can blast a hole in a line and open the throttle in the broken field."

My heart was in my stomach as I thumbed to Don Kern. "A speedboy who can sweep the flanks and catch passes, number *six draft pick* who at his scintillating best. . . ." That was enough. I closed the book. I was getting ill. "Scintillating"? Dear Lord, the Colts had used their first, third, and sixth draft picks just to get rid of me. I now remembered what Emlen Tunnell had told me. "The first three years are the hardest. If you can make those three years, you play ten." This would have been my third year.

A great many changes had taken place during the off-season. Six starters were absent from last year's roster. Three had been traded, and three had retired. Every great team has a hub, or core, of players around which the team forms its own personality. Usually the hub is comprised of six to twelve players, who are leaders. They dictate the standard of excellence with which the team will perform. These men are invaluable in setting the tone or style for the rest. It is from this hub that the character and quality of the team emanates. The remainder of the players are the spokes, and together they form the wheel. Our wheel size had been cut nearly in half.

Alan Ameche, now retired, had been a big part of the hub. Ameche was a leader. He had a dry sense of humor and a spirit of adventure that I would greatly miss. His lightheartedness cleared the air of any tension, his subtle wit had been refreshing. Until I joined the team he had been the player most frequently fined by Ewbank for violation of team rules.

All the money that we paid in fines was donated to a crippled children's hospital in Baltimore. The year before, Ameche and I had been principally responsible for the new whirlpool installed at the hospital. Alan had speculated that the children there had changed their nightly prayers to "God bless Mommy, God bless Daddy, and God bless Mr. Ameche and Mr. Hawkins." In the absence of Alan, the poker games would be fewer and far less fun.

After I read the press guide a couple of times, it was clear what was necessary for my survival. If I were to make this team, I would have to be at my very best at everything I did. Weeb's words were haunting me: "The more things you can do, the better chance you have of making the team." I made up my mind that getting rid of me was not going to be as easy as they thought.

At the start of each practice we ran a full, fast lap around the field to loosen up. Every day Weeb would scream out, "Don't anybody be last." Common sense would dictate that someone had to be last, unless we all tied for first. But I ran my heart out and finished first.

I volunteered for anything. If Weeb needed a halfback, I was a halfback. If he asked for a fullback, I was just that. If he called out for a tight end, I was a tight end. I took it upon myself to learn the plays at five different positions. I developed the nickname "Odd Jobs." My eagerness to stay with the Colts was apparent. They were going to have to run me off, because I was not going to leave. Nothing was beneath me or too degrading. Had they asked me, I would have doubled as a ball boy. I was bound and determined to get in that third year.

From the way I was volunteering for everything, I expected some resentment from my teammates. Instead, a trace of respect was starting to show.

20

Aman cannot play the game of football without a clearly defined philosophy to fall back on. Although John Unitas was my hero and I would gladly have killed for him, he would not do as a role model. He was a moderate beer drinker and a good husband and father. He would stop off and have a couple of beers with us after practice, but afterwards he always went home for dinner.

I was looking for someone a little more swashbuckling, someone that I could pattern myself after and use to develop a philosophy about this game I was playing. The man I most wanted to emulate was Bobby Layne.

Layne was the most respected and talked about player of his day. Bobby went first class, and the men who played with him went first class as well. The highest-paid player in the game, he allocated a large part of that salary to entertaining his troops. He picked up most of the checks. Bobby liked night life, late hours, and games of chance. He liked the sound of jazz music, the click of poker chips, and the tinkle of ice in a glass. He made no excuses for his life-style, nor did he try to hide it. Regardless of the time of day or night, he always went in via the front door. He lived life on his own terms.

He played the game of football twenty hours a day. On the field or in the bars, it was still football to him. Bobby didn't sleep more than three or four hours a night. He claimed he just "slept fast." There were only two kinds of players, he believed, stayers and leavers. Layne was a stayer and he *demanded* that his teammates be stayers as well. The stayers were the players who closed the bars. Layne believed that only fourteen good players were needed to win football games—if they were the right fourteen. Bobby *insisted* on fourteen stayers. He demanded a great deal of himself and of the people who played with him. In short, Bobby felt that life was to be lived hard, fast, and full. He was a star, and he was treated like one. He paid the price for that stardom in more ways than one. His philosophy had more impact on the game than that of any other man of his time, or since.

Any mention of Bobby Layne would be incomplete without the mention of his coach, Buddy Parker. Parker and Layne were both Texans, who had grown up just sixty miles from each other. In a sense, Bobby was responsible for Parker being a head coach, having recommended him for the job in Detroit in 1951. The relationship between the two was incredible. They agreed on everything. Buddy Parker recognized the importance of a quarterback's leadership, and so did Bobby Layne. Layne was the undisputed leader of his team.

Neither man believed in rules or fines. Both were positive thinkers and strong believers in an individual's personal character. They both believed in self-discipline. If a player had to be watched or prodded, they reasoned, they couldn't win with him, anyhow. Together they won back-to-back championships for Detroit in 1952 and 1953. Parker resigned in 1957 to take the coaching job at Pittsburgh. He traded for Bobby in 1958.

Where Layne was pragmatic, Parker was superstitious. Buddy not only would not stay in a room numbered thirteen he would not even stay in a room whose numerical equivalent was thirteen. He would not put a hat on a bed, and the sight of a black cat drove him to distraction. Immediately after any loss he would cut his tie and shoelaces in half.

With Parker and Layne things were pretty much a matter of black and white. They were steadfast in their respected beliefs, Parker with his lucky and unlucky theory, and Layne with his stayers and leavers. This is how we happened onto John Campbell and Jimmy Orr. They came in a trade with Pittsburgh that year.

Jimmy Orr was single when he joined Layne and the Steelers in 1958. A hard drinker and night carouser, Jimmy was a good disciple for Bobby. Jimmy *was* a stayer. With Layne throwing to him, Orr was Rookie of the Year in '58, and went to the Pro Bowl in '59. When he returned to Pittsburgh for the '60 season, however, Jimmy was married and didn't get out as often. This, of course, didn't set well with Bobby Layne, and things were never the same between the two again. Layne quit throwing to Jimmy, and in 1961 Orr was traded to the Colts.

John Campbell was a linebacker who played his college football at Marquette. During the four years he had attended Marquette, his team had failed to win a game. During the 1960 season the Steelers had lost three straight games that Buddy figured they should have won. He attributed these losses to bad luck, and he decided that he was going to get to the bottom of it. He called a team meeting and ordered each Steeler player to write down his name on a sheet of paper, along with his combined won-and-lost record for the four years he had attended college. When he went through the papers he came upon "John Campbell, Marquette, 0–40."

"Here it is!" Buddy screamed, "Campbell is the black cat that's responsible for all this. Hell, Campbell doesn't know what it is to win." As soon as that season was over, "Black Cat" Campbell was traded to us.

I was still on the roster when I sprained my ankle in our last preseason game. It was a bad sprain, and the trainers estimated I would be out of action for at least four weeks. The Colts put me on injured waivers, which meant that I was no longer a part of the team. The one advantage to this was that the Colts would have to pay my salary until I was healed. That was my loophole for survival.

Two weeks prior to our opening game the Colts broke camp. We couldn't move into Memorial Stadium until the major league baseball season was over, so we practiced at a military school fifteen miles west of Baltimore. I was sharing a room at the Boxwood Motel with John Campbell.

On the Monday before our opening game, John had taken his playbook and left for practice. Three players had to be cut that day to reduce the squad to the thirty-six-player limit. I was sitting on the edge of the tub soaking my swollen ankle in Epsom salts, when the door to the room burst open. It was Campbell.

"What's wrong?" I inquired.

"The son of a bitches cut me, that's what's wrong. You'd better not go out there because they'll cut you, too," he warned. He started packing his clothes.

"They can't release me until my ankle is well," I informed him, showing him my swollen, black-and-blue foot.

"Then you better keep it swollen or you're gone," he said. At that, he soaked a towel in the tub, tied a large knot in the towel, and started beating it against my injured ankle.

"What in the hell are you doing?" I asked.

"Making sure the ankle doesn't lose that swelling," he said.

That made sense to me, so we took turns beating on the ankle until the swelling had increased almost twenty percent.

Ed Block, our trainer, was baffled. The discoloration was slowly disappearing, but the ankle remained mysteriously swollen. I beat my ankle with that towel for the next three weeks, until injuries hit both Tom Matte and Jerry Hill, at which time, suddenly and miraculously, my swollen ankle was healed.

Our season more or less ended the third week in Baltimore against the Minnesota Vikings. I was still on the injured reserve list, and standing behind the bench in street clothes, when Unitas came to the sideline with an injured finger on his throwing hand. There was absolutely no expression of pain on his face, just that deadpan look that he wore on game days. The middle finger on his right hand was dislocated in the shaped of a Z.

Ed Block gently put it back in place. John just stood there like a man having his nails done: no grimace, no emotion, just that stone-cold stare. Then he trotted back to the huddle and threw a long pass on the next play. He had an incredible tolerance for pain.

The year before, he had practiced and played with an ankle that was so swollen he could barely get his foot into those black high-top shoes. In 1957, he had broken three ribs and had a collapsed lung. Yet he missed only two games.

John played the rest of the year, but his finger never healed. We finished the season with an 8–6 record, well behind the Packers. Green Bay beat the Giants for the championship, 37–0. It was Vince Lombardi's first championship.

Vince Lombardi had somehow convinced the Packers that they were winners. He was serving notice to the Colts and the rest of the league that his team would be doormats no more. In just two short years Lombardi had transformed a group of losers into the league's best. It was amazing.

21

When I reported for the 1962 season, I found that there was a different attitude among the Colts. No longer was this a loose and fun-loving group. The poker games were harder to put together, and the hardcore beer drinkers were thinning out as well. A tenseness, an air of urgency, hung over the training camp.

I didn't have to be told that our owner, Carroll Rosenbloom, was upset. He was surly about finishing out of the title picture for the second straight year. Carroll rewarded his teams handsomely for winning, and he was equally harsh about losing. Winning to Rosie was winning the world championship, and nothing less would suffice. Thus was his ego.

He was a fine football owner, but he could see that his dynasty had come to a close. He was not happy with this development and it was easy to read his moods through his coaches and the front-office people. Carroll was a powerful man, and he could make his presence felt.

Keith Molesworth, our personnel director, was getting the heat. He had an outstanding draft in 1955, but since then his drafting had been questionable. This year's No. 1 draft choice was even more questionable. The Colts had surprised everyone by selecting Wendell Harris, a halfback from Louisiana State.

Scouting was not as sophisticated an operation then as it is today, but on this pick Molesworth outdid himself. Wendell was listed as a 6'1", 215 pound, 9.9 sprinter. He had been labeled as a "can't miss" performer on offense or defense, who could also handle extra points and field goals. But Molesworth had never actually seen Wendell Harris play. The story was that Molesworth

had a great dislike for crowds, so quite often he would not go to
football games. He had checked into a hotel in Baton Rouge, read
about Wendell in the paper, listened to the game on radio, and
then watched a Big Ten game on TV in his room.

As luck would have it, Wendell turned out to be 5'10" and 170
pounds, and had run a 9.9 as a sophomore when he weighed 150
pounds. Now he ran a 10.3 or 10.4, could not play offense, and could
not kick. Such was the science of scouting in the early sixties.

The inescapable truth was that the Colts had been drafting and
trading poorly, while the Green Bay Packers had been very pru-
dent in those areas. In 1959, the Colts finished the season with
eight All-Pros, while Jim Ringo was the Packers' lone all-league
player. Just three years later, in 1962, the Colts could boast only
two All-Pros, while the Packers had no less than ten All-Pro performers.

Carroll Rosenbloom was nobody's fool. He knew that the life-
blood of any team was the college draft. He had seen the cracks
in the veneer, and had already taken steps to prevent them from
widening. Rosie was a good football man, but he was a *great* businessman; he never wasted a favor on anyone unless there was
something in it for him. He knew that Molesworth was the weak
link in his organization. He also knew that general manager Don
Kellett's health was declining and that sooner or later he would
have to be replaced.

Bert and Upton Bell were the sons of former League Commissioner Bert Bell, Sr. Bert, Sr., had coached Carroll at Penn; it
was he who was responsible for Carroll's having bought the Colts.
Bert, Jr., was working in current commissioner Pete Rozelle's
office in New York and Upton was just finishing school at LaSalle
in Philadelphia. Carroll knew both of these boys were bright and
knowledgeable, so, repaying a debt to his old college coach, he
hired Bert, Jr., in the spring of 1961 and Upton joined him that
summer. Carroll had gotten two good football men and as a bonus
had tied up the well-respected Bell name.

The older brother, Bert, had grown up with pro football. Since
childhood he had worked in the front office with his father. When

he was ten years old he had drawn up the league schedule. He had the same reverence for the game as his father did. After high school, he attended Notre Dame, Penn, Villanova, and two other schools. Finally he graduated from the New York School of Typing in 1960.

Sports were his life. Bert had gone to work in the league office with interim commissioner Austin Gunsel. When Alvin "Pete" Rozelle was voted in as commissioner, the league office was immediately moved from Philadelphia to New York, much to Bert's dislike. So when the call came from Rosenbloom in the spring of 1961, Bert packed an assortment of clothes, all of them black, and hastened to Baltimore, where he vowed he would wear nothing but black until the Colts won another championship. This earned him the nickname of "Blackie" for years to come.

The first year he worked in the ticket office, and the next year was moved to assistant publicity director. He had a head for business and a solid understanding of the game. He was learning every facet of the Colts' operation, and he was the heir-apparent to the general manager of the Colts.

Of the two Bell brothers, Upton was the better athlete. He had been a ten-flat sprinter on the track team in high school, a basketball player at LaSalle, and he still stayed in good condition. He started in the ticket office, too, but by the fall of '62 he was scouting college players on the side. Upton was a free spirit with an eye for talent.

The Packers were the world champions, but the Baltimore Colts were still America's team. Everywhere we went people turned out to see John Unitas. It seemed that every young man wanted to play for the Colts. Wherever we were scheduled, youngsters would beg for a tryout with the Colts.

Don Kellett was a master of public relations, and when people asked for tryouts, rather than disappointing them by saying no, he would allow them to run against Upton. If they could beat Upton, then they would be invited to camp. Outside of Moore and Lyles, Upton was the fastest person in the organization, and he would take on all comers. After Upton beat them, Kellett would call them aside and explain that Upton only worked in the ticket office, so if they couldn't outrun him, they really had no chance in the pros. No one ever complained.

The Colts had decided to change Lenny Moore into a running back. This did not help my chances of making the team. However, the fact that I could play so many positions was really an asset. It mattered not how poorly I played them, I was still a body. Meanwhile I had also started returning punts, adding to my versatility.

In the next-to-last preseason game, I severely sprained my other ankle, and had to stay on the sidelines for at least four weeks. It was getting to be ridiculous; I had not been in the league four years yet, but had already been put on waivers three times. My life in football was like a yo-yo.

This time, however, I didn't have to use the old towel trick. Lenny Moore cracked his knee cap and would be out of action for over a month. The Colts needed a halfback, and fast. My ankle quickly healed and I responded rapidly.

I have never been sure whether winning builds character, or whether it takes character to win. I do know that the Colts lost a lot of character when Artie Donovan and Jim Mutscheller retired before the start of the '62 season. The respect and leadership they offered could not be replaced.

Vince Lombardi once made the statement that every team needs an educated clown. For the Colts, Artie was just that. Now thirty-seven years old, he had been there from the start. He had served his country in the South Pacific during World War II and was fighting the Japanese when I was eight years old! A four-time All-Pro, "Fatso" was the heart and soul of the Colts. He had been a starter for twelve years, the most popular and beloved member of the team, and in many ways the very conscience of the Colts.

The Colts retired Artie's number and jersey at our opening game with the Rams. Artie was dressed out in full uniform, wearing his jersey number 70 for the last time. When Donovan cried through his speech and then trotted off the field to the dugout for his final time, 45,644 spectators were bawling their eyes out and every member of the team was crying as well. I doubt that there was a dry eye in the stadium. I had never witnessed anything as touching or tender in sports.

Inconsistency would be the only valid description of the Colts' performance that year. We would win two, then lose two, win one and lose one. We finished the season with a 7–7 record, in fourth place in our division behind Green Bay, Detroit, and Chicago.

I was a little confused as to how the Packers were beating us. In our two games with Green Bay, we had beaten them statistically, but still they had won both games. Unitas, Berry, and Moore had all missed games because of injuries that year, and our once quick-striking offense had slowed to a halt.

On the other hand, the Packers had had their share of injuries, too, but they didn't seem to matter as much. Paul Hornung was lost for a good portion of the year, but he was simply replaced by Tom Moore, a young man from Vanderbilt, and the steady, consistent Packer offense hummed right along. You could scarcely tell the difference between a starter and his replacement. They were interchangeable parts of a very effective machine.

It was perplexing to me how Lombardi's simple, basic little offense could function so well. Little by little, Lombardi had instilled something into this team in three short years. Bart Starr had turned into a confident field general. He no longer resembled the frightened young quarterback I had known in 1959.

Weeb Ewbank's downfall started in Los Angeles at midseason. At the Tuesday meeting before the Ram game, he announced that Lenny Moore, Orr, and I were being fined a hundred dollars for curfew violation. It was no big thing, until Lenny made it one. He argued that the reason he was late getting in was that no cab driver in Los Angeles would pick him up because he was black. It was a ridiculous excuse, and it caused laughter from the team, but Lenny was vehement about it. When Weeb refused to rescind the fine, Lenny stalked out of the room, announcing that he would not play another game for Weeb. Three or four black players went along with Lenny, thus creating a touchy situation. Rosenbloom was summoned from Hawaii to quiet the insurrection. As usual he settled this volatile situation quickly, but in so doing he had undermined Weeb's authority to discipline his own team. Ewbank's days as coach of the Colts were numbered. This was the first display of black unity in pro football.

The Packers went on to a 13–1 season and once again beat the Giants for the World Championship, 16–7. That game was played in near-zero temperature, with gusting winds that brought the windchill factor down to minus forty-one degrees. To win a game under those conditions takes class. It just might have been that Vince Lombardi and his Packers were outclassing not only us, but the rest of the National Football League as well.

22

The pro game was starting to change. Another league had been formed, and Al Davis was now coaching the Oakland Raiders in that other league. The player limit had been raised from thirty-six to thirty-seven. Paul Hornung and Alex Karras had been suspended for betting on games. Other than amphetamines, the use of drugs was all but unheard of at the time, yet Big Daddy Lipscomb had died of an overdose of heroin that spring. At the suggestion of Buddy Parker, Bobby Layne had called it quits at Pittsburgh. In Cleveland, Blanton Collier had replaced Paul Brown. Perhaps the biggest change was right here in Baltimore.

After three years without a championship, Carroll Rosenbloom decided it was time to make a coaching change. It didn't surprise anyone that he let Weeb Ewbank go, but when he hired thirty-three-year-old Don Shula to replace him, he did cause some eyebrows to rise. It wasn't that Shula wasn't qualified; he had played seven years of professional football, two with Cleveland, four with the Colts, and a final year with the Redskins. Before joining the Detroit Lions in 1960 as an assistant coach, Don had worked with defensive backs at Kentucky and Virginia. He was clearly a coach on the rise, with a reputation for functioning as a coach even on the field during his playing days. Still, he was just thirty-three years old, and nobody had ever hired a coach as young as that. As usual, Rosenbloom knew what he was doing.

I decided to visit Baltimore and meet Don Shula when I talked about my contract with Don Kellett. After four years, my salary was now at $14,000. Kellett gave me my customary $1,000 raise, but Shula was less kind. Don Shula was friendly enough, and he looked me straight in the eye when we talked. It wasn't so much the way he spoke to me as what he said that hurt. He had studied the films of the past year and had evaluated the talent on hand. I was welcome to report to camp, he said, but in all honesty he didn't think I could make the team. He was not counting on me for the coming season.

I returned home and contemplated my next move. I had not yet finished school, and I did not want to go to work. The American Football League had started in 1960, but nobody paid very much attention to it. Weeb had just been hired as coach of the New York Jets and I felt certain I could play for him, but who wanted to play for that "other league"? No self-respecting NFL player wanted to play "minor league" football. That other league was for either washed-up players or those who couldn't make it in the NFL.

I decided to report to the Colts and take my chances. There was something that I liked about Shula, and, besides, things had always worked out for me in the past. I did, however, make up my mind to stop this senseless roller coaster of emotional stuff. I had paid my dues, and it was time to start enjoying professional football. From now on if I didn't make it through the final cuts, then I would begin worrying about it when I was given the ax, and not before. I was going to relax and have fun.

When I reported to camp I discovered that R. O. Owens had been badly injured in an automobile accident on his way to Baltimore but that Shula had penciled him in as a backup to Raymond Berry. On the first day of camp he approached me with a warm, knowing look and told me that I was now a receiver. By the warmth in his smile, I knew that he had found a way to keep me. Well, if I was to be a pass receiver, who better to study under than Raymond Berry?

Raymond wasn't much to look at, but what he didn't know about catching passes wasn't worth talking about. He was the most detailed, precise person I had ever known. He was a perfectionist. With Raymond Berry football was a full-time profession. He spent eleven months a year at it. During the month of January he put football aside, answered his mail, and rested. The rest of the year was all football.

Raymond was a physical wreck. He was almost blind, needing

contact lenses to function. He was tall, frail, and slow. He had a bad knee, a bad back which required a brace, and one of his legs was shorter than the other. He resembled the sort of person who was pictured on an Easter Seal stamp. So unathletic was his appearance that he had appeared on "What's My Line," the television quiz show, and stumped the panel as to his occupation.

Raymond had come to the Colts in 1955 as a twentieth draft choice. His father had coached him in high school and he had attended Southern Methodist University. In his first year with the Colts he had caught only thirteen passes. The next year, however, he teamed up with Unitas, a man with very little more physical endowment, and together, through tireless hours of practice, they became the best passing combination the game has ever known.

I listened to everything Raymond had to say. He was meticulous and organized. He washed his own practice pants, and on the road he carried his own scales with him to monitor his weight. He had a drill for every conceivable type of pass. He was busy during every minute of the practice sessions. He would practice catching low balls, high balls, balls thrown behind him, and deflected balls. To any other receiver in football a dropped ball was one that he could not get both hands on. To Raymond, a dropped ball was one that could be touched with one hand only. Anytime that Raymond dropped a ball in practice, he would catch that same ball for twenty times without a miss before he left the field.

In a preseason game Raymond had gotten one hand on a deflected pass that was thrown behind him. He was running one way and dove headlong backwards, but he couldn't hold onto it. It was an impossible pass to catch, but I laughingly told Jimmy Orr that I was willing to bet that Raymond would have us practicing that catch on Monday.

That Monday when we reached the practice field Raymond had already dug a pit, and at his own expense had ordered a truckload of sawdust. All week we practiced diving catches of deflected passes, with the sawdust coming out of our ears. I never managed to catch one, but as I recall, Raymond hung on to two or three.

Football was fun under Don Shula. He had a good sense of humor and a great appreciation for determined play. He called me aside one day and took me into his confidence. "Alex," he said, "I scouted you in college and I rated you a 'can't miss' player on offense or defense in the pros. That just goes to show you how wrong a guy can be." He trotted off laughing, leaving me with the thought that Shula was a guy who could laugh, and better still, he could laugh at himself. Finally I had found a leader with a real sense of humor.

He was a down-to-earth person, who believed in working hard but in leaving his work at the office. Just a few years earlier Shula had been a defensive back for the Colts. He had been a teammate and roommate of several of the players. They knew him, and respected him as a shrewd and competitive player. Never greatly talented, he had stayed in the league by hard work and determination, and he seemed to appreciate players of a similar mold. As a matter of fact he even seemed to prefer them over the naturally talented ones. I always knew where I stood with him. After a player did his work, his time was his own. In a sense, Shula was a cross between Weeb and Buddy Parker.

The Colts had drafted well that year. We had eight or nine rookies who made the team. Bob Vogel, John Mackey, Jerry Logan, and Fred Miller would all soon be starters. Vogel, our number one pick, had been hand-picked and selected to replace Jim Parker at offensive left tackle.

Vogel was different from the rookies I had seen in the past. There was a new breed of players entering the NFL, and Bob was the first one that caught my attention. He was a nice kid, serious, studious, intelligent, and quiet. He was sane and civilized, and his hobby was classical music. Football was a money-making proposition to him. He viewed it as a business opportunity. His body was his marketable commodity, and he was going to protect it. He was the first player that I ever saw who wore gloves to protect his hands. When he was hurt he would not practice. After practice, Bob might have a beer or two but he wouldn't stay for long. He would go home to his wife; they did things together. Imagine that!

Shula had taken the "one-of-the-boys" approach to coaching

that first year since he was younger than several of the players; he avoided the "holier-and-wiser-than-thou" theory and stuck to being a straight shooter. To ease any possible strain that might occur or exist, he had made Marchetti and Pellington player-coaches. He was feeling his way.

His attitude toward me was renewing and refreshing. I felt absolutely no pressure about my job, and I was responding rather well. Some people need pounding, while others need petting. I loved being petted.

Just before the start of the 1963 season, Shula made a trade with Detroit for a placekicker and linebacker named Jim Martin. Jim had beaten the Colts with his kicking for the last several years, and was at the end of a fine career during which he excelled for twelve years with the Lions. He was thirty-nine years old, but his legs were still those of a twenty-year-old. Life had not been an open box of candy for Jim. He had joined the Marines straight out of high school, and had fought in hand-to-hand combat in some of the toughest battles in the South Pacific.

After the 1961 season he had retired as a player and coached at Denver in 1962 in that other league. He convinced Shula that there was still some life in that thirty-nine-year-old leg. If you play long enough, he claimed you would have your finest hour just before you finish up. He referred to it as the "last gasp before dying." He could not have been more accurate.

That year he was voted Comeback Player of the Year. He kicked twenty-four field goals and was second in the league in scoring, with 104 points. His kicking provided the winning margin in five of our eight wins.

Jim was like a breath of fresh air to the Colts. He fit right in, and his positive attitude was contagious for a number of young players. He was a team player first and foremost. Like most of the players of the fifties, he was passionate about the game, and appreciative of the opportunity to play it again. His one year away from playing football had taught him that the real world could be cold and cruel. When a younger player would complain about something, or get down in the mouth over his prospects, Jim would offer his sage advice: "Play as long as you can, boys, it's a cold cruel world out there on the outside."

The 1963 season started out uneventfully enough. A combination of youth, injuries, and fumbles resulted in our losing three of our first four games. Yet even with Carroll Rosenbloom looking on closely, Don Shula refused to panic. He stuck to his guns, showing a great deal of poise and character for a young first-year coach.

Along about the middle of the season, Wendell Harris came to me and suggested that the two of us talk to Shula about putting ourselves on the special teams. At that time they were referred to as the suicide squads, owing to the number of injuries and operations that resulted from the kicking game. At first I thought Wendell was crazy. Nobody wanted to be on these teams, and absolutely no one ever volunteered for that kind of work.

Wendell's reasoning was that neither he nor I was doing anything but sitting on our rear ends on game days. He was embarrassed by not contributing something, he said. Sooner or later people were going to get tired of us just standing around and doing nothing. He went on to explain that the big slow players who were on the special teams would be easy to avoid in the open field. He closed by adding that he needed the action, and felt like he was cheating on his "pill."

The pill he was referring to was an amphetamine tablet that was used by many players in those days. Amphetamine is a drug often referred to as "speed" or "uppers." The characteristic effects of the drug are a feeling of euphoria, a false sense of security, irritability, hostility, and more aggressive behavior on the part of the user.

When I thought about it, Wendell's idea made sense. Besides, Wendell was fearless and someone had once said that "a man with no fear belongs in a mental institution or on special teams." I knew how I was going to break the wedge and get to the ball carrier without too much danger. I would let Wendell do it.

I decided to run the plan first by Bill Saul, a reserve linebacker who was kind of goofy himself. Saul was a surly person, with an attitude that could best be described as "I came uninvited and I don't plan to leave." He just giggled at the notion and assured me that if Wendell and I would volunteer, he too would.

After practice I went to Shula with the idea. At first he told me I was crazy, and that we would get killed. The more he talked against it, however, the funnier he thought it would be. So, after letting the idea flit around in his head, he reached the conclusion that even if all three of us were maimed, it would be no great loss to the team.

So the following Sunday we premiered our new act, and it worked. Eluding these bigger, less agile would-be-blockers in the open field was no problem, and they in turn were easy prey to our blocks. Linemen were not accustomed to open field maneuvers, and they found themselves at our mercy. This kind of thing did wonders for our confidence and sense of self-worth. All three of us were now contributing something to the team. At first it was reflected in field position alone, noticed only by the coaches, but the more successful we became, the more people volunteered to join us. Near the end of the season both Unitas and Marchetti were commenting on our daring and would applaud us as we came off the field. Approval from these two men was like being knighted.

No other team in football seemed to be following our lead. We found ourselves dominating other teams in the kicking game, and they were making no moves to counter us. On every exchange of the ball, we were bettering the opposing team by ten or more yards. Not only that but an *esprit de corps* was building among our troops. The scheme was suddenly turning into a giant morale builder. Our intentions had been to con Shula, but this stupid pill-conceived plot was actually working.

Everybody remembers where they were when President John F. Kennedy was killed on Friday, November 22, 1963. We were flying over Texas on our way to play the Rams when the pilot announced that the President had just been shot and killed in Dallas. There was much debate as to whether the game on Sunday would be played or not. Finally it was announced that the game would go on as scheduled.

Before the game there was a ceremony in memory of Kennedy.

Ordinarily we stayed in the dressing room, but that day the teams were lined up along both sidelines in numerical order for the playing of the anthem. I was lined up directly in front of Wendell as the national anthem was being played. Suddenly Wendell tapped me on the back and spoke in the most serious manner, "That's the most beautiful song I've ever heard," he said. "They should play it before every game."

Meanwhile the Packers and Bears were making it a two-horse race. Chicago had allowed us only ten points in two games. Without anyone that resembled a quarterback, the Bears were winning with their defense. While they were not scoring many points, they were giving up even fewer. Vince Lombardi had set the pace and standard of excellence, and "Papa Bear," George Halas, was answering his call.

The Packers finished the season with an 11–2–1 mark, but it was not good enough, because the Bears lost only one game and beat the New York Giants for the championship, 14–10, in New York.

After the title game Halas was asked if he was finally going to retire. Halas was shocked. "Retire from what? I've never worked," he said. When informed that he had been a player, coach, and owner of the Bears for forty-three years, Halas responded, "Work, purely defined, is doing something when you would rather be doing something else. This is all I've ever wanted to do." Football was George Halas's life.

23

When I reported to camp for the 1964 season I read in the Colts' press guide, "Alex is one of the league's more valuable utility men, more trouble shooting is on tap for the Hawk this year." I should have known at once that this was going to be an unusual season.

Shula was wasting no time establishing himself as his own man. With only one year of head-coaching experience, he had taken complete control of his team. Vince Lombardi once said, "a team expresses a coach's personality and its own personality. All of us are takers, but if a person can't add something to what he takes from others, he should get out." Getting out was the furthest thing from Shula's mind; he was just getting started. He had studied under Paul Brown and Weeb Ewbank, and their systems were similar. Shula accepted most of what he had learned from them, but now he wanted to add a few ideas of his own.

Just before our first preseason game, he took me aside and told me he was going to do something new. He was making me a captain. I was to be the captain of the special teams. In those days teams had only two captains, one for offense and one for defense. To have three captains was unheard of. I was flattered, but also embarrassed. Everybody knew that Unitas and Marchetti were our captains. Scarcely anybody in the league even knew who I was, and I could just imagine walking to the center of the field with those football legends and having to introduce myself to men like Bill George and Joe Schmidt. I could just see them breaking up from laughing at my presence. So I thanked Don for the honor, but graciously declined.

Shula didn't argue with me about it. He simply repeated I was going to be a captain. I informed Jim Martin about what was going on, and he almost died laughing. Take the initiative, he told me. Walk right out there and offer your hand and ask the other team's captains who *they* are. "Act like they should know you and pretend you don't know them," he said. I figured I had nothing to lose, so I'd try it.

The official came to the sidelines to greet us. He shook Unitas's hand and said cordially, "Hey, John, how are you? Hey, Gino, how's things?" Then he turned to me and said, "Captain Who?" I could hardly get "Captain Hawkins" out of my mouth. When we went to the center of the field to meet the opposing captains, I felt naked. It was a repeat of the same conversation. "Hey, John, Hi, Gino, Captain Who?" It was highly embarrassing, and it went on for the entire year. "Captain Who" became the first special team captain in the history of professional football.

Jim Martin had been right about his "last-gasp-before-dying" theory. The year before he had been fantastic, but his kicking in training camp had fallen off. Shula and every other Colt had been hoping Jim would find the range, but as the season approached, it was clear that Jim was nearing the end as a kicker.

Much to the sorrow of every Colt player, Shula managed to trade Jim to the Redskins. I drove him over to Washington. He reflected on his years in pro football with much warmth and veneration. Here was a man who really loved the game. He talked about the affection that existed between players on those championship Detroit teams. He couldn't say enough about Bobby Layne, and of the closeness that winning brings to a team. I felt that somehow he would never be that happy again. I hoped I was wrong.

Fran O'Brian, a Redskin player, owned a bar in downtown Washington, so Jim suggested we stop there. He was sure it was a hangout for the Redskin players. He didn't know where he was going to live, but he felt certain that some of his new teammates would be able to tell him where he was most likely to find a suitable place.

Among members of a losing team close or lasting friendships rarely develop. Turnover of personnel is usually rapid. Washington had not won a divisional title since 1945. There were two

Redskin players in Fran's bar. Jim Martin was a well-known and highly respected player, yet neither of the two said hello or even offered to talk to us. To them he was just a newly acquired body who might be taking their jobs, although neither was a kicker. Finally, Jim went over, introduced himself, and asked where was the best place he might find to live. Neither of the two had any suggestions for him, nor did they welcome Jim to the team or invite him to join them. I dropped him by a hotel and drove back to Baltimore thinking that it just might be a cold and cruel world out there.

Don wanted fiery, competitive people on his team. During the off-season he had traded with the Minnesota Vikings for a linebacker named Steve Stonebreaker. Stoney brought with him stories of life on an expansion team, and of the ways of the "Dutchman," Norm Van Brocklin, coach of the Vikings. He also brought a fierce desire to win football games. Stonebreaker was a full-time player; his competitive attitude was infectious. The hub of the Colts was being rebuilt.

Living with the "Captain Who?" label took humor and some imagination. I could not afford to give the appearance of being serious about anything. No doubt Shula believed that superior special teams had added another dimension to our football team, but perhaps the greatest value was from a morale standpoint. The new approach enabled players who were not yet seasoned enough to be regulars to show their courage and desire for the game.

The selection of the performers on the special teams was being left up to me, although Shula did have the good sense to retain veto power. Shula and I were on the same frequency in the matter. We were looking for the same type of players. It takes relatively little skill to cover kickoffs and punts; what is required is a willingness to be reckless, bold, fearless, and also somewhat crazy.

The Colts had just drafted a linebacker named Ted Davis, who had been thrown off the team at Georgia Tech for kicking an opposing player in the head. I thought he would fit in just fine with my group, so I asked for and got "Kick'em-in-the-head Ted."

The following Monday brought more surprises to the Colt family.

Knowing that I was living alone, Shula called me aside and asked me to room with a player he had just traded for. The player in question was a rookie from Oklahoma whom the Giants had given up on, even though he was their first draft choice. His name was Joe Don Looney.

From all accounts, Looney was a likely candidate for the rubber room at the laughing academy. Never has a man's last name been more appropriate. I had heard stories of Looney, and considered him too great a challenge even for me. I passed on rooming with this strange person with the explanation that I never turned the lights off in a room with anyone crazier than I was. I did, however, volunteer to look after him.

I suppose that the players of the fifties were more naive than those of a later era. We didn't question much; we accepted many things as they were. Perhaps we felt that not everything was meant to be understood. Joe Don Looney, by contrast, was a radical departure from the fifties; he was a product of the sixties. He had questions, and demanded answers. Joe Don was a freak. He was too dangerous to live with, but too exciting to be far away from, so I moved him into the room next to mine.

He had grown up in Dallas, Texas. His father had played for the Eagles, and now refereed NFL games. Joe Don knew he was different even when he was in the first grade. When the twenty children in his first grade class were let out in the schoolyard for an Easter egg hunt, Joe found and claimed all twenty eggs. He did not understand why his teacher made him give all but one back. He had not cheated, he said; he just knew somehow where the eggs were hidden.

In the fall of 1960, Joe Don had enrolled at Texas. The next spring he transferred to Texas Christian. He spent the fall of '61 and spring of '62 as a junior at Cameron Junior College. In the fall of '62, he made All-American at the University of Oklahoma. He was thrown off the team in his senior year for punching a coach.

He was drafted No. 1 by the New York Giants in '64, and he served three months at Fort Dix before reporting to the Giant training camp. The Giants' coach, Allie Sherman, should have known something when this twenty-year-old stepped off the bus dressed in green jeans, blue blazer, yellow shirt, red tie, brown shoes, white socks, and no belt.

He was not popular with his teammates in New York. He stayed in his room and played Motown music. His few friends were blacks. He would not allow the trainer to tape his ankles or treat his injured thigh. It was his body, he insisted, and he knew more about his own body than anyone else. He refused to practice, but played catch with the children who watched the practices.

The final straw came when he was fined a hundred dollars for being fifteen minutes late for an eleven o'clock bed check. The following night, Joe was in bed at nine o'clock. When the bed check was made, he explained that, if the rate was set at a hundred dollars a quarter-hour, the Giants now owed him seven hundred dollars, because he had gone to bed two hours early. He was traded to us the next day.

He had read dozens of books on nutrition, and resented trainers telling him about something that he felt that they knew little about. He was the first football player I knew who lifted weights regularly and took vitamins and food supplements. When I looked at the condition he was in, I couldn't argue with him. Coaches and trainers resented him ordering spaghetti or pasta for the pregame meal instead of steak and potatoes. (Joe said the body burns up carbohydrates when anybody exercises, and they were feeding us proteins.) He seemed certain about it. I told him to be quiet and eat his steak. Joe Don was a stallion with a brilliant smile and electric eyes.

If you were to design the perfect fullback, you would draw a likeness of Joe Don Looney. He was big, fast, and wild, at 6'1" and 225 pounds. He had 9.5 speed and the agility of a gazelle. He was the Herschel Walker of his day. He would be a worthy addition to the special teams.

Just when I thought things were leveling off, Shula called me aside again. This time he asked me to room with Lou Michaels. At first I thought he was testing my sense of humor, then I realized he was serious. Poor Don Shula, in just his second year of coaching, had gone completely crazy. A cold fear ran through me;

if this kind of thing continued, I would be the sanest person on the team. That was a frightening prospect. What could Shula have been thinking? Was he trying to create an out-patient clinic for wayward players? Why, our team picture would soon be on display in every post office in the country.

Lou Michaels had been drafted by the Rams. While in Los Angeles he had a run-in with a policeman, and it had taken nine officers to subdue him. The cops were all too happy to see him relocated in Pittsburgh. I had just read in the newspaper where Lou had broken a teammate's jaw in a bathroom scuffle in Pittsburgh's training camp. Now Shula was asking me to room with him.

"No, no, a thousand nos!" I pleaded. "I do not mind walking on the razor's edge, but I have to draw the line. While I may appear to you as unbalanced, I assure you that I am only pretending to be insane. I will do my best to look after Lou and introduce him around, but I will not live with him." The next day Lou reported and I got him a room at the Boxwood, far down the hall and on another floor.

The '64 season was close at hand and I was listed on the depth charts as third-team wide receiver, flanker, fullback, halfback, and tight end. Since there were only two quarterbacks, I was the only person on my third team.

The players limit had been increased that year from thirty-seven to forty players. Jimmy Orr had insisted that the change had been brought about in order to keep me out of the ranks of the unemployed. Since everybody was healthy, there was no need for me to practice. Shula had told me to be quiet and stay out of everyone's way. I spent a lot of that time talking to the kickers.

One afternoon about eight of us were having an after-practice beer or two at a bar down the street from the Boxwood. After a couple of hours, we were down to four drinkers. An hour or so later, there was only Lou and myself, sitting side by side in the same booth. Lou was on the outside to my right, and he was lefthanded.

Without thinking, I had inadvertently referred to him as a dumb Polack. Lou took exception to the remark, and informed me that he was about to remove my teeth. While Lou was pivoting his body into a position where he could belt me with his large left fist, I had just enough time to think of a way to save myself. Where the idea came from I don't know, but I took the offensive. "Lou," I said, "you can hit me if you want to, but hasn't anybody told you?"

"Told me what?" growled Lou.

"Hasn't anybody told you that I own the team?" I said.

"You don't own the team, Carroll Rosenbloom owns the team, " he insisted.

"Carroll and I own the team, Lou," I shot back. "You've heard of player-coaches, haven't you, Lou? Well, I'm a player-owner. You've been with the team three days. Have you seen me do anything in that time?" I asked.

"No, I guess not," he said, now showing a little uncertainty.

"Carroll called me the other night about you, Lou, and told me you were available. He said that you could kick as well as play defensive end and that he'd like to give you a try, but he was afraid you were a troublemaker. I told Carroll there would be no more problems. I would be right there to check on you personally, and if you screwed up, even once, that I would send you back to Swoyersville on the first available bus. I won't even give you plane fare, Lou." He could go on and hit me if he wanted to, I told him, but just as sure as he did, he had better pack his bags, because he would be leaving on the first running dog back to Pennsylvania.

Lou could say nothing. He didn't actually believe me, but he just wasn't sure. He stared at me for a minute, then got up and left.

The next day I got to practice early, and I told Gino, Freddie Shuback, the equipment manager, and Bert Bell what had happened. I asked them to drop the hint of my ownership around Lou. I stayed away from Lou that day. After practice Gino made the remark just loud enough for Lou to hear, "It looks like the Hawk's got a good team this year." Bert Bell happened by and said, "The Hawk's going to be happy, we've sold out again this year." Freddie Shuback gave Lou a pair of socks and told him, "Don't let the Hawk know I gave you these." That did it; as far as Lou was concerned, Alex Hawkins was a player-owner of the Baltimore Colts.

24

At Bert Bell's invitation, I moved into the second floor of his rowhouse on Abel Avenue, not far from Memorial Stadium and two blocks from Sweeney's. The second floor consisted of two unfurnished bedrooms and a bath. I went to a used furniture store and purchased a twelve-dollar rug, a four-dollar lamp, a twenty-dollar queen-size mattress, and a thirty-dollar king-size box spring. I borrowed a light bulb from Bert and four towels, two bars of soap, and four rolls of toilet paper from the Colts. The shower curtain was an open-house gift.

Bert lived on the first floor. His household goods consisted of a living room with a card table and six chairs, one spare tire, and a piano with twenty-eight keys. He had traded his garage to a neighbor for the piano and one free lesson. His bedroom was furnished with a bed, a TV set, a lamp, a dresser with a mirror, and a clock-radio that controlled the room. When the alarm buzzed, the lights, radio, and TV went on and the toilets flushed.

There was no heat, so as the cold weather approached, Bert's dates got heavier. His wardrobe consisted of twelve different outfits, for sport, dress, and leisure, and two pairs of shoes. All of these were black. His black hair was heavily Vaselined in the ducktail style of Elvis and Fabian.

Bert had a nickname for everyone. I became "No. 25" and "Hawkie." We were a perfectly lovely duo. Living with him was a learning experience. He was a throwback to an earlier time. He greatly admired his father, and, like him, he worshipped the game of pro football. It didn't matter whether we were eating breakfast, standing at a bar, or sitting across the card table, the conversation always ended up with football. Through my association with him I received a thorough education in the game.

The Bells were members of the old guard, made up of Bert Bell, Sr., Art Rooney, Tim Mara, George Halas, and George Marshall. These were the men who had introduced the pro game, and they were responsible for building it into the giant enterprise it was fast becoming. To these men, professional football was almost a religious obligation. They considered themselves trustees of the sport, whose function was to protect and nourish the fortunes of the sport.

Ironically, all of these men were heavy gamblers and colorful promoters, but when it came to what was good for the game their integrity was bedrock solid. Pro football was not a business to them; it was a way of life.

Bert Bell, Jr., became my gridiron guru. His stories of the early days of pro football were exciting, packed with humor and romance. My two favorite characters in his stories were Bert Bell, Sr., and Art Rooney. As different as night and day in family backgrounds, they were welded together in unshakable friendship by the game of pro football.

De Benneville Bell, Sr., known as Bert, was a man born into Philadelphia main line society, a product of a wealthy political family. His father was once attorney general of Pennsylvania, and during the 1890s a member of the Intercollegiate Football Rules Committee; his grandfather had served in Congress, and his brother sat on the state supreme court. The Bell family had both money and position.

Bert himself was the black sheep of the family. What he had loved was sports and gambling. He played quarterback on the University of Pennsylvania football team. To the horror of the rest of the family, he married an actress from the Ziegfield Follies. After graduation, he coached at the University of Pennsylvania for a time before buying the Philadelphia Eagles in 1936. For five years, he split time as owner, coach, publicity and advertising chairman, as well as ticket manager.

Once he rented Philadelphia's Municipal Stadium, which seated

102,000, and won his Eagles the dubious distinction of playing before the largest absentee audience in pro football history: not one single paying customer showed up. Only the press was present to witness the game.

After the 1940 season, he swapped the Philadelphia franchise for the Pittsburgh Steelers, and was co-owner with Art Rooney. His one-year coaching record there was 1–9–1, giving him a lifetime coaching record of 11–53–3. In 1943, because of wartime travel restrictions and a shortage of manpower, the Steelers were merged with the Eagles, and the team was named the Steagles. A colorful nonconformist, Bell was clearly not a coach, so in 1946 he became Commissioner of the National Football League.

A successful gambler who would bet $20,000 on a horse race at Saratoga, he was one of the best three or four bridge players in the country. Bert was a high roller, but he would not tolerate betting on football games. He was a strong, fair person, who defended the weaker owners from the stronger ones. Often he took the side of a player against an owner. He was once quoted as saying, "The one thing we can't forget is that this game was built and made popular by the players. We owe them everything. I don't think that any group of athletes in the world can match pro football players for honesty, character, and strength."

He had a genuine love for professional football and a burning compulsion to keep the game healthy. "Television has made the pro game what it is today," he declared, "but it can ruin it just as fast if we are not careful about over-exposure."

On October 11, 1959, Bert was attending the Philadelphia-Pittsburgh game in Franklin Field when he died of a heart attack. At one time he had owned and coached both teams, and had played his last college game in Frankin Field in 1919. The following Wednesday, October 14, he was to have signed the papers to purchase the Philadelphia Eagles for his sons Bert, Jr., and Upton.

The Rooneys, on the other hand, first came to Pittsburgh from Pennsylvania's rural coal country. Art's father founded the Rooney Saloon, which fast became the watering hole of the city's Irish sportsmen and politicians. Art was one of the city's better amateur baseball players and boxers, then he turned pro and fought at carnivals for a short while before going into politics.

Art's real love was not football, but horse racing. It was through handicapping horse races that he came to own the Pittsburgh Steelers. During a two-day stretch, one at the Empire City track and another at Saratoga, he turned two twenty-dollar wagers into a $250,000 payout. In 1933 the Pittsburgh franchise was being offered for sale for $2,500 and with this racetrack winning he purchased the franchise for the city. For the first twelve seasons the Pittsburgh franchise lost money, and Rooney's prowess at the track was essential to its survival.

In his attitudes toward the NFL, Bert Bell, Jr., had been schooled by the old guard, and he passed their thinking on to me. Without knowing it, I soon became the youngest old codger in the league. Bert was a Damon Runyonesque person, and I came to know most of the characters and nightlife people of Baltimore. There was no organized crime in the city; they tried their best but they just couldn't find anyone organized enough to run it. Monday nights we went to the club fights at the steelworkers' hall. Tuesdays, when they were in town, we went to the Baltimore Bullets' games. We sat with the bookmakers who were gathered together in the stands. Wednesday night was poker-playing night at Bert's. Thursday night was the big party night at Sweeney's. Friday nights were movie nights and early to bed. My routine was pretty well hammered out.

After losing the opening game in 1964 to the Vikings, we got on a winning streak and by the middle of November we had clinched our divisional title. When we were winning, the days went by so fast that I felt like I was having breakfast every fifteen minutes. The emphasis on the special teams was working well for us and the Captain Who business had captured the imagination of the city. I had vaulted into a semi-celebrity status. Two people who sat behind our dugout even started a Captain Who fan club, and before the season was over the membership had mushroomed to four.

One morning I returned to my apartment in the rowhouse to find Bert asleep in my bed. When I asked him why he was there instead of in his rooms, Bert told me to go down and look in his bed. Then he told me how he had to get Lou Michaels out of jail that evening.

It seemed that at about 4:30 A.M. Lou had been involved in an automobile accident near the Block. I marched into Bert's room and switched on the lights. There was Lou, fully clothed and covered with blood. His tongue had been nearly severed in half, and he had three cracked ribs. When I awakened Lou and demanded an explanation, Lou started crying, "Of all the people in the world to see me this way, it had to be you," he moaned.

"What were you doing on the Block at that time of night?" I demanded.

"Visiting friends," he said.

"Listen to me and listen good," I yelled, "We've got a great shot at the title, and you have to go and screw things up. We've got a big game in just two days, and you are our only kicker. You are *not* going to miss a day of practice, and you *are* going to kick."

At practice that day I stood beside Lou while he practiced field goals and kickoffs. Although he was in terrible pain, he never let on. So as not to insure the wrath of the player-owner he played on Sunday. Don Shula said something to me about being a rotten son-of-a-bitch, but he enjoyed it as much as anyone.

On Tuesday, Nov. 24, I was at an election party at the Gridiron Club when I got a call from the Baltimore police. The calling officer asked whether I spoke Looney language. I realized that what he meant was whether I could communicate with Joe Don. "At times," I replied.

"Well, you had better get on over to his apartment, because he's in trouble, and when we left here he said that if we came after him we had better bring a dozen men," the officer told me.

As soon as I hung up, there was another call, from general manager Don Kellett. He informed me that Joe Don had kicked down a neighbor's door and had beaten up two men in the apartment. The injured parties had sworn out a warrant for Joe Don's roommate, but said they wouldn't prosecute Joe Don because they were Colt fans. He told me to go over and stay with Joe Don so that he wouldn't create further problems.

When I arrived at Joe Don's, I found the door locked. Joe was inside, with a barricade in front of the door. Finally I persuaded him to let me come in. Joe and I were both big Barry Goldwater supporters and he explained that he was upset over the presidential elections and had gotten drunk. Joe Don was not a big drinker; in fact, he almost never drank. When he did, however, he invariably got into trouble. He and Flynn, his roommate, had been invited to dinner by two girls in the same apartment complex, he said. They had knocked on the wrong door, and when they were refused entrance, they had taken matters into their own hands. Joe went back to his apartment and put on his "quick starts"—his tennis shoes. Then he knocked down the door and waded into the two guys inside. He didn't feel it was right for Flynn to go to jail while he went free. We sat up most of the night talking.

The 1960s had brought about changes in attitudes, and Joe Don was a full-blown product of the sixties. That night he got out pictures and maps of an island off the coast of Australia, which he and Flynn and two other friends were buying on the installment plan. In five years the island would be all theirs. I asked Joe what he was going to do with the island after it was theirs. The four of them were going to build a boat, he said, pick up some healthy chicks, and go there and breed. What they intended to do was to start a "super race."

Joe finally fell asleep, but I stayed there with them for the rest of the night, pondering the meaning of this new breed of athlete. I was delighted to see the morning sun appear over the rooftops of East Baltimore. When I told Shula that I would not turn off the lights in a room with a person crazier than I was, I had meant it.

By winning eleven straight games and sewing up our division with four games to go, the Colts were once again on top of the world. We always knew where we stood in terms of popularity when we went out to the West Coast. If there were a lot of Hollywood people in our dressing room after the Rams game, we knew we were "America's Team." That year we had a lot of them.

After the game in Los Angeles, John Unitas and I were sitting in a restaurant having dinner with Max Baer, Jr., and Robert Mitchum's son, Jim, when Hollywood columnist Louella Parsons approached our table. I had no idea how important Louella was, and Unitas was without interest in such matters. He did not like pretense of any kind. John loved children, and would stand in the rain, sign autographs, and pose for pictures for as long as they wanted, but he would not have driven fifty miles to meet the president of the United States.

When Louella approached our table, Mitchum and Baer almost turned the table over to greet her. Louella Parsons addressed John from the rear. "Mr. Unitas, I have always been a big fan of yours," she gushed, "and I would like to take this opportunity to meet you."

Looking straight up and over his head, he replied, "Sure, Louella, sit your ass down and have a beer." Louella dropped her cane and did a 9.5 sprint out of the restaurant. John's response might appear to have been rude, but he was so untouched by success and so unimpressed with stardom for himself or anyone else, that it was just a natural thing for him to say.

After our two wins on the Coast, we decided to take in Las Vegas before returning to Baltimore. The Colts seemed to be invincible, and meanwhile off the field we were playing fast and loose. This bunch of renegades Shula had assembled were on fire; we were making a shambles of the rest of the league.

Jimmy Orr and I had gone to Vegas the year before. We had met a few of the casino people, and didn't feel like tourists. Although the NFL did not approve of our being in Vegas, it had not been placed off limits. Naturally, Vegas took care of the bill for everything: rooms, meals, drinks, women, anything. It did not hurt business one bit to have Unitas at the tables. As for me, I just loved the idea of being in a city with no clocks.

We were at the tables when it was announced that Wendell Harris and Joe Don Looney had just arrived, full-blown drunk in

Bermuda shorts with no change of clothes, and they were looking for us. I hastened to the entrance and there found Joe Don terrorizing a room-service waiter in the hall. He had the waiter backed up against the wall and was doing monkey flips and headstands and bounding around in a crouched position like a chimpanzee. After calming Joe Don and locating Wendell, we got them a room and put them to bed around nine o'clock.

Shortly after midnight, I saw Wendell. He was dressed in a nice shirt and a pair of slacks that had been folded twice at the cuff and were still too long. Joe Don had cornered a guest in the hotel, Wendell explained, and told him to take off his clothes, because he needed them for Wendell. The guest complied, and now Joe Don was somewhere outfitting himself. It was time to leave Vegas; we were having too much fun.

We finished the regular season with twelve wins and two losses, bettering Green Bay by three-and-a-half games. We were easily the class of the NFL, and were looking forward to the championship game against the Browns in Cleveland.

All week we studied films of the Browns' defense. The Browns had one of the worst defenses in football that year, with the weakest secondary in football. Unitas should have a field day. We couldn't help but feel confident.

On Thursday, as was my custom, I talked to Bobby Boyd about the Browns' offense. Strange as it may seem, most players are poor at assessing another team's overall talent. They study only the person they play against. I had confidence in Bobby's ability to view the overall picture. To my surprise, he informed me that the Browns were good—very good.

To beat the Browns we all knew we had to contain Jim Brown, the greatest runner in the game. Jim Brown was going to gain one hundred yards or better, that was a foregone conclusion. The objective was not to let him run wild.

Bobby warned me that Gary Collins, the Browns' flanker, was a fine receiver, and that Paul Warfield, on the other side of the line, was probably the most dangerous receiver in the game. I told Bobby to relax; I was confident our offense could score thirty points or more. "They have no chance of stopping us," went my immortal words. My only concern was the weather in Cleveland. A frozen field could neutralize the game and favor a strong running team. There was no confusing the playing conditions of Cleveland with the climate at Miami Beach on December 27.

On the morning of the game Orr and I gathered in Bobby Boyd's room, as was our custom. Superstition runs strong among athletes, and that had been our routine for the past couple of years. The first thing we did on game days was to check out the wind. The reason Unitas threw the easiest pass to catch in football was that he had a "hole" in his throw; by this, I mean he did not throw a perfect spiral. Quarterbacks like Babe Parilli and Frank Ryan, who threw the perfect spiral, were better in the wind, but the ball they threw was "heavy" and harder to hold on to. A strong wind always affected Unitas adversely.

When I looked out the hotel window, a flag across the street was standing straight out. The wind was the first thing Orr mentioned at breakfast. It was blowing heavily, and as game time approached it continued to get worse. When we got to the stadium we found that the ground wasn't frozen, but the wind coming off Lake Erie was horrible.

An athlete's mental attitude is based on confidence. The slightest sense of doubt can be disastrous. I can't speak for everyone on the team, but Orr and I had reservations.

The first half was scoreless, but in the third quarter Collins caught two touchdown passes and Lou Groza kicked a field goal, to give Cleveland a 17–0 lead. Time and time again, Jimmy Orr worked his way open, only to have the ball blown away by near-gale-force winds. The delicate precision between Unitas and Berry was literally gone with the wind. Even more astonishingly, Jim Parker, our great offensive lineman, was being repeatedly whipped by Jim Kikinski, a rookie tackle. It was all over, and we could feel it. It mattered not that Collins caught another bomb in the fourth period, or that Groza connected on yet another field goal. We never really threatened. The Browns walked away with a 27–0 win and the world championship.

I never felt sicker or more bitter over a loss in all my life. We had been shut out by the Cleveland Browns! I could not accept the fact. How could a team that had averaged scoring better than thirty points a game be held scoreless by the Browns? It was humiliating; it made no sense, no sense at all. I knew it would be bitter whisky I drank that night—which it was.

Libby had spent Christmas in Manning and had come up the day after to share in the victory celebration. She was staying with Dottie Unitas, John's wife, and they had watched the game together. Neither John nor I liked losing, and perhaps we took it harder than some people. Hardly a word was spoken. When we walked into the house, Dottie was polishing the floors and Libby was pretending that she was sewing. John and I went downstairs to his bar stool and pool table, and replayed the game over and over, well into the night. Finally, around 3:00 A.M., we decided we hated every player on the team, and that the two of us were the only decent people left in the world. A football player lives from game to game. A victory is good for a week, and so is a loss. We carry the feeling of elation or despair with us until the next game. Now there wouldn't be another game until September, so the rage and hatred were just starting to boil.

The next day Libby and I drove back to Manning. I had put off having to grow up during the off-season for the past few years by going back to college. I had been raised to finish anything I started. It had taken me nine years to do it, but the previous year I had graduated from the University of South Carolina.

We had built a lake house on the Santee in 1961. We had been spending most of our weekends there, and we planned to live there in the off-season. Now we had two children, a four-year-old son and a three-year-old daughter. Lake Marion was a great place to raise children and get to know our family.

For the next two weeks and more I refused to see or talk to anyone. I couldn't get that Cleveland game out of my mind. Talk about the agony of defeat—that 27–0 pounding was indelible. I couldn't erase the disappointment. It was wrong; it shouldn't have happened. I felt certain of that.

25

Living full-time in a small Southern town is a very different matter from visiting there on the weekend. I loved the outdoors, and now I had the time to enjoy it. It was paradise. There was so much at my disposal, and so many things to do. As the shock of the defeat wore off, I began to enjoy being there.

I rearranged my schedule completely. Depending on the season and time of year, I got up early and went fishing or duck hunting, then returned to the lake house and had breakfast with the children. After breakfast I watched "I Love Lucy," "Andy of Mayberry," and "The Real McCoys" on the television and then took a nap until lunchtime.

After lunch I drove the seven miles to the local country club to play golf. The dues were only $160 a year, there were less than forty club members, and fewer than thirty of them played golf. I could play eighteen or thirty-six holes and still get back to the lake by five o'clock to fish or hunt until dark. Then I had dinner with the children and went to bed. It was a complete departure from my Baltimore life-style, and I learned to enjoy it as much or even more.

Let me give an example of how small the town was. One day a friend from Baltimore was driving through town on his way to Florida. He stopped to get gas in Manning and asked the owner whether he knew where I could be reached. Without a moment's hesitation, he was informed that I could be found at the seventh hole of the golf course, practicing my sand shots. He not only knew who I was, he knew where I was. When my friend arrived I was swinging away in the sand trap.

During the week I had the lake almost to myself. There was always someone to go fishing or hunting with, and some kind of fish was always biting.

The winter months featured the finest rock, or striped, bass and crappie fishing in the world. In late March, April, and May the bass fishing was the greatest in the country. The bass would average four or five pounds apiece. The bass-boat had not come along yet, and depth finders, trolling motors, and 150-horsepower outboard motors had not yet made anyone who could afford them an expert bass-master. During the summer months we could fish for bream and white bass, and usually catch our limit in less than two hours. And in the winter I could set my alarm for 5:30 A.M. and be shooting ducks in the back of the slough by 5:45.

If this wasn't enough, we were also members of Home Lake, a private club on the Black River Swamp. The Black River was teeming with bream, warmouth, red breast, and jackfish. Quail, deer, and wild turkey were also abundant in season.

In short, it was a sportsman's dream. I would cash a ten-dollar check every Monday, and the following Monday have change left over. Occasionally we would have friends down for weekends, but more often than not we would play bridge with local people. Libby, of course, was an excellent bridge player. Making friends with the residents of Manning was no problem. South Carolinians were the friendliest people in the world.

J. B. McCord, the town mayor, was the best shot with a rifle or pistol of anyone for miles around. Ralph Cothran was a lawyer and the best golfer in town. Charles McCord built the best boat and was recognized as the best one-armed golfer in town.

The men drank, but rarely in front of women. Bevo Bradham was the town drunk, but only because he wouldn't work. I thought it strange, but perhaps telling, that Bevo was Libby's favorite person.

"Little Brother" Eadon was the town fool. In point of fact, he was no fool at all, but he would act like one on the weekends. I called him "Do Right," which he never did, until one day several years later he just gave in, grew up, and started doing right. He was, and is today, a wonderful person.

Howard Elkins was vice-president of the bank. Howard brewed his own beer, but was careful whom he told about it. Howard was my friend. Randolph ran the marina. His son, Jack, had a fatal disease, but he wouldn't accept it, so apparently it just went away. Herman and Roosevelt were two black brothers who launched boats, cleaned fish, and told jokes to white people for tips.

Dr. Harvin was a good old-fashioned doctor who charged one dollar for an office call and two dollars for a house visit. For as long as he practiced his rates remained the same. Uncle John was the city manager and Miss Rose was a schoolteacher. The two of them began going with each other at fifteen. For fifty-five years they saw each other every night until Uncle John died. No one ever asked them why they didn't marry.

Jehu Jackson was the sheriff. His brother Scott had played football at Clemson.

Marian McKnight had been the beauty queen, but when she became Miss America in 1957 she moved to Hollywood and got married. Judge James Hugh McFadden kept six cold beers in Keith Josey's soda box at the service station.

There were four Jewish families in Manning. My sister-in-law was the only Catholic.

Robert E. Lee was the town's richest man. He was a contractor who spent a lot of time out of town. His dog, Major, always traveled with him.

Miss Polly and Miss Pansy ran the dress shop. Libby's Aunt Tora was the best-looking woman in town. After college she came back home, moved in with Dr. and Mrs. Harvin, and went to work for the doctor. She never dated, but I was the only person ever to think that was strange.

There were persistent rumors that a local preacher was having an affair with a member of his congregation, and that one of the doctors was fooling around with a nurse, but nothing ever came of them. Every few years one of the high school girls would get pregnant, but the father would always marry her and everything would be all right. Life went on as if nothing had happened.

People in small Southern towns have a way of keeping things in perspective. They know that no matter what happens things will somehow get back to normal, and since they will all be staying there and living together, it is better just to gossip about things for a while and then put them away and go on about their lives. They have perfected the art of forgive and forget.

South Carolina was not one of the richer states, and Clarendon County was not one of the more prosperous regions of that state. Blacks outnumbered whites by nine to one, there was almost no industry, and farming was the major occupation. Since the labor supply far exceeded the demand, jobs were hard to come by and wages were low, often in violation of the minimum-wage standards. My mother-in-law, Mrs. Bagnal, worked with the welfare department. She had a maid, Viola Sweat, who came six days a week. Viola came to work at 7:30 A.M. and worked until 4:00 in the afternoon. She washed, ironed, cleaned, and cooked for twelve dollars a week. Our children's nurse, Gertrude, worked from 3:00 P.M. until 7:00 P.M. for fifty cents. She worked all day Saturdays for a dollar.

My father-in-law, J. Scott Bagnal, was born in Manning. His wife, Thena Egeria Mims Bagnal, was born in nearby Pinewood. For all practical purposes, they had never been out of Manning, except for an occasional visit to Sumter, some twenty miles away, for dinner, or a vacation trip by automobile. Neither of the two ever found any reason to venture out. Mr. Bagnal was a rural mail carrier and farmer; he had bought his farm from his in-laws shortly after his marriage.

Mr. Bagnal had seen so many changes in his lifetime, I wondered how he had kept his sanity. He remembered the first automobile that came through Manning. He served in World War I, but never got closer to action than Spartanburg, South Carolina. He witnessed the change from propeller-plane flights to jets to rocketships.

He smoked three packs of cigarettes a day and, if the count could be known, probably went through a pint of Old Crow bourbon a day. He was a sneak drinker who hid half-pints in tackle boxes, behind the toilet, in his car, and under the couch. His health was excellent and his mind razor-sharp. He could still recite nearly every batting average in major league baseball and predict which team would win the NBA.

He maintained that longevity and good health could be attributed to his life-style. He arose at 6:00 A.M. and drank a Coke. Then he ran his mail route (during which he drank another Coke) and finished by 10:00 A.M. After finishing his work, he stopped by the Sinclair station and had his third Coke of the morning with Coon Land, his lifelong friend. He would be home for midday dinner around 11:00 A.M. and start reading one of the two daily newspapers. After dinner—not to be confused with lunch—he would sit in his chair, watch the noon news on television, finish one newspaper, and then nap until the heat cooled.

About three, he would drive to the farm to check on Doot, Cooter, and Blease. These three "darkies," as he referred to them, lived and worked on the farm. They had been born there and stayed there; it was all of life that they knew. Each family had a two-bedroom wooden structure with an open fireplace. They paid no rent, ate off the farm, and were welcome to live there as long as they behaved. I was never sure what that meant.

Doot was the foreman and his orders were respected. One day I saw Cooter with a bandaged head. When I asked him what had happened, he smiled sheepishly and referred me to Doot. Doot told me that Cooter had been drinking and had misbehaved over the weekend, and he had to hit him in the head with an ax. "My God, Doot," I asked, "you didn't really hit him in the head with an ax, did you?"

"Don't be worried, Mr. Alex, I only hit him with da dull end," he replied.

Doot, Cooter, Blease, and their families still live on that farm. They would not consider leaving the place where they were born and grew up. They understood life on these terms.

I had no practical sense about anything mechanical, nor did I understand its applications. There is no telling how many times I had to send for help to get my car started or pulled out of a ditch. The workings of an outboard motor were a complete mystery to me; many times the locals had to tow me off the lake, or fish me out after I had turned over a boat. Sometimes I ran out of gas or had motors explode on me. Mothers and wives gave a sigh of relief when I got their children and husbands back safely. In short, I was a menace to the community, tolerated because of Libby and the fact that I was a pro football player.

When Libby saw that I was not putting on an act and that I was actually just as helpless as I appeared, she started doing everything for me. Here was a Southern lady, who was not supposed to have enough sense to open a door or lock the house, doing everything from changing tires to working on motors. She could fix broken fishing reels and repair guns. She could fix a toaster oven, repair a television set, or fix a watch or camera. She even knew a little about plumbing. Given three days of good training, I have no doubt she could have run the entire space program.

Approximately once a month the clean, quiet life would start to be boring and I would excuse myself for a weekend and go to Baltimore, Charlotte, or Columbia for a tear. Meanwhile I began to notice a change in some of my old friends. Those poor souls who had finished school, gotten married, and taken jobs as salesmen, teachers, coaches, and bankers were beginning to advance themselves in life. Initially they had taken jobs that paid five or six thousand dollars a year. They were now making almost as much money as I was for playing football.

Even so, I couldn't envision myself living a "normal" existence. I needed more excitement. How could my friends possibly take life seriously, when all they had to look forward to was more of the same? I could not imagine myself performing the tasks that they had to perform to earn a living. The only future that I looked forward to was the opening game of the next NFL season.

26

Most of the Colt veterans had reported early for the '65 season. Our attitudes were in every case identical: this year we would take no prisoners. This was a vendetta year, to square things for that performance in Cleveland. Everyone had taken that loss to heart. We had all been embarrassed, and we wanted to atone for it. That bitter loss to the Browns had pulled us together as a team.

Bill Pellington and Gino Marchetti had retired, leaving a huge void in the defensive leadership. A Gino Marchetti simply cannot be replaced. He had been an All-Pro selection for eight years in a row. He was, simply, the greatest defensive end who ever played football. Gino had virtually revolutionized pass rushing. Back when we were playing only twelve games a season, he was already getting forty to fifty sacks a season. There were never less than two men assigned to block him, and often three. A quiet man, he was a leader by example. Bobby Boyd, Jerry Logan, and Jimmy Welch would somehow have to make up for the lost leadership.

In terms of personnel we were not a great team, like the 1958 and 1959 Colts, but we were a very good team. We had a team spirit that helped to make up the difference.

The night before our first practice we had a team party at a local bar. About ten o'clock Bobby Boyd warned me I'd better leave, because Lou Michaels had switched from beer to Scotch. Lou never got mean on beer, but he did on Scotch. I glanced around at Lou and sure enough, he had that angry glare. It seems that Art Rooney, the Steelers' owner, had revealed to Lou that I did not really own any part of the Colts. Lou felt he had been made to look like a fool, and he was not at all happy about it. I could see that my leverage as supposed owner-player was gone.

I was rooming with Billy Lothridge, so I went to him and suggested that we leave. When we got back to the dorm we locked our door. Normally players don't lock their rooms, but we did that night.

About 10:45, the players started coming in and a water battle started in our hall. Suddenly there was a knock on my door. "Who is it?" I asked.

"It's Lou," a gruff voice answered.

"What do you want, Lou?" I asked.

"I want you to open the door so I can tear your little blond head off," came the answer.

"Let me get this straight," I said. "You want me to open the door so that you can tear my head off, is that right?"

"Yes," said Lou.

"Well, then, I am not going to open the door," I responded.

"I can come right through the door," Lou said.

I informed him that it was very thick door, and I also asked Lothridge for a weapon in the event that he did. Billy handed me a wooden shoeshine box, which was the nearest thing we had to a blunt instrument.

"Well, you've got to come out sometime," he said as he sat down on the wet hall floor.

"Not until breakfast," I informed him.

"I'll just wait," he replied.

About that time John Sandusky, an assistant coach, came by for bed check. "Why aren't you in your room, Lou?" John asked. Lou told him he was waiting for me to come out so he could tear my little blond head off. Sandusky, who was just as leery of Lou as I was, went to get Shula.

I heard Shula tell Lou that if he wasn't in his room in two minutes, he would be fined $500. The best way to reach Lou was through his billfold. So he left. Shula knocked on the door and I let him in. "What did you do to Lou?" he asked.

"He found out I don't own the Colts," I told him.

"Don't worry," he said, "I can take care of that." Shula left.

The next morning before breakfast, Shula sent for Lou. He told

Lou that I had some pretty serious mental problems, and that I probably thought I did own the team. You can't afford to let a sick man get you into trouble, Shula told Lou. He suggested to Lou that it would be better just to humor me. The thought that I might be crazier than he was thrilled Lou Michaels.

When I entered the training room that morning Lou was getting taped. He greeted me like a long-lost friend, placing his massive arm around my neck very playfully, while making small circles around his temple with his other hand to indicate that I was crazy. "Hawk is my good buddy. Not too bright, but still my good friend. Did you really think I was going to hit you last night?" he joked.

"Naw, Lou," I lied. "I knew you wouldn't do that, there was never a doubt in my mind." From now on I would have to be on my toes with Lou, but Shula had once again bailed me out.

For the first time, the Colts and I were having contract problems. I had asked for a $5,000 raise, and they had offered me $2,000. That "other league" had started a price war, and even rookies were demanding more money and getting it. Joe Namath, a quarterback from Alabama, had just signed with the Jets for the unheard-of salary of $400,000. We all knew that was a ridiculous figure; nobody was worth that kind of money. Unitas was the best in the game, and he was making only $100,000. Still, if prices were going up, I wanted my share of it.

Don Kellett would not budge. Finally Shula came to me and told me I had better sign, because the Colts were going no higher. After having lost the championship game, Rosenbloom was not feeling charitable.

No Colt player had ever played out his option, and there was always the threat that if I didn't sign, I would be traded to Pittsburgh. Nobody wanted to be a Steeler. I finally agreed, but only after Shula gave me his word that if an expansion team was awarded to a Southern city, he would make me expendable.

The college draft that year had brought us Mike Curtis, a fullback from Duke and a natural linebacker. Away from the football field Mike was a quiet, well-mannered, intelligent young man, but when he put on a uniform, he took on an entirely different personality. He became quick-tempered, hostile, and hypertensive. He was the most combustible young man I had ever known. Something about the smell of a locker room seemed to transform him into a stalking, raging animal.

Jimmy Orr's theory was that when Mike was conceived his mother had mistakenly taken a Dexedrine tablet, thinking it was a birth control pill. Whatever the reason, he was big, fast, mean, and quick, and even more importantly he had madness about him. I knew he would do well on the special teams if I could just keep him pointed at the enemy instead of turning on me.

As the regular season approached the attitude of the '65 Colts was something to behold. Usually we didn't care much about preseason games, but this year we took a genuine satisfaction in winning all five of them convincingly. There was a closeness about this team, a dedication of resolve. We were a loose, reckless, daring outfit that I'm sure Shula was proud to present in his image. We were ready to start the 1965 season.

27

I moved back in with Bert in my penthouse apartment on Abell Avenue and we resumed our schedule, with only moderate changes. Since this was not one of the more desirable neighborhoods in Baltimore, burglars would occasionally drop by after the lights were off. Bert had already warned me not to acknowledge them by waking up; frequently they carried guns. With Bert it was a game, because there was nothing of value to steal. He was wondering when the news would get around the criminal community that we were deadbeats, he said. We slept with our money under our mattresses.

It seems that the Colts' publicity department was struggling for ways to describe me these days. The press guide note read, "The Hawk is a tough, daring performer at any position. As a leader of the suicide squad, the Carolina cottontop instills spirit, enthusiasm, and pride into his mates." I could live happily with that distinction.

The year before I had offered a hundred-dollar prize for the special team player who graded out highest. The hitch was that I was the one grading out their performances. There were a lot of close seconds, but somehow I always finished first.

We opened the '65 season with a win over the Vikings, followed by a 20–17 loss to the Packers in Green Bay. We became even more determined, and promptly went on a winning tear.

In Washington, right before the Skins game, Raymond Berry told me to get ready. He had pulled a muscle in warmups and felt he might not be able to play. Shula was informed of it, but elected to go with Raymond even so. Like any child, I was hurt. I had developed into a fairly competent receiver, and Unitas had confidence in me. I knew I was not the receiver Raymond Berry was, but I felt that I was a better receiver on two legs than Raymond was on one.

In our 38–7 win over the Redskins, Raymond caught only one pass. After that game, I had made my feelings known to Cameron Snyder, a sportswriter and friend, who printed it in the morning newspaper. The next morning I got a call from Shula's secretary. She said Don wanted to see me right away.

When I entered his office Shula was livid. That great stone jaw of his was set and there was fire in his eyes. Since I had not yet read the newspaper, I wasn't sure what he was mad about. I found later that I had not been quoted, but the context of my story was in print.

Shula showed me the papers and demanded, "Is this your shit?" I glanced at the first couple of sentences and realized that Snyder had quoted me. "Yes," I answered. "He wasn't suppose to have printed it, but those are my words."

"Well, you asshole, we've got a good thing going and you try to screw it up with shit like this."

"He wasn't supposed to print that," I argued, "but it's the truth. I am a better receiver when I'm healthy than Raymond is when he's hurt."

"That has nothing to do with it," said Shula. "What you're doing is second guessing my decision, and I won't have it. Now get your ass out of here. I don't want to see you any more today. From now on, keep your mouth shut."

Shula knew all too well that I've never been able to keep my mouth shut, but he was serious, so I left.

On my way home I did some heavy thinking. Over the past couple of years I had watched other receivers around the league, and I felt strongly that I was better than several of them. I knew I was not better than Lenny Moore, Jimmy Orr, or Raymond Berry, but I was better than some of the other receivers who were starting for other teams.

It was at that moment that the Peter Principle—that everyone gets promoted until he goes beyond the limits of his competence

—set in. No one could ask for better treatment than was given me by Shula and the Colts. I had been given full semi-celebrity treatment by the coaches and everybody in the city. However, this was no longer enough. I wanted to be a regular.

Meanwhile we continued on a roll, winning our next three games. Our offense was scoring over thirty-two points a game, and our defense giving up less than eighteen points. Our special teams were doing just as well. We were averaging almost ten yards per punt return, and giving up less than two. Each of our kick-off returns gained thirty-two yards, and we were limiting our opponents to less than twenty. Going into the Viking game in Minnesota we had reeled off six straight wins.

Nobody ever knew what to expect when playing a Van Brocklin–coached team. Minnesota was one of two teams whose stadiums had both benches on the same side of the field. This allowed us to stand just a few feet away from the stormy Dutchman and watch and listen to his coaching tirades and sideline theatrics.

There are a number of ways to describe the Dutchman. He was brilliant, fiery, stubborn, sometimes vicious and vitriolic. He was quick-tempered and viper-tongued, and always extremely colorful. Van Brocklin had been a great player, and like all great players he expected everyone to be as good as he had been. He had a deep respect for professional football, and definite opinions on how it should be played. Sometimes these feelings were so strong that they were self-destructive.

The Vikings had a rookie cornerback named Earsell McBee, who would be defending against Jimmy Orr and Lenny Moore. Earsell was no match for these two, and the Viking defensive coach, "Gummy" Carr, who knew this, went to the Dutchman and asked him to use a zone defense. He might just as well have asked him to burn water. It wasn't that he didn't want to; he couldn't. The Dutchman hated the zone defense. It went against his principles. The Dutchman had a huge ego and a strong will. If he thought it was wrong, it *was* wrong. The case was closed. Gummy begged him, and tried to reason with him that Earsell was not ready to go against Orr and Moore, but the Dutchman's mind was made up. He told Carr that Earsell was a man, and he expected him to play like a man. There would be no zone defense.

Unitas's back was ailing, and Gary Cuozzo was making his first start as a Colt quarterback. We beat the Vikings that afternoon 41–14, with Cuozzo throwing five touchdown passes. Four were at the expense of Earsell McBee. After the third touchdown, Carr once again pleaded for the zone, but the Dutchman had already spoken. I was standing not five feet from Norm when Cuozzo completed the fourth touchdown pass. Van Brocklin cupped his hands and hollered onto the field, "That's it, McBee, you son-of-a-bitch, set a record."

On December 5, the Bears came to Baltimore, bent on revenge for an earlier defeat. The Bears had two No. 1 draft picks that year and they had used them well, drafting linebacker Dick Butkus with one and running back Gale Sayers with the other. Talk about impact players, these two were something special. Sayers was the entire Bear offense, and on defense Butkus was a one-man gang.

Despite the fact that we had dominated play on special teams for the past three years, no other teams had followed our lead in putting an emphasis on special teams. Then George Halas put Dick Butkus in the wedge and Gale Sayers returning kickoffs and punts. We didn't know which one to fear most. Butkus was like a tank running fearlessly at us at full speed. Sayers, the most dangerous runner in the game, followed behind him with lightning feet that seemed to touch the ground only every ten yards. I was praying for a low-scoring game, because I did not look forward to kicking off very often.

Pro football had never previously seen the likes of Dick Butkus. In just his first season he had become the most dominating, intimidating player of all time. No previous linebacker had played the game like this man. He was a bear who walked like a man. In addition to having all the physical requirements, he was also the most intuitive and instinctive linebacker who ever lived. It didn't matter what position you played, you always felt his presence. Two blockers were always assigned to him, but it was futile. He warded off blockers as if they were gnats.

Before the game was done, Butkus had intercepted two passes and caused and recovered four fumbles as the Bears mauled us, 13–0, for our second loss of the season.

Just before the first half ended, Unitas was sacked and was late getting up. In six years of playing with John this was only the second time I had seen him stay on the ground. I knew he was hurt and went onto the field along with the trainers. When we got to John he was still down, holding his knee, trying in vain to get up on his feet. Once again Doug Atkins stood over him after Earl Leggett had sacked him and said, "Well, boy, I guess that's it for you today." This time he was right. John had torn the ligaments and cartilage in his right knee and was finished for the year. With two games to play and a half-game lead in our division, we would face the Packers next week with Gary Cuozzo as our only quarterback.

28

When they came to Baltimore, the Packers were 9–3, while we were now at 9–2–1, with a half-game lead. A win over Lombardi would clinch our division championship.

Paul Hornung ran for three touchdowns and caught scoring passes of fifty and sixty-five yards, and the Packers beat us for the second time, 42–27. Hornung, who had been benched the two previous games for poor performances, was once again the Golden Boy.

Bear Bryant once made the statement that most games are decided by only five or six plays. The secret to coaching was to have the right players on the field when these plays occurred. Did Lombardi know something we didn't? In our first game, Max McGee, a money player, had beaten us. Now it was Paul Hornung who came to the front. It really made me stop and wonder what it would take to beat Lombardi.

In the third quarter Gary Cuozzo left the game with a shoulder injury, and Tom Matte, who had been a quarterback in college, filled in for him on that series. Gary returned and finished the game, but X-rays later revealed that Cuozzo had suffered a shoulder separation and would be unable to play again that year. That left us a half-game behind the Packers with one game to play and no quarterback.

On Monday, Shula got on the phone and tried to locate a signal caller. First he contacted Lamar McHan, who had played with us in '63, and was familiar with our offense. Now retired, McHan was back farming in Arkansas. He had a terrible fear of flying. Shula asked Lamar to come to Baltimore that day so he could work out with the team on Tuesday. We would then fly to Los Angeles on Wednesday, and after the game we would return to Baltimore. During the time Shula was talking, McHan was calculating the number of air miles ahead of him. Even with the possibility of a championship at hand, Lamar told Shula that he just couldn't make it, because his wife was having people over for bridge on Saturday. Then he hung up the telephone.

Back to the drawing board went Shula, and by Thursday he had wrangled a deal with Pittsburgh for their quarterback, Ed Brown. Ed had already planned to retire after the '65 season, so this would be his last game of football. He had quarterbacked the Bears and Steelers, and had been the Steelers' starter when Layne retired.

Brown was cut in the mold of Bobby Layne. A hard person and hard liver who liked his fun, he had agreed to play the last game of his career on his own terms. Those terms were that he could take his girlfriend with him, and that there would be no bed check. All conditions were agreed upon, so with his girlfriend on one arm and a Scotch and a Drambuie in his hand, Ed Brown joined us in Los Angeles on Thursday evening. Damn the torpedoes—full speed ahead.

On Saturday, December 10, we lined up against the Rams in the coliseum with the loosest team ever assembled. We had everything to gain and nothing to lose, and we had the sympathy and attention of the sporting world. Brown, having been with us just a little over twenty-four hours, completed a sixty-eight-yard touchdown to John Mackey during his time at quarterback, and Tom Matte rushed for ninety-nine yards when he was at quarterback, and we held on to beat the Rams 20–17. There was nothing to do now but wait for the outcome of the Sunday game between the Packers and 49ers.

No one really thought the 49ers would beat the Packers, so about half the team decided to watch the game on TV in Las Vegas. Bobby Boyd and I were rooming together in a suite at the Desert Inn. Saturday evening had been good to me; I couldn't lose at the tables. Whatever I played, I was on a roll. I actually became bored with winning, and went from table to table trying to find someone who could beat me. Anyone who has ever been on a winning streak can appreciate this feeling. At blackjack I was hitting seventeen and getting a four. Ten the hard way, at dice, was routine. When I ran out of tables I had already beaten, I went to bed an eight-thousand-dollar winner. My money clip was so loaded with hundred-dollar bills that it would not hold any more. At last I knew what I was going to do after football! Las Vegas was just too easy.

The next morning we set up a bar in our suite to watch the Packers-49ers game. Some of my teammates had not fared as well at the tables, so I quickly loaned out four thousand for walk-around money. There was now room enough in my money clip for tonight's action.

The Packers got off to an early lead, but, surprisingly enough, the 49ers were making it close. The closer it got, the faster we drank. When the game ended in a 24–24 tie, we were delirious. We were jumping up and down on the beds, hugging each other, and laughing at how funny this whole season had been, when the phone rang.

It was Shula, back in Baltimore. He was telling us to get back to town; we had tied Green Bay, and would have to play them next week for the title. When I asked him if he wanted us back that night, he told me we should stay where we were that evening and catch the early flight Monday. It would take a couple of days to figure out what we were going to do, anyway, Shula said. Because he had not played enough games for the Colts, Ed Brown would not be eligible for post-season play.

We showered and headed downstairs for the tables. I thought I might be able to win my teammates' money back for them, now that I had mastered Vegas!

About nine o'clock I went looking for Orr and Boyd, because I was having a temporary cold streak and needed the money I had loaned them to regroup. Their respective financial positions had also reversed, and they both paid me in full.

When I woke up the next morning, I immediately went for my

money clip. It was there all right. Inside the slip, where $100 bills had previously bulged, was one lone quarter. I was sick, and turned to look at Bobby, who was rolling around dying laughing at my poor dumb soul. "Come on, Whitey," said Bobby, "Let's get dressed and get back home, we've got another game to play."

At our Tuesday meeting Shula came up with what were perhaps the most epic lines of his career. "Gentlemen," he said, "Wilson will be starting in place of Berry, Hawkins will be starting ahead of Orr, and Tom Matte will be our quarterback against the Packers. If they can't take a joke, fuck 'em." The entire squad broke up with hysterical laughter, and with that attitude still alive, we went to Green Bay to determine the conference championship.

Shula had no choice but to go with Matte as our quarterback. Tom had played quarterback at Ohio State under Woody Hayes, but Hayes's teams almost never threw the ball.

Tom Matte became a folk hero that year for his gutsy and heroic performance under the most adverse conditions. On the surface Matte was a calm, cool, deliberate individual, but just under the surface he was a furnace of nerves and fears. From the moment he took his first snap from center, Matte was a wreck. His peptic ulcer flared up and afterward he consumed gallons of Maalox to quiet the bleeding ulcer.

He taped the odd-number plays to his left wristband and the even-number plays to his right wristband. His voice was shrill and high-pitched, like a man whose shorts were too tight.

Orr and I alternated taking plays in from the bench. Orr had a strong Southern accent and mine was a nasal-muted Appalachian. Neither was understandable. We would enter the huddle and report the play to George Preas, a tackle from Roanoke, who could decode both Southern and Appalachian. George would recite the play so that everyone could understand it, and Matte would then yell "break."

On the first play from scrimmage Don Shinnick picked up a Packer fumble and ran it in for the score. On that play Bart Starr had been injured, and would not return to the game. So now we led the Packers, 7–0, and they were down to one quarterback. Our defense allowed the Packers nothing, and at halftime we went into the locker room with a 10–0 lead.

In the third quarter, Hornung scored to make it 10–7. Then on fourth down, and with just two minutes to play in the game, the Packers lined up for what would prove to be the tying field goal.

I always watched the kicker's own reaction to see if the kick was good or not. From the sidelines I could tell if it was long enough, but I had no idea whether it was through the uprights. Immediately after the kick, Don Chandler, the Packers' kicker, grabbed his helmet with both hands and turned his back disgustedly on the goal. When Chandler turned away I knew the kick was wide. Then suddenly he turned and started jumping up and down; the official had ruled that the kick was good, and the score was now tied. The game went into overtime, and after 13:39 minutes, Don Chandler kicked a twenty-five-yard field goal to beat us 13–10. It was only the second overtime game played in the NFL.

Later, back in Baltimore, the end-zone movie shots of the controversial tying field goal showed clearly that Chandler's kick had been wide by a good two feet. We played the kick over and over again, and each time it looked wider, but nothing would change the outcome of the heartbreaking loss.

The film was of course sent to the league office, but there was no statement issued. Pete Rozelle's offices on Madison Avenue were strangely mute about it. The following year, the uprights were lengthened ten feet, to the height they are today. It was the league's subtle way of admitting that a mistake had been made, but it was no consolation to us.

After the game we were having a beer in the airport when Shula remarked, "I guess I'll be reading in the papers that I can't win the big games." Sure enough, the next day some of the press and at least one owner were alluding to that premise. The one owner was Carroll Rosenbloom.

Don Shula had done the finest job of coaching ever witnessed in the NFL. He had taken the Colts to the playoffs under the most adverse conditions imaginable. Shula had learned a lot that year.

Out of necessity, he had discovered how to be flexible and innovative, and how to adjust his system to the personnel available.

The next week, the Packers defeated the Cleveland Browns for the NFL Championship. It was Vince Lombardi's third World Championship, and he was being heralded as the finest coach in the land.

As for me, I went on back to Santee, looking forward to the expansion draft.

29

Late one afternoon in February I had just returned from fishing when Libby came running out of the house, telling me that Shula was on the phone. I hurried to the phone, knowing that something had happened. Somehow Libby always knew when something was wrong, while I never did. She was standing in front of the sink, her lower lip was twitching, and tears were mounting in her eyes. Her entire body was trembling.

"What's happening, Shoes?" I spoke into the phone.

"Well, you got your wish," I heard him say. "I put your name on the expansion list and the Falcons claimed you. Alex, you have no idea how much confusion there is with an expansion team. You're not going to like it down there, but you'll have to make the best of it. You asked for it and you got it, but at least you'll get a chance to be a starter. Good luck, Hawk, we'll miss you."

I was scared, but excited and happy. I thanked him for making me available to the Falcons, wished him luck, and hung up the phone. Libby ran to me and broke out sobbing. I started laughing and told her it was what I wanted, it was the opportunity I had been waiting for. I had no illusions of becoming a star, but it was my chance to prove that I was better than many of the other receivers around the league.

"Are you sure this is what you want?" she asked me.

"I am absolutely certain," I replied. I was never any good at making decisions, but once the die was cast I could live with anything. Or so I thought.

I sat down and tried to collect my thoughts. In July I would be thirty. Thirty was the magic mark for receivers and running backs. Every year past it was borrowed time. If you were a quarterback, a field goal kicker, or an offensive or defensive lineman you could play a few years longer, but thirty was the cut-off year for the likes of me.

I was getting along in life, and had still not worked or found a permanent home for the family. Libby was a Southern lady, and wanted very much to stay in the South. If Atlanta was anywhere near as fine a place as Orr had described, it would be a nice community to settle down in. My son, Steele, would soon be starting school, and it was time for me to stop playing gypsy.

About the middle of April, I got a call from Orr, inviting me to the opening of his new restaurant in Atlanta. He said it would be a good time to meet some of his friends. Orr picked me up at the airport and he gave me my first real look around this bustling city —my new home. We drove past the new stadium that was already home for the Braves and would soon house the Falcons. Then we cut through the downtown section and drove on out Peachtree Street northwest to the Buckhead area. He said, "Señor, this is the only place to live. It's all happening in the northwest side of town. You've never had it so good. You won't ever want to leave this city."

Orr checked me into a motel and we picked up Unitas, Matte, and Bobby Boyd, who had come down from Baltimore for the occasion. We had been so close over the years that it was painful to think that I would not be seeing them in training camp that summer. All good things have to come to an end, however. As I dressed for the evening I thought about something Big Lou had once told me. "Be careful of what you want, because you just may get it."

When we got to Jimmy Orr's restaurant the place was overflowing. Having played his college ball at the University of Georgia in Athens, Orr was in his element. To top it off, the Colts had been the most popular team in the South. Most of our games had been televised throughout the region, and Unitas, Boyd, and Matte were as celebrated in Atlanta as they were in Baltimore. Even "Captain Who?" was pretty well-known. As sad as it may seem, Alex Hawkins was to be the biggest name to join the newborn Falcons. With Orr on one side and Unitas on the other I entered the restaurant a full-blown semi-celebrity!

Jimmy Orr had indeed married well. His wife was from a

wealthy, established Buckhead family, and his friends and business partners were the same. These were the young lions of Atlanta, the movers and shakers of the city. There were no Johnny-come-lately types here; the people present were the mainstream, the old money. I had stumbled into the social register of the city.

Three of Jimmy Orr's partners, I. M. Sheffield, Alfred Thompson, and Richard Hull, had grown up together, gone to school together right on through the University of Georgia, and belonged to the same country clubs. More importantly, they all belonged to the Piedmont Driving Club.

The PDC was so exclusive that you did not join, but were born into it. If you were not fortunate enough to do that, you had to marry into it. Numbered among its members were the wealth, power, prominence, and prestige of the city of Atlanta. It was and is the social backbone of the city. There were no blacks or Jews in the Piedmont Driving Club.

As I met and mingled with the elite of Atlanta, I found myself totally awestruck. This was a far cry from my Baltimore crowd. These were the most handsome and cordial people I had ever met. Santa Claus had truly doubled back on me. As the evening progressed, I was more and more overcome by the attitude. With this crowd anything was possible. Everyone was so positive; these people didn't have a worry in the world. Everyone was optimistic. Just when I thought I had met the nicest person in the world, an even nicer person would appear. There was no question about it, Atlanta would support a pro football team. This city would support *anything*.

The Falcons had broken all previous records for ticket sales in the NFL. In just fifty-four days, with no promotions, they had sold 45,000 season tickets. Everyone was wild with excitement over pro football coming into the South. I felt sure that first night that I had finally found a home.

We were all seated having dinner when I was approached by a medium-sized, ruddy-complexioned, abrupt man named Rankin Smith. He introduced himself as my boss, the owner of the Atlanta Falcons, and arrogantly snapped, "You're not going to hold me up about signing a contract, are you?" I thought it was a poor time to discuss business, but I replied that although I would expect a raise over my previous contract, I was not going to hold him up. I told him that I had requested the transfer and was very much looking forward to playing in Atlanta.

When he departed I turned to Orr and asked, "What's with that guy?"

"Don't pay any attention to Rankin," Jimmy said, "he's a good guy, but he drinks too much." From that time forward, the relationship between Rankin Smith and Alex Hawkins went straight downhill.

The next day Orr, Unitas, Boyd, Matte, and I played golf at the new Atlanta Country Club. It was not yet open for play, but since all of my new friends were the only members we played there anyway. At the turn I was notified that I had just been voted in as a member. These were my kind of people. This was the life-style I had been born to enjoy. Since birth this was what I had been searching for: rich, beautiful, happy people to share my life with. I could not wait to tell Libby how happy we were going to be in Atlanta.

Meanwhile, in the spring of 1966, some unusual developments were taking place in professional football. That other league, the AFL, hadn't been taken very seriously until they started playing hardball. In April the American Football League turned to thirty-seven-year-old Al Davis, then the coach and general manager of the Oakland Raiders, and asked him to become commissioner of the AFL. For an all-out war they couldn't have picked a better man.

Al Davis was a man who usually got his way. He loved a fight. His methods were often unorthodox, but his results were impressive. He was a man you would rather have in your tent pissing out than outside your tent pissing in. He knew football. Al was born in Brooklyn and was street-smart and tough: the perfect adversary for a smoothie like Pete Rozelle.

Within only a couple of months, Davis had signed seven of the top quarterbacks in the NFL to AFL contracts. On June 8, 1966, Rozelle agreed to merge the NFL with that other league. He was clearly no match for Al Davis in a street fight.

30

The city of Atlanta had been working to secure a football franchise for several years. In 1964 Billy Bidwell had considered moving his St. Louis Cardinals there but the deal had fallen through. The next year, on June 7, 1965, J. Leonard Reinsch, president of Cox Broadcasting, was awarded an AFL franchise contingent upon exclusive stadium rights.

Pete Rozelle, who had been moving deliberately in Atlanta matters, now caught fire and hopped aboard the next plane south to protect his league's claim on the Empire City of the South. Rozelle met with Arthur Montgomery, chairman of the stadium authority; Ivan Allen, mayor of the city; and Carl Sanders, governor of Georgia. On June 30, Rankin Smith, a roommate of Carl Sanders in college, was awarded the franchise. All the aforementioned were members of the Piedmont Driving Club. The price of the franchise was $8,500,000.

Rankin Smith was president of and major stockholder in the Life Insurance Company of Georgia. Although rich and affluent, until he purchased the Falcons he was relatively unknown. A successful businessman, he was totally uninformed on football matters. To staff the franchise he relied heavily on the advice of the league office. What they had against Rankin Smith is unclear to this day. In any event, what they didn't do to Mr. Smith, he did to himself.

Eyeglasses do not help a man in the dark, but Rankin took it upon himself to hire the head coach. Both Paul Brown and Vince Lombardi were interested in the head coaching job, but both wanted part-ownership. Rankin was not interested in giving up ownership, so the interviews continued. At length Rankin interviewed Green Bay assistant Norb Hecker. Rankin had asked Lombardi about Hecker, and Vince had told him that Norb was not yet ready for head coaching responsibility. For Rankin Smith, that was enough; he figured that Lombardi had said that because he did not want to lose Hecker. It was a classic case of a vain and inexperienced man trying to outsmart a simple, honest one.

In January Norb Hecker was named head coach of the Falcons. Rankin also named his accountant, Frank Wall, vice-president and treasurer. The league office was responsible for recommending Bud Erickson as assistant to the president. Together this group comprised the strangest and most ill-advised front office in the history of the NFL. Not a single one of these men was qualified for the position he held. The Falcons were well on their way to their gloomy destiny from the start. It was the blind leading the blind, as together they stumbled down a dark, dead-end street.

I reported to the Falcon training camp in Black Mountain, North Carolina, the first week in July. Black Mountain is a small town about thirty-five miles east of Asheville. Pro teams always try to locate their training camps in out-of-the-way, secluded areas, but the Falcons had outdone themselves.

I had driven up two days early to survey the place that I would be living in for the next ten weeks. It took me a full hour to drive the thirty-five miles from Asheville because the roads were under construction. Now here I was. To my left was Sewell's Beer Joint, the only one in town. It could seat six people at a time. A sign on my right marked the entrance to the Blue Ridge Assembly, a Baptist retreat that would house the Falcon football operation. In just a matter of days this place would be forever remembered and referred to as "Camp Run Amuck."

I gazed in disbelief as I followed a winding little road about a mile uphill to the Falcon quarters and training site. To my left was a large wooden structure, which was the sleeping quarters. On my right were the training and dressing rooms. About fifty feet above that were some steep steps that led up to the dining room. Following the horseshoe road, I saw a couple of wooden buildings, which were dormitories for camping children and little old ladies who were attending religious seminars.

As I continued on down the hill, a practice field was on my right.

I pulled over and parked the car to inspect the field. It had just been built that spring. The authorities had come in, cut down 300 trees, planted grass, lined the field with lime, and erected two goal posts. The rookies had been practicing for almost a week, and by now the grass was almost gone. The field itself was full of rocks and as hard as Peachtree Street. The large mountain pines on three sides of the field blocked off any possible breeze.

I hurried back to my car, drove straight back to Asheville, and checked into a motel. I picked up the phone and called Shula in Baltimore. When I heard his voice at the other end of the phone, I quickly pleaded, "Shoes, you've got to get me out of here. I can't stand it."

"Is it tough down there?" he asked.

"I don't know, I haven't reported yet, but I can already tell you I can't live here for ten weeks."

Shula reminded me that he had warned me about expansion teams, and went on to tell me that there was nothing he could do about it now. The only way I could return to the Colts was on waivers. He told me just to try to make the best of things, and reminded me again that I had asked to be sent there.

I dressed and went out to see what Asheville had to offer. I had already seen Black Mountain and the Blue Ridge Assembly, and knew there was nothing doing there. Asheville was a beautiful area, but it was not exactly Las Vegas. I had dinner and was back in the room by eleven o'clock. This was going to be a long, hot summer.

The next day I reported to camp vowing to make the very best of the situation that I could. I had brought with me two things I could rely on: the pass-receiving skills and knowledge that Raymond Berry had taught me, and the attitude and life-style that I imagined to be Bobby Layne's. Since I really wasn't sure who I was anyway, I would try to combine the two personalities; on the field I would be Raymond, and off the field I would be Bobby—if I could find a place to practice being him.

Forty-two veterans had reported from other teams. Eighty-eight rookies and free agents had been signed, swelling the total to a hundred thirty players. Before this season was over another forty to fifty players would come and go.

The first evening in camp I was late for bed check, and good-naturedly fined a hundred dollars by head coach Norb Hecker. Hecker was a handsome and likeable soft-spoken guy and he had aligned himself with the most amiable and fun-loving group of assistants you would ever want to spend ten weeks with in Black Mountain. Norb stayed out of the way during most of the practice sessions, while Tom Fears handled the offense and Hall Herring ran the defense. Although the Falcon offensive and defensive playbooks were identical in content to the Packers', I felt sure this operation would be nothing like the one in Green Bay.

The first few days were grueling, with a tremendous amount of time spent on conditioning. The dreaded grass drills seemed longer than I remembered them being at Green Bay. I was sure that this would be reduced in a day or two, but to my surprise the drills started getting longer and longer. The practice sessions were getting longer each day, too.

Every morning a practice session schedule was posted, with a list of what we would be doing that day. The practices usually called for being on the field an hour and forty minutes. Each day, however, a coach would get an idea of something additional to work on and the practice schedule would be modified to allow for the new drills.

It wasn't long before our one-hour-and-forty-minute practices were lasting two-and-a-half to three hours. By the start of the third week I was a mental and physical wreck. I had vertebrae problems in my back, and that stonelike field had compounded them. My thirty-year-old legs were tired and hurting.

We had not been given a night off since we reported to camp. Our free time amounted to two hours each night, which was just enough to visit Sewell's and throw down three or four beers. Pretty soon I found myself sitting in those rocking chairs on the front porch of the dorm, rocking and feeling older by the day. I wondered what Bobby Layne would have done under the circumstances.

The days were long, and the nights even longer. Each day there was more of the same: grass drills and calisthenics. All the emphasis was on conditioning. Norb Hecker saw no reason to deviate from the Lombardi system; it had been successful at Green Bay, and there was no need to change or modify it. There was no first or second unit. If we needed a guard or receiver, any of a dozen guards or receivers stepped in. Consequently there was no working on the timing of a team as a unit. The precision timing between quarterback and wide receiver as I had known it in Baltimore was out of the question. Well, I would just have to make the best of it.

The Falcons had been awarded two picks in each of the first five selections of the college draft. In the first round they had selected Tommy Nobis and Randy Johnson. Nobis was a linebacker from Texas, and it was no surprise that he turned out to be a fine player. Randy Johnson was a quarterback from Texas A&I, with a great throwing arm; it was obvious that he would develop into the starting quarterback. A fourth-round pick was Ken Reaves, a cornerback from Norfolk State. He was a natural at the position, and would later develop into one of the league's best.

Aside from those three picks, the rest of the Falcons' college draft was a complete washout. The remaining twenty-two players were physical mysteries.

The strangest choice of all was the sixth pick in the draft, Charles Casey, a pass-catcher from Florida. Charlie had received a $100,000 signing bonus. He reported to camp with an injured leg, which never healed.

Our trainer, Clint Huey, was from the old school. A cardinal rule in pro football was that you should never get on the wrong side of a trainer. To a football team a good trainer is invaluable; he acts as healer, both mental and physical, and becomes the liaison between the coach and player as to the character of a given player. Trainers often know more about the mental and physical makeup of an individual than the coaching staff does. Clint Huey had already decided that Casey was dogging it. Casey became Clint's special project; he set out to make Casey's life miserable until he suited up. Since Casey claimed he couldn't run, Clint put him on a stationary bicycle and made him ride it fifty miles a day.

One day I was alone with Casey in the training room. I had no respect for him, either. His signing bonus was more money that I had made in seven years of pro football. I asked Casey why he refused to practice. He stopped riding the bike long enough to tell me that he hated football and was not ever going to practice. The only way he would lose his $100,000 bonus was if he quit the team, and he informed me that he was not about to quit. He would ride that bike to Czechoslovakia if necessary to keep his money, he said. "Sooner or later the Falcons are going to realize this," he predicted. It was the first time I had ever heard an athlete admit he was playing the game for money alone. The game of pro football was changing. Finally Casey was released.

Our first preseason game was in Atlanta. We rode an old bus to the airport in Asheville. The major airlines were on strike, but the Falcons had chartered a small plane from Southern Airlines that would take half the team to the playing site, then return to Asheville and pick up the other half. If you were scheduled to ride on the first plane, you stood in high graces with the Falcons. After the game in Atlanta, which we lost to the Philadelphia Eagles, we returned to Asheville that same night, then went on by bus to Black Mountain. There was a bed check at 1:00 A.M. This was absurd; there had been no time away from football in three weeks. We were not given a single night out, and had no place to go if we got one. In Baltimore we had been allowed Wednesday nights off, and were often free from Saturday night until noon on Monday. It was apparent that Norb Hecker was trying to out-Lombardi Vince Lombardi.

I returned to the dorm that night, got my car, and headed back to Asheville. The Bobby Layne in me was winning out. I had heard of a private club that stayed open most of the night and served mixed drinks. When I arrived I found most of the Falcon front office officials and some of the coaches were there. "Never go in the back door" was Layne's credo, so I went in the front door and joined them. This flagrant violation of team rules and policies shocked and outraged them. The next day I was startled when nothing was mentioned of the incident.

Eventually we started getting Wednesday nights off from seven to eleven, but there was still nowhere to go. The two hours it took to drive round-trip to Asheville and back ate up most of the time. There were three players on the roster from each of the twelve NFL teams, and we compared notes on how each team operated its respective training camp. It was mutually agreed that the Falcons had their own way of doing things.

Every training camp has a certain following of local girls, who like to get to know the players. They are referred to as camp followers. We had our camp followers, too: Shovel Face and Pocahontas. They were at every practice, and were outside the dorms or at Sewell's every evening. No one ever learned their real names.

Poco was an Indian girl of very loose morals. With 130 players to choose from, she had no preferences, so her dance card was always full. Shovel Face could have been an attractive girl, except for her flat features that made her look like she had been hit in the face with a spade. I've since thought it strange how relative things are, because each week that went by made Shovel Face and Poco more attractive. The first week in August, I told Shovel Face that she should consider entering the Miss North Carolina beauty contest. She modestly declined, saying, "Shit, I ain't that purty."

The last week in August, I told Poco she could do better than Black Mountain. She argued that she felt like she had been doing pretty well there, considering that the airlines were on strike and it was difficult bringing in more would-be Falcon players. I couldn't refute that fact; Poco had had a great training camp.

Nothing changed in regard to the practice sessions; they only became more and more grueling. Hours turned into days and days seemed like weeks as we struggled on with no break from the norm. Morale became a problem. My own light and carefree spirit had died after only three weeks. My disposition had turned sour, my attitude negative. The relationship between Hecker and myself was plummeting downhill. Just before our first preseason game it got worse.

After a bad three-hour practice, Norb made the receivers, running backs, and quarterbacks stay after practice. We lined up on the goal, facing the other goal post, got down in a three-point stance, and at the sound of his whistle we ran until he blew the whistle again. Then we started all over again. This was a new drill to me. The stop-and-start thing went on and on. We had gone up and down the field four times, and players were dropping to the ground like dead fish on a beach.

Hecker had escorted this leader of dissent to his breaking point. I quit. I took off my shoulder pads and started walking away. With less than a dozen players still responding to the whistle calls, I dragged myself off the field. I expected to be reprimanded as I walked away. Instead nothing happened. Hecker merely kept blowing his whistle until the remaining players reached the other end of the field, then he announced that practice was over. I kept waiting to be called in and admonished or released, but instead nothing happened. The tension between the two of us continued to mount.

The isolation and confinement were getting to everyone. Even the most laid-back, easygoing players were starting to break under the ordeal. One afternoon, I was going by Bill Jobko's room when he called for me to come inside. Bill was a veteran linebacker from the Vikings, and the most even-tempered person on the squad. "Alex," he said, "I think I'm in trouble. See that spiderweb in the corner of the room? I've been watching that spider spin his web for several weeks."

"What's wrong with that?" I asked.

"I'm starting to enjoy it," he said. Bill was honestly worried about himself.

Players began leaving in the middle of the night. No one ever returned. A mutinous attitude was beginning to surface. Instead of making the best of things, I was now making the worst of them. I had come there to play football, and the Falcons were running a camp for drill sergeants.

On August 27, we played our final preseason game in Columbia, South Carolina. We finally won a game, and spirits were rising, until we returned to Black Mountain and found it abandoned. The Falcons had not planned to break training camp until September 9, but the cooks and waiters had all gone home.

The next morning I was approached by one of the four college students who had agreed to stay on. He asked me what I enjoyed eating. "Why do you ask?" I inquired.

"I'm the new cook," he answered.

"Can you cook?" I asked.

"No, but I figured that we can survive if you like canned soup."

In the two weeks that followed, the Falcon players lost an average of fifteen pounds apiece. Finally, on the Friday afternoon of September 25, just two days before our opening game, we broke camp, ending the largest, longest, and most bizarre training camp in the history of the NFL. Talk about burning bridges: on the last day of camp a couple of players set fire to a wooden bridge at the Blue Ridge Assembly. Returning to Black Mountain was unthinkable!

31

The Falcons were the fifteenth team in the league, so we were scheduled to play every team in the NFL during our fourteen-game schedule. Our opening game was against the Rams in Atlanta. The mayor of Atlanta, the governor of Georgia, and the commissioner of the NFL were there, along with 54,418 fans, to welcome the debut of the Atlanta Falcons football team. Before we took the field a live falcon was to be released in the stadium. Our mascot was to circle the field three times and land back on its trainer's perch. I watched that bird as it circled the field once, then flew out of the stadium, never to return. Our mascot had abandoned us before the first snap. It was a preview of things to come.

We played the Rams close, but ended up losing, 19–14. A strange thing happened in that game. In fact, strange things were to happen in nearly all of our games. We had the ball just off the infield dirt when a player came on the field with a play from the bench. It was a sweep to Deacon Jones's side of the field. Everyone knew a sweep wouldn't work against Jones. The play lost two yards. The Falcon bench was clapping their hands with approval as another play came in, this time on a piece of paper. The player bringing in the information gave it to Randy Johnson, our starting quarterback. He knelt down in the dirt and diagrammed a play that we had never seen before. It was then that we realized why we had run the sweep. The idea was to move the ball over the infield base path. That way we could use the infield sand to diagram the brand-new play. Of course the play didn't work.

The next week on the opening kickoff in Philadelphia we lost our kicker, Wade Traynham. He actually missed the ball sitting on the kicking tee, and tore all the muscles in his leg on the miss. We lost that one to the Eagles.

The third game was against the Lions in Detroit. Harry Gilmer was coaching the Lions, and was sending in plays with alternating fullbacks. Joe Don Looney was one of the fullbacks. He was as talented and temperamental as ever. The Colts had traded him to the Lions. This was his third team in as many years.

In training camp he had refused to practice and would not leave his room. Joe Schmidt, a great linebacker and team captain, went to Looney's room to counsel him. "Joe Don, I have been with the Lions for twelve years. In all that time I have never missed a practice or been late for a meeting."

"Are you serious?" said Joe Don, "You mean in twelve years you have never missed one practice?"

"That's right, Joe Don, not a single day," he said proudly.

"If that's the case," said Joe Don, "pull up a chair, because if there ever was a guy who needed a day off, it's you!"

Despite this, Joe Don had stayed with the Lions, and was having a great first half against us. By halftime he had gained nearly a hundred yards and scored a touchdown. In the second half Joe Don did not step foot on the field, but the Lions still handed us our third defeat.

After the game, I was walking out to the buses, when standing there waiting for me was Joe Don Looney. I walked up to him and was shaking hands when he announced that he was in trouble again. "What for?" I asked, "You had a hell of a first half. Why didn't you play in the second half?"

"Well, I didn't like the idea of Harry Gilmer using me as a messenger boy sending in those plays. In the second half I refused to take the play in. I told Harry that if he had any more messages to send that he could call Western Union." Gilmer's sense of humor was not as keen as Joe Don's. Looney was suspended the next day.

Dallas beat us for our fourth loss, 47–14, and the fifth week of the season we played Washington in the nation's capital. The Redskins, led by none other than Joe Don Looney, beat us 33–20. Joe

A friendly game of chance aboard an airliner. Left to right: Bill Saul, George Preas, John Unitas, myself, and Gino Marchetti.—*Courtesy John Steadman*

Raymond Berry catches a pass.—*Courtesy Weeb Ewbank*

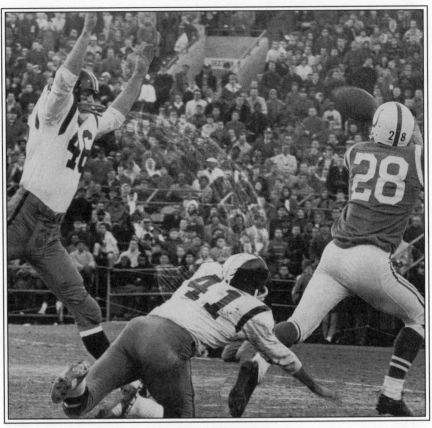

Jimmy Orr catches a pass.—*Courtesy Weeb Ewbank*

Captain Who? catches a pass.

Carroll Rosenbloom's guests, the night before a game. Left to right: Jim Parker, John Unitas, Lenny Moore, George Preas, myself, Dan Sullivan, Bill Pellington, Tom Matte, Jimmy Welch.

Carroll Rosenbloom alone with his thoughts, shortly before a game with the Giants in Yankee Stadium.—*Courtesy Weeb Ewbank*

Norm Van Brocklin, with earphones, and Harmon Wages.—*Courtesy* Atlanta Journal-Constitution

Atlanta Falcons observing the progress of a game. Left to right: Don Talbert, Frank Marchlewski, Junior Coffey, Errol Linden, and myself.—*Courtesy Bob Verlin*

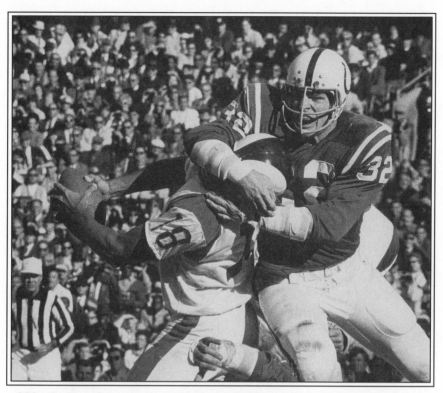

Mike Curtis is here shown in the act of gently sacking the Rams' Roman Gabriel.—*Courtesy Chuck Hickey*

Touchdown against the Los Angeles Rams. The tackler is Irv Cross.

Me and my street-people, at the Timonium State Fair. Left to right: Henry Amos, Rocky Thornton, myself, and Willie Metzger.—*Courtesy Joseph A. DiPiola, Baltimore Sun Papers*

Rocky Thornton and myself at ringside. Boxing always turned Rocky on.

Coach Don Shula and myself after the Colts-Vikings game, 1964.—Baltimore
News-American

This story in the *Baltimore News-American* delighted Shula and the Colts
management.

The New York Jets' Joe Namath, shown here with Billy Mathis protecting him, stuck with Weeb Ewbanks' game plan in Super Bowl III, and it worked all too well.

The Hawkins family, back home in Atlanta: Alex, Steele, Elizabeth, and Libby.—*Courtesy Bob Verlin*

Don had just been acquired by the Skins, and with just two days of practice had rushed for well over a hundred yards and scored another touchdown. In just three years Joe Don had now played with four different teams. He was such a troubled person that I really wasn't sure that he wouldn't find himself playing on yet another team before the season ended.

Meanwhile, I had proven my point. I was not only a starting receiver, I was the fourth leading pass-catcher in the league. Still, losing games week after week was hard for me. I wasn't used to it; in my entire life I had never played on a losing team in any sport. Until my first game with the Falcons I had never entered a game thinking I was going to lose; I could not get over how easy losing came to some of these players. I began to wonder whether being a starter was worth the emotional price I was paying.

I missed being with the Colts. I missed the feeling of being with winners. When I was with the Colts, large crowds turned out to greet us. Newspaper reporters, TV and radio people, and fans hailed us and called us by name.

Here it was very different. No one was ever around. When we went into a city you would have thought a leper colony had landed. The Colts had "Let's go all you Baltimore Colts." Washington had "Hail to the Redskins." In the first year the Falcons had no tradition and no fight song. Ken Reaves, our rookie cornerback, came up with one in jest. It went like this:

We are the Falcons,
Mighty, mighty Falcons,
Everywhere we go-o,
People want to know-o,
Who we are, so we tell them . . .
We are the Falcons,
Mighty, mighty Falcons.

Losing is no fun.

In training camp everyone had agreed that we had enough talent to win three games, but no one had expected that one of those three would be with the 49ers. They were right; the 49ers clobbered us 44–7. Then the Packers whipped us 56–3. Next the Browns clubbed us, 49–17, for our eighth loss.

In our ninth game the Baltimore Colts came to town with Unitas, Orr, Berry, and Moore. A record stadium crowd, 58,850, turned out to see what, if anything, their local team could do against the South's favorite team. We went in at halftime with a 7–6 lead and the Falcon fans gave us a standing ovation. In the second half the Colts scored thirteen points and shut us out to win 19–7, but compared to our previous games it was a moral victory. This had been our most successful loss so far.

I had torn a medial ligament in my knee, and was scheduled to be operated on the next day. Sunday night it occurred to me that three Falcon players had been operated on for knee injuries and had not played again since then. I declined the operation and tried to play on. I figured that I would have the knee repaired after the season was over—in Baltimore.

The following week we beat the Giants for our first league win, 27–16. The next week we were to play the Bears in Chicago. Saturday afternoon we had boarded the plane, but bad weather kept us circling O'Hare field for over two hours. The pilot finally landed in Milwaukee about eight o'clock.

Milwaukee is about eighty miles north of Chicago, and none of the coaches were on the team plane. They were all out scouting college teams. This left Bud Erickson in charge of getting the team to Chicago. As assistant to the president, next to Rankin Smith, Bud was the highest ranking Falcon official. He was a fine person, but in all honesty there were more capable people in this country than Bud. He was simply not a decision-maker or a leader of men. When we got off the plane he made the decision for everyone to meet in the bar until he could figure out how to get to Chicago.

Nearly one hour later Clint Huey and I were sitting together with Billy Lothridge and Billy Martin when Bud rushed up to us in near panic, asking for advice. He had not been able to secure another plane. We suggested he call a bus company and drive on in. He liked that idea and went rushing off again, but not before announcing that everyone was to stay in the bar until he returned. Some of the players had friends and relatives waiting for them in Chicago, and were already getting cabs and heading off on their own. The rest of us were just sitting there, ordering drinks, and laughing at how pathetic the situation had become.

It was after 10:00 P.M. when Bud came rushing back in the bar with a triumphant look on his face. Like a general, he took control and ordered everyone outside. He had rented about twenty cabs to take us to the train station, for a train which would finally take us to Chicago.

This operation went well enough, and after boarding the train we made our own preparations as to what would follow, should none of the coaches make it to the game. We agreed that Whitey Zimmerman, our equipment man, would handle the defense. Clint Huey, our trainer, would work with the offense. We also voted unanimously to disallow curfew fines, since we would not reach the hotel until well after one in the morning. As it turned out, the coaches made it to the game, and we lost our tenth game to the Bears.

The following week in Bloomington, Minnesota, we won our second game of the season. A "norther" had come in the night before the game, and the temperature had dropped below zero. The tarpaulin had frozen to the field and it had taken the ground crew all night to get it off the playing surface. On the morning of the game over six inches of snow had fallen on the frozen field, and footing was impossible. We could get no traction by wearing cleats, and tennis shoes did not work well on snow. This, of course, went in our favor and was a bad break for the Vikings, because adverse playing conditions tend to neutralize teams.

The headstrong Dutchman, Norm Van Brocklin, head coach of the Vikings, had been once again feuding with his quarterback, Fran Tarkenton, and for whatever reason had decided to go with second-team quarterback Bob Berry. I suppose he wanted to see if Berry was tough enough for these conditions. We intercepted five passes and beat the Vikings 20–13. Van Brocklin's decision to go with Berry would prove to be a costly one. At season's end it would cost him his job. Losing to an expansion team does not endear a football coach to an owner.

The next Sunday we made it two in a row. The three victories tied a league record for wins in a season by an expansion team. With one game remaining against the Steelers, we had a chance to set a record. But Pittsburgh swamped us, 57–33. The season was over.

As I cleaned out my locker the following Monday, I looked long and hard at the empty stalls in the Falcon dressing room. It had certainly been an interesting, if not fulfilling, season. I had come here to prove I could be a starter. I had done just that, and my forty-four passes caught were not all that shabby a performance, considering I had missed two games. Still, it had not been a rewarding season for me. If I had discovered nothing else, it was the undeniable fact that I would rather be a backup receiver on a winning team than a starting receiver on a losing one. Expansion teams were everything Shula had told me they would be: heartaches.

As I walked past the empty stalls to the door for what I was sure would be the last time as a Falcon, I looked at these names: Rector, Rassas, Silvestri, Wolski, Sherlag, Sieminski, and Szczecko. Names that rang no bell, names that had never been heard of, and names that would never be heard of. Most of these players had never known the feeling of being a part of a winning organization, the unique emotion of feeling special about yourself, of being something that is special, a winner.

If you are part of an organization such as the Colts, there is the proud feeling of walking down the street and being recognized, and hearing your name as they whisper, "there goes so and so." The idea of being ushered in the back door of a sold-out event, while others stand out front in a line. Of finishing dinner and asking for the check and having the waiter say, "That's on the house," or "Mr. X at a nearby table picked it up." Of walking in a bar and not being allowed to pay for anything. The proud feeling and confidence of never being alone, because people won't leave you alone. It's an almost God-like feeling.

Most of the Falcon players had never experienced it and most of them never would. Except for a couple of Green Bay rejects and Larry Morris and myself, nobody on this team wore a championship ring. None of them ever would.

It made me wonder even more about the common draft. A player spends twenty-one or twenty-two years becoming the best college football player in the country, and then is drafted and has to play on a team that never wins. I thought of these first-year players who would never see a second year, and the second-year players who would never see a third. At least they had gotten a shot at it, which most never do. I thought of Taz Anderson, not quite thirty, but already limping from five knee operations. Before he was through he would have twelve.

There was Larry Morris, eleven years in the league, most valuable player in the 1963 championship game, nearing the end of a great career, having to undergo the humiliation of being relegated to the kick-off team—put in the wedge, no less. There was Billy Lothridge, so intense a competitor that he played safety with one kidney, knowing that an injury to that kidney would have cost him his life. There were Tommy Nobis and Randy Johnson, so young and talented, yet in all likelihood they would never know the feeling of being a winner.

And then I thought of Alex Hawkins. To hell with this. One losing season was more than enough. My choices were all too clear. I would either have to retire from the game or find a way to get back to Baltimore.

32

Meanwhile, that year the Packers had won the Western division crown. Dallas had just won its first Eastern conference title. On January 1, 1967, these two teams played for the championship of the NFL and the right to participate in the first Super Bowl.

It was Vince Lombardi against Tom Landry, as Bart Starr threw four touchdown passes for a 34–27 lead with just over two minutes remaining. Don Meredith then took control and passed the Cowboys to inside the Green Bay one-yard line. With first and ten from the one, Dallas failed to score in the next four plays, the last ending in an interception by Tom Brown. Once again Green Bay had shown the mark of a championship team. It didn't seem to matter what it took to win a big game, Lombardi's Packers always responded.

On January 15, 1967, the Green Bay Packers were to play the AFL's Kansas City Chiefs for the world championship, in what would later be referred to as the Super Bowl. The only thing accidental about this game was the title itself. Owners had first suggested that it be called "The Big One" or "The Final Game." Pete Rozelle offered his customary compromise by suggesting they call it the "N.F.L.-A.F.L. World Championship Game." Finally Lamar Hunt, owner of the Kansas City Chiefs, blurted out the name "Super Bowl" in a joint meeting of the NFL and AFL owners. His young daughter had used the term to describe a toy he had brought her earlier. Super Bowl it would be.

For two weeks Pete Rozelle and his PR staff had hyped this game as a great matchup between the old NFL and the avant-garde, upstart AFL. This game had already been planned in June of 1965, as part of the merger agreement. No one was really taking the game very seriously, as nobody truly believed that parity existed between the two leagues. The smart money was going on Green Bay, and the Packers were favored by eight to ten points.

The Chiefs left Kansas City on January 4 for Long Beach, California, where they would be training. The Packers practiced in Green Bay in subzero temperatures until January 8, when they left for their training site in Santa Barbara.

Vince Lombardi was uptight over this game. The practice sessions in Santa Barbara were reminiscent of his training camp. Vince went back to the basics. Whenever a feeling of uneasiness or uncertainty touched Vince, he always returned to the basics. The schedule, the conditioning, the seclusion, and the discipline were getting to the Packers. They were edgy, some of them mean as hell. This was exactly what Vince had wanted. He had once made the statement, "To play this game you must have fire in your eyes, and there is nothing that stokes fire like hate." Harnessing and dispensing hatred was Lombardi's strong suit.

The Chiefs by contrast were tentative, cautious, and scared. They weighed their statements to the press. They were careful not to offend the reigning World Champion Green Bay Packers. All of them, that is, with the lone exception of Fred "The Hammer" Williamson. The Hammer was a defensive back who alleged he would inflict personal physical damage on any Packer who entered his territory. Openly and repeatedly he denounced the Packers to the press. Talk like this did not belong in football; these kinds of statements were customary only in wrestling.

The league office could not have been more pleased with him, however, because the forthcoming contest was not getting the fans excited. Ticket sales had been slow; Rozelle, a marketing wizard, knew that people wanted to go mostly where they couldn't get in, and the coliseum seated 93,000 with tickets priced at six, ten, and twelve dollars. A less than sellout crowd would look bad on TV. A week before the game, less than half the tickets had been sold. On January 10, five days before the game, a burglar had broken into the Chiefs' headquarters in Kansas City and made off with an undisclosed amount of cash. They left behind 2,000 tickets to the Super Bowl game.

The media hype continued.

From the *New York Times*, January 14:

"I plan to spend tomorrow afternoon in front of my TV set," said Senator Robert F. Kennedy (D.-NY). "Vince Lombardi is an old friend of mine. We're for Green Bay all the way."

"I'm sure it'll be a good game," said Mayor John V. Lindsay of New York City, "but I don't plan on watching it. I have so little time with my family, we're going to spend the afternoon playing tennis."

LOS ANGELES, January 14 (AP):

The Super Bowl Committee announced today that 1,049 press credentials had been issued for tomorrow's game. The breakdown is 338 for newspapers, magazines and wire service reporters; 262 for TV and radio staffs, 170 for photographers; 88 for press box officials; 78 for league officials; 73 for communications services and 40 for sideline services.

NEW YORK, January 14 (UPI):

The National Broadcasting Company has announced that 18 one-minute commercials during the telecasting of the Super Bowl game tomorrow will cost each sponsor $70,000.

NEW YORK, January 14 (AP):

The Columbia Broadcasting System has announced that 18 one-minute commercials during the telecasting of the Super Bowl game tomorrow will cost each sponsor $85,000.

Kansas City coach Hank Stram was busying himself brainwashing his troops, saying what an honor it was to be representing the league. All he was expecting of them was a good showing.

Vince Lombardi intended to uphold the honor of the NFL and all the players and coaches that had come before him. His conversation with his players was to the point: "Nobody is going to leave that stadium until the job is done. I'll keep you there all day, all night, all week if necessary, until you win."

From the *New York Times* of January 15:

Ten Apollo astronauts from Houston led by Walter Schirra were escorted into the stadium as a group and then, with diplomacy typical of a government agency, split up. Five went to sit on the Green Bay side of the field, and five on the Kansas City side.

Just before the kickoff, after the field had been cleared of 313 musicians, 30 baton-twirlers, several glee clubs, and a few floats, 4,000 pigeons were released into the air. Sixty-three thousand people had shown up to see which team would walk away with the winners' share of $15,000. The losers would receive $7,500.

I had returned home from Baltimore, where Ed McDonald, the Colt physician, had repaired my injured knee. I had arranged everything and was preparing a full day of TV football. Like so many others, I was awaiting the slaughter of the Chiefs. I had never seen this other league play, not a down. These players were so anonymous that they had their names displayed on the backs of their jerseys.

The Packers won the toss and received the opening kickoff. I had already made bets that The Hammer would be nailed before halftime. On the second play of the game, Boyd Dowler injured his shoulder and was replaced by thirty-four-year-old Max McGee. Max was a "big game" player, and had been instrumental in beating us many times in the past. It dawned on me that this was the first time in seven years that I had ever pulled for the Green Bay Packers.

Nine anxious minutes went by before McGee put Green Bay ahead with a thirty-seven-yard touchdown grab. I was shocked when Kansas City's Lenny Dawson found Curtis McClinton open in the end zone to tie the game in the second quarter. Green Bay came right back on a twelve-play, seventy-three-yard drive as Jim Taylor, led by Thurston and Kramer, bolted into the end zone to put the Packers ahead 14–7.

A Kansas City field goal made it 14–10 at halftime. What in the world was going on? I had fully expected the proud Green Bay Packers to rout these men from nowhere, but the Chiefs were making a game of it. This was embarrassing to me personally. I spent the halftime pacing the floor, inventing names to call Vince and his green-and-gold group. To make matters worse, The Hammer was still on his feet. What had happened to the famous Green Bay pride?

In the third period, Willie Wood ran an interception back to Kansas City's five yard line, and Pitts put the Packers ahead 21–10. I gave a sigh of relief as Max McGee caught his second touchdown pass to widen the margin to 28–10. This was more like what I had expected.

Early in the fourth quarter, The Hammer got clawed. Fred Williamson was carried off the field unconscious. Justice was served as Green Bay scored yet another touchdown. The Packers ended it at 35–10. Vince Lombardi had just won his fourth world championship in six years.

I felt a little better about it when Vince Lombardi, in a post-game interview on TV, said, "Kansas City has a good team. But it doesn't compare with some of the teams in the NFL. Dallas is a better team. That's what you wanted me to say, isn't it? There, I have said it."

"You're damn right that's what I wanted you to say!" I stormed. For one half at least, this bunch of ragtag castoffs who had to wear their names on their jerseys for identification had made the Super Bowl a football game.

33

If I could choose one time and place to suspend life in, it would be Atlanta, Georgia, in the spring of 1967. Despite how I felt about the Falcons, Atlanta was great. "Great" is probably the most over-used word in the English language. It is the most over-used word in sports, which was why someone had to come up with the term "super." It was necessary to have lived in Atlanta at that time to fully appreciate what "great" means. The city that had risen out of the ashes of the Civil War was now bursting at the seams. There was no stopping the place.

What do you look for in a city? Atlanta had it. Leadership was strong, stable, harmonious, and united. Carl Sanders was the governor and Ivan Allen was the mayor. Mills B. Lane was the leading banker. Lane was good-natured and likeable, and in his banking practices most liberal. Bob Woodruff was chairman of the board of the Coca-Cola Company. His checkbook was thick and his heart was charitable. He made things happen.

John O'Chiles was the leader in real estate. There were no natural land barriers to prohibit growth in any direction. Atlanta was growing so fast that anybody could drive around the city, throw a hat out the car window, buy the property it landed on, and double his money in six months.

Because Atlanta has the highest elevation of any major city in the East, the climate was marvelous. The rolling landscape, covered with towering trees that shaded manicured lawns, was teeming with flowering dogwoods and azaleas. With just less than a million people, the city was large enough to get lost in, and small enough to be found.

Atlanta featured the most beautiful women in the world. Every

spring the graduating classes of every school in the Southeast gal-
loped their way to Atlanta. This was the happiest, richest, and
most fun-loving city I had ever lived in. Every day was a holiday,
and every night was New Year's Eve. It was a never-ending cocktail party that started at noon and went on until the sun rose the
next morning.

Jimmy Orr's was the "in" place at the time, and it was my headquarters. My new friends were the "beautiful people" of Atlanta.
Jimmy Orr had been right when he told me I would never leave
this city. We had rented a house, just north of the high-rent dis-
trict of Buckhead. The children were starting school. Everybody
was growing up but me.

There were about two dozen of us who got together for lunch
almost every day. They had all either inherited money or operated
successful businesses. Rarely did anyone work after lunchtime.
The saying among them was, "if you can't get it done by noon, the
job's too big for you." They were free spenders and fun lovers. I
was acting the part, but they were living it. I would have to figure
out how I was going to be able to afford running around with my
friends.

We played golf every Wednesday, Saturday, and Sunday. Every
weekend there was a cocktail party at one of the fashionable Buckhead homes. Once a month we had a three-day golf outing in
another city. One month it would be in Sea Island, the next month
in Augusta, then Jacksonville, or the Highlands of North Carolina.
There was golfing and gambling, drinking and laughing.

The Buckhead area was the place to live. It was the home of the
old money. The wives of the Buckhead Boys were things of beauty.
Almost without exception they were beautiful and charming, well-
bred and mannered. They handled the affairs of the family and
allowed their husbands a long, long leash. The Buckhead Boys
used all of it.

Southern women tend to humor their husbands. They treat
their men just as their mothers had treated their fathers—like
children. This was fine by me, since I was used to being a child
and preferred the role. Although they generally acknowledged
the husband as leader of the family unit, do not let that deceive

you. Silently and skillfully the Southern lady rules the roost. As long as the family unit is not threatened, a Southern woman is a sweet and gentle creature. But when the nest is endangered, look out. That sweet, charming, harmless soul can turn into a fire-breathing dragon.

From the standpoint of common sense, it is probably true that women are smarter than men. It has been said that a man's best friend is his dog, while a woman's best friend is a diamond. Now have you ever needed to raise some money and tried to hock your dog?

What I am trying to get at is the fact that I was in the fast lane, and flying. I was running so fast that it was as if I was trying to get even with the city of Atlanta for not having entered my life until so late.

Most of the Falcon players were young, and many of them were unmarried. For them, there was only one place to live at that time, Peachtree Town Apartments. The PTA was located just off Peachtree Street, less than a mile from Orr's restaurant, which was just short of Buckhead.

This 116-unit complex was developed by Don J. Davis, known to the tenants as "Mr. Daa-vees." Don was a good developer, a great promoter, and the pied piper for young people. In his youthful army Don had enlisted about fifty, whom he referred to as Daa-vees' Raiders. With these people as a steady nucleus, he could assemble a party in less than an hour at any time of the day or night. Over a dozen Falcons, four or five Braves baseballers, and an assortment of airline stewardesses, secretaries, and teachers lived at the PTA. As in Las Vegas, locks and clocks were not necessary.

One evening that spring I had just closed Vic's, a late night restaurant nearby, when I decided to have one more cocktail. I kept a bottle at a teammate's place in the Peachtree Town. When I arrived wearing my golf shoes, the lights were on and the door was open. I walked in, poured myself a drink, and went upstairs in search of life.

I walked into my friend's bedroom and there, in bed, buck-naked, was my teammate with his fiancée, sound asleep. I climbed in bed between them still fully clothed and wearing my golf shoes. I picked up the phone and called Libby. A sleepy voice answered and inquired, "Where are you, Alex?"

"Libby, you won't believe this, but I'm in bed with a naked man and a naked woman," I said. There was a pause at the other end of the phone for about four beats, and finally she said, "Come on home, Alex, it's late." How much longer would I put up with this kind of nagging?

I was living my life as if there were no tomorrow. It was the only way to get the full measure out of it. The more outrageous my behavior, the more popular I became. I was fast becoming more and more talked about. I thought this was good. Libby did not share these beliefs.

Along about June a professional football player begins to get anxious. It's that way with all of us. Ask the wife of a football player, and she will tell you that the month of June is hellish on her. A player will get nervous, irritable, and short-tempered. He is prone to unpredictable fits of anger with no apparent cause. I was a creature of habit, and more predictable than most, so it was strange when nothing happened that year.

June meant nothing to me. I was a civilian now. The month came and went, but nothing changed. In a sense I was pleased. I was thirty years old and had been lucky to have played for eight years. That was enough for me. Playing with the Falcons had warped my attitude toward football. Last season had been no fun, and I had too much respect for the game just to play it for the money.

The second week in July I was lying on the beach in Sea Island pondering my future. I tried to project as far ahead as September. They would be kicking off another season, but this time without me.

Suddenly I jumped up from my lounge chair and started running down the beach. I ran for about a mile, and I discovered what bad physical condition I was in. I walked halfway back, then ran the remaining distance back to my chair.

"What was that all about?" Libby asked me.

I started picking up my things. "Get packed," I said, "we're going back to Atlanta. Why did you let me get this far out of shape?" I demanded. "Don't you know I have to report to training camp in three days? It's time to play football."

34

The NFL had a facelift in 1967, although cosmetic surgery might be a more accurate term. Conforming to the merger agreement of 1966, New Orleans was awarded a franchise, giving the NFL a total of sixteen teams. The AFL was to add one team for 1968 and two more before 1970.

The NFL announced that starting in 1967 it would divide its sixteen teams into four divisions, two each in both the Western and Eastern Conferences. The winners of each division would play for the conference titles at the end of the season, and then the conference winners would play for the NFL championship and the right to meet the AFL champions.

The Western Conference was split into a Coastal Division—Atlanta, Baltimore, Los Angeles, and San Francisco—and a Central Division—Chicago, Detroit, Green Bay, and Minnesota. These lineups were assured for 1967 and 1968.

In the Eastern Conference for 1967, there were the Federal Division—Cleveland, New York, Pittsburgh, St. Louis—and the Capital Division—Dallas, New Orleans, Philadelphia, and Washington. In 1968, New Orleans and New York would switch divisions.

Now if this all sounds complicated, let me simplify it. What Pete Rozelle and his Madison Avenue marketers were doing were creating more winners, and thus more playoff games. The fewer teams eliminated from the championship race, the more fans would remain interested throughout the season. Through expansion and reorganization, Rozelle was simply creating more with less. Whereas in 1965 the NFL had one championship game, there were now three.

The AFL would decide its champion in a playoff game, and the winner would then face the NFL champion in the Super Bowl. The bottom line was that where we had been accustomed to one playoff game, we would now have a total of five. This of course meant more games, more money, more TV exposure and revenue. Pete Rozelle had proven himself to the owners. They now had complete confidence in Pete's ability to market their product in the TV world.

I knew it was going to be a bad year when Norb Hecker threatened to take away my BB gun. We had been in camp for about two weeks when Norb opened the meeting with, "Who shot out the big light in the front of the dorm?" Since I was the only one with a Red Ryder air rifle all eyes turned on me. "Was that some of your doings, Hawkins?" he asked.

"No," I said truthfully.

"If I see any more lights shot out or get any more complaints from the maids, I'm going to take that gun away from you," he said. I thought it was strange for a head coach to threaten to take away a thirty-year-old pass receiver's BB gun. But then again, I was getting accustomed to the Falcons doing strange things.

For whatever reason, Rankin Smith had promoted his accountant, Frank Wall, to the position of vice-president and general manager of the football team. Frank wasn't a bad guy, but he didn't know the first thing about football. Unfortunately, Frank thought that he did. Then there was the college draft. The Falcons had traded their No. 1 pick to San Francisco for wide receiver Bernie Casey. Bernie never reported to camp, choosing rather to stay on the West Coast and paint. So much for the No. 1 pick.

Their second round pick was Leo Carroll, a defensive end from San Diego State. Leo was a Tiny Tim freak, and one night he just disappeared, leaving behind his collection of Tiny Tim albums. So much for the second pick.

Randy Matson was their fifth pick. Randy was a shot-putter who hadn't played football since his freshman year. Apparently he never intended to play, because he also never reported to the

Falcons. And who will ever forget their thirteenth choice, Sandor Szabo?

If there was a method to this madness, it had somehow eluded me. Out of seventeen draft choices, not one of them made the Falcon team. The '67 draft had been a total disaster.

After last year's debacle at Black Mountain, the training camp had been moved to Johnson City, Tennessee, where we were the guests of East Tennessee State University. Conditions there were much improved.

I had reported in the worst condition of my career, but was gradually working myself into playing shape. I was not on the friendliest terms with Norb Hecker. In his job as head coach he was irritable and uncertain. I don't know if it was the poor draft or the absence of Tom Fears that bothered him most.

Fears had been named the head coach of the fledgling New Orleans Saints. The previous year Tom, with an outspoken personality and a large ego, had handled the offense. An outsider would have sworn he was the head coach. With Fears gone, Norb, a more retiring personality, had asserted himself as offensive coach. He simply did not have an ego large enough to take the lead as an active, vocal head coach.

In our last preseason game we were beaten by the newly formed Saints. After the game, owner Rankin Smith came into the dressing room and delivered the most blistering tongue-lashing I had ever heard directed at a team. As a team we didn't know what to make of this sudden tirade, although to be honest about it, his words were so slurred that we could scarcely understand him. It was as if New Orleans owner John Mecome had personally beaten him.

Earlier in the preseason, we had played and beaten the Miami Dolphins. Rankin had boasted to the press that he would jump in the Miami River if we lost to Joe Robbie's Dolphins.

These new owners that Pete Rozelle had selected seemed to have embarked on an ego trip with their new toys. They were not football people, but "rich kids" who had turned the NFL into a personal issue. Each loss was a personal attack on the losing owner's self-esteem. Back when there had been only twelve owners unity and humility was never a problem. Now that was all changing. The competition was no longer confined to the playing field. Pro football was beginning to alter a number of lives. A new wave of owners had taken over the league, and I did not like what I was seeing.

When we returned to Atlanta from training camp I had to call Libby to find out where we were living. While I was in camp she had bought a new home. Although I made all the important decisions in our family, such as what movie we were going to see or who would be first to read the sports section of the newspaper, I left the minor decisions up to her.

We opened the 1967 season against the Colts, in Baltimore. John Unitas put the season in perspective as he passed the Colts to a 31–7 halftime lead. In the second half Shula called off the dogs and the Colts coasted on in for the win.

Our second game was against the 49ers in San Francisco. Libby had flown out to the coast on Wednesday with Rankin and several of our friends. She had never visited the West Coast and I didn't know when she would get another opportunity, because this would definitely be my last season. Anyone who is not playing to win is playing for the money, and as a result I was feeling cheap. San Francisco beat us 38–7 in a game so dominated by the 49ers that they had rolled up 517 yards to our 97.

After the game Libby and I flew over to Las Vegas for the evening. I had notified all the team officials except Norb Hecker that I would not be returning on the team plane. I was particularly irked with Norb at this time, because he had benched me in favor of Tommy McDonald, a receiver he had picked up on waivers from the Rams. It would not even be inaccurate to say I was pouting. I had asked to be sent to Atlanta so I could become a starter and I wanted no part of sitting on the bench on what would prove to be a 1–12–1 team.

At Tuesday's practice, Norb called the team together and the conversation went as follows: "Where were you Sunday after the game, Hawkins?"

"I went to Las Vegas," I answered.

"Did you have a good time?" he asked.

"Yes, as a matter of fact, I did," I said.

"Did you have a thousand dollars worth of fun?"

"Well, I don't know about that," I said. "Why do you ask?"

"Because that's what I'm fining you for not coming back on the team plane," he said. It was a nit-picking thing to do , as there was no rule that said that anyone had to return on the team plane.

After practice I asked Norb if I could see him in his office. When I walked into his office, he was seated at his desk staring at a sheet of paper. It must have been the stats on the 49ers game, because he never looked up. "Norb," I said, "I think this has gone as far as it can go. I know you're not happy with me, so why don't we just end this thing?"

Norb never even so much as looked up. He agreed, saying that he had already spoken with Shula about me, and that they were working on some way to get me back to Baltimore. The next day I was waived by the Falcons. It was the fourth time in nine years that I had been placed on the waiver list. The next two days I waited for someone to contact me, but the phone was silent.

Finally I called Shula to see what was going on. He told me that two other teams had claimed me, and that he was talking to them about withdrawing their claims. "Why don't you trade for me?" I asked, "Don't you want me back?"

"We want you back, Hawk, but we don't want to give up anything for you. Let's face it, you ain't no bargain at any price! The Colts got you from the Packers on a nothing-for-nothing trade and we're trying to swing the same deal." It seemed my price had been established years ago.

Two more days went by and finally it was Shula on the phone. "You can come on up, Hawk, we made what everybody considers a fair deal for you."

"What did you have to give up for me?" I asked.

"Nothing," he said as he hung up the phone.

35

Gentlemen, let me have your attention. I'd like to introduce a new member of our football team. You older players already know him, and you younger players soon will. He is a player who will dissipate himself horribly but can still play the game. Don't any of you try to emulate him. Say hello to the Hawk." With that, Don Shula went on with the meeting, and I was once again a member of the Baltimore Colts.

The introduction Shula had given me had clarified things. Obviously he did not expect me to change into something that I wasn't. I was a flake, all right, but one whom he knew would work hard and play hard. I was not there to be a role model, I was there to play football, and to help in any way that I could to bring a championship back to Baltimore.

Back then pro players didn't think of themselves as role models. John Unitas was the only one who was doing commercials or endorsements of any kind. We judged ourselves only by how we played the game. Television would soon change all that.

I can't say how happy I was to be back with the Colts. I felt ten years younger and forty pounds lighter. The monkey had been taken off my back, and there was spring in my legs, a smile on my face, and laughter once again in my heart.

There were, however, a number of changes in the Colts' organization. Bert Bell, Jr., had resigned as business manager the previous year. In a dramatic but sincere announcement, he had said that he could no longer lend the Bell name to the crass commercialism that had invaded the pro game. He had taken a job with a newspaper and was writing a column, not always flattering to the Colts or Rosenbloom.

Steve Rosenbloom, Carroll's son, had assumed Bert's position. Upton Bell was now personnel manager. Chuck Noll was the new defensive backfield coach. Chuck came to the team with excellent credentials, having played linebacker and offensive guard at Cleveland under Paul Brown, then having moved on to San Diego where he had coached under Sid Gilman for the past six years. Only a few days were needed for everyone to realize that Chuck was head-coach material.

General manager Don Kellett had resigned his position and retired to Florida. For fourteen years he had been the best general manager in pro football. The Colts had honored him by announcing that an award of $5,000 would be given in his name to the Colt player voted by the press as most exemplifying the spirit of the Colts.

Nineteen sixty-seven was the first year of the common draft. The NFL and AFL had held the first combined player selection of college men, thus eliminating the competitive bidding of previous years. The Colts had proven that there was enough talent to go around if a team knew what it was doing.

Unlike the Falcons' draft, Upton Bell's draft had been sensational, considering the available talent was being spread pretty thin. Eight rookies had made the team. Bubba Smith and Rick Volk, their number one and two picks, were quality players who would move right in as starters. When I had come into the league in 1959 there were 430 players. Now there were well over 1,000 players in pro football.

Throughout training camp Raymond Berry had been troubled with injuries. A rookie from Alabama, Ray Perkins, had been studying behind Berry. I was once again a third-team wide receiver, fullback, halfback, tight end, and flanker. I was insurance against injuries wherever. In my absence Jimmy Welch was now captain of the special teams. That was just fine by me. What mattered was that I was back with the Colts.

John Unitas was remarkably healthy, for the first time in years. He was throwing the football better than I had ever seen him do. The offense was averaging over thirty-five points a game, and when the Rams came to Baltimore for our fifth game of the season the defense had allowed only one touchdown in the last three games. We were unbeaten and the Rams had lost just one game.

Los Angeles was coached by George Allen. He had taken over the year before and had molded the Rams into a good, solid team. This was the only team in our division that we *had* to beat. The Rams had come up with a great defensive team, a good but not great offensive team, and exceptional special teams. After the Colts had dominated special teams for the past four seasons, George Allen had finally recognized their importance. He had taken away our hole card. Now, coaches are not rocket scientists, but it was amazing to me that it had taken four years for someone to figure it out.

Berry was out with an injured leg and Ray Perkins, his replacement, left the game with a muscle pull. Just that abruptly I was the starting receiver. Shula's insurance policy was working out, as I set up two touchdowns with catches and got into the end zone with another. Had we won the game, I would probably have been labeled the star, but as it was we had to settle for a 24–24 tie. We still had a one-game lead over the Rams.

The following week we were once again tied, this time by the Vikings. A tequila-drinking Mexican-American quarterback named Joe Kapp had come down from the Canadian League to provide leadership for Bud Grant's Vikings. After seven years the Vikes were finally making their move.

Raymond Berry was out for six weeks, leaving me to back up Perkins. Jimmy Orr had been hurt in the first game and Willie Richardson had replaced him. My value to the Colts was greatly enhanced. Since I could play both right and left, I was backing up both positions. I caught five passes against the Redskins as we squeaked by them for our fifth win. After seven games we were still undefeated, holding on to a one-game lead over the Rams who had also suffered another tie.

I was delighted to be back in Baltimore and playing for a winner. As usual, I found myself over-indulging. I didn't want to discredit Shula's description of my dissipation, to be quite honest. I ran the streets and bars like a mad dog. The harder I ran, the better I played. I was on a roll and taking every advantage of it. I felt certain Bobby Layne's three hours of sleep was excessive. Like Layne, I was becoming a legend in my spare time. I had made so many friends in the city it was hard to get around to all of them. I had to work long hours and late nights. There was no better place to do that than the Gridiron Club.

The Gridiron Club was an historic two-story wooden structure which had been the clubhouse for the old Hillendale Country Club. The golf course itself had been sold to a developer to accommodate some apartment buildings. Because of its historic significance the clubhouse had been spared.

An enterprising man named Hugh Elliott, a bricklayer by trade, had taken a lease on the property and had turned it into what some people would call a restaurant and bar. When the Gridiron Club opened in 1963, it did well. The rib-eye steaks were the best in town. After a couple of years the dinner business had fallen off until by 1967 it was only a bar. But, ah, what a bar! Only the most colorful, daring, devil-may-care customers socialized in this bar. None but the most spirited of the Colt players dared enter these doors. In fact Bobby Boyd and I were the only Colts who were reckless and foolish enough to go there.

The proprietor of this institution, Hugh Elliott, or "Joy Boy" as his friends referred to him, was an ex-featherweight boxer. His record as a professional fighter was 21–3. Joy Boy ran the place like a boxer-bricklayer would run it—recklessly.

The bar featured a shuffleboard, and Joy Boy was one of the best shuffleboard players in the city. Even though he was a dynamite player, he was a poor gambler, so he rarely won. He would often negotiate himself into a losing position. Anyone who has ever seen a scratch golfer consistently give away so many shots that he can't win will understand. Hugh was one of those. He was simply too competitive to win. He didn't care about money, it was winning that turned him on.

Naturally, if Hugh won too often he would eliminate his competition. This is where Bobby Boyd came into the picture. Bobby was not a regular, but from time to time he felt it was his duty to stop by and entertain Joy Boy. Bobby was not only a competitor, but he also wanted the money. He was an early arriver and an early leaver, while I always arrived late and left early the next morning. Many was the time that I left the Gridiron Club and went straight to practice.

One night I ended up at the Gridiron Club, and during the course of the evening I had managed to acquire a large cut above my left eye. Hugh drove me to Union Memorial Hospital where eleven stitches were required to close the cut.

That morning I reported to practice wearing large, dark sunglasses. Shula walked over to me, removed my glasses, saw the cut, and demanded an explanation. I told him that I had an early breakfast and the man sitting next to me said Weeb Ewbank was a better coach than Shula. At that I had hit him, he had hit me back, and that explained the cut. Shula understood. He grinned, fined me two hundred dollars, and went on about his business. If you couldn't play for Shula you couldn't play for anyone.

On Halloween night before the Packer game, Bert Bell and I were playing poker in the backroom of a barber shop on Taylor Avenue. The game was no secret; it had been going on for almost twenty years. Bert and I had played in the game off and on for the past three or four years. This time the door flew open shortly after 4:00 A.M. and four or five policemen dressed like lumberjacks burst into the room. The leader of the group blew his opening line when he announced, "This is a card game . . . I mean a raid." Since all of us knew it was a card game, we thought it was a Halloween prank. This notion was quickly dismissed when he countered with, "Everybody freeze, you're under arrest."

One of the officers pointed a camera at the assembled group, but the camera didn't work, so another officer went out in search of another camera. When he returned thirty minutes later his camera worked no better. Regrettably, a picture was never taken.

We were marched outside and ushered into a police van. Unfortunately, the van was not large enough to accommodate ten card players, so the lookout man, Larry, offered to drive four of the arrested players to the police station in his car. En route the police van ran a red light, but Larry was not about to do so. The driver of the van, sensing a break was in the making, returned to find Larry still obeying the stoplight. When we finally arrived at the bailiff's office, it was closed. Thirty minutes later we were being photographed, fingerprinted, and booked. It took the police four-and-a-half hours to finally get us officially arrested. It was the story of my life all over again; I couldn't even get arrested gracefully. After posting fifty-five-dollar bonds we were released. The court date was set for November 17.

While I was being booked I called Libby to tell her the news of my most recent misadventure. She told me that she would tell the children and explain to them that it was just a misunderstanding. She assured me that she would handle everything on that end. "Alex," she said, "I do wish that you would grow up soon; the children are, and things are getting to be embarrassing to them."

Later she told me that when she walked the children to the bus stop to go to school, they were greeted with a chorus of "Your daddy's in jail, your daddy's in jail." The family had taken it in stride. Libby would surely make the mother's Hall of Fame.

I hurried to the stadium to inform Shula of the incident. He had a solemn frown on his face as he told me he had already heard about it on the 7:00 A.M. news. "What were you doing in a barber shop at 4:45 in the morning?" he asked.

"Look," I said, "you know how bad I hate to wait in lines."

"This is serious," he said, "Rosenbloom has already talked to Rozelle on the phone. The league office is investigating."

He picked up the phone in his office and dialed Carroll Rosenbloom. He handed me the phone and I began, "Carroll, I know this looks bad but . . ."

"Shut up," he explained. "Let me do the talking. I've already spoken to Rozelle about it and he's upset. Everybody in the game was all right except the dealer, who had been arrested thirty-three times on gambling charges. You know what your contract says about affiliation with known gamblers. You know what he did to Hornung and Karras. Alex, you're in big trouble, and frankly

I think you'll be suspended for life. Now do exactly as I tell you and I'll do everything I can to help you. Go to your friends with the press and tell them that you didn't know anybody in the game and you were there as a guest of Bert Bell's."

"But, Carroll," I said, "That just isn't the truth. I've played in that game dozens of times."

"Alex, if you want me to help, you'll do exactly what I tell you. Your career depends on it," he explained. That sounded strange. I had never thought of football as a career. It was simply something I had done all my life; hell, it *was* my life.

I put down the phone and told Shula what Carroll had said. I told him that Bert was my best friend and I couldn't lie about something like that. Shula said it was a decision that I would have to make on my own. "By the way," he said, "what were you doing playing with a guy with thirty-three arrests?"

"Shoes," I answered, "When you're up at that time of the night it's tough enough getting up a game, much less screening the applicants."

I was confused; I couldn't understand why they were taking this so seriously. I didn't consider myself a bad guy. All I was doing was playing poker. When I thought back to the people who built this game, almost every one of them was a gambler. Art Rooney had bought the Steelers with money he had won at the race track.

I had been brought up to believe that good character was more important than a good reputation. Character is what you are. Reputation was only what other people thought you were. It was apparent that Rozelle and I differed in this respect, because he was of the opinion that reputation was all-important. If people perceived you to be bad, you may as well be bad. It was a relatively new thought, and it was generally being accepted on Madison Avenue. The age of image was upon us.

After practice I went out to have a beer with Larry Harris and Cameron Snyder, two writers who covered the Colts for the *Sun* papers. They, too, were concerned. After two or three beers we had still not come up with a solution to my situation. After four or five beers, it came to me. I said, "You know I'm not a criminal. A fool, yes, but a criminal, no. Listen, you guys, you've always protected me in the past. I've got an idea. Let's just turn this whole thing into a joke." Larry looked at Cameron and they stared at each other for a minute.

"That might just work," Cameron said. "Get on the phone and talk to Steadman and Tanton (the two sports editors of the papers). Let's get everybody in on this. It could be fun."

The next day, the sports pages were covered with write-ups and pictures of me. The captions were hilarious with lines like "The Hawk is always best when the chips are down." I was especially adept at handling the "inside straight" routes. Another picture bore the caption, "The Hawk is our Ace in the Hole."

All week long the newspapers poured it on, until by game time on Sunday the Alex Hawkins scandal had been laughed into oblivion.

36

Because of the uncertainty of my status, Shula had elected to go with Ray Perkins against the Packers on Sunday. Jimmy Welch, the special teams captain, had been lost for the rest of the year, so despite my arrest Shula had reinstated me as special teams captain.

My nickname had been changed from "Captain Who?" to "Captain Daybreak." At the coin flip that preceded the game, Bobby Boyd had refused to allow me to make the call. He said I was already in enough trouble over gambling.

We were trailing the Packers 10–0, with just over six minutes remaining, when Shula sent me into the game. Nobody ever beat Lombardi's Packers in a situation like this. I had been having a hot hand, and I suppose Shoes felt he might as well play it. For whatever reason, the Colt offense, which had been unable to move all day, suddenly came alive. Unitas put his magic to work and completed five straight passes, the last one to me for a ten-yard touchdown. The extra point was wide but a trace of hope remained when Rick Volk recovered Lou Michaels's onside kick on the Packers' thirty-four-yard line.

John missed on a couple of passes, and then with thirteen seconds to play hit Willie Richardson for the winning touchdown. It was the first time Shula had beaten Lombardi in their last six encounters.

The real story of the game was Richardson's catch, but not in the Baltimore papers. All at once I became the inspirational hero of the victory. A large picture of my touchdown catch ran in the morning paper with the caption, "The Poker Faced Hawk Shows His Winning Hands." I was quoted as saying that the victory was "in the cards." It was too good a story for the Baltimore writers to let go. I might add that they were the same people who would select the winner of the Don Kellett Award of $5,000 to the Colt player who most exemplified the spirit of the Colts. I had been buying their drinks since returning from Atlanta, and the award now loomed as a possibility.

I was looking forward to our game with Atlanta the following week. The floundering Falcons were starting to skid, and it might be fun playing against my old mates. On the way down to Atlanta, an old passage came to mind: "Don't be dismayed by good-byes. A farewell is necessary before you can meet again and meeting again after moments or a lifetime is certain for those who are friends."

An article in Monday's Atlanta *Constitution* sports page read:

"HE'S NOT FOR ME" . . . NORB ON ALEX

"I don't care if he catches 40 passes a game, he's still not going to play for me."

That was Norb Hecker on Alex Hawkins here late Sunday, right after the Colts' 49–7 win over Atlanta. Hawkins, the late Falcon, had come alive, so to speak, by grabbing three passes for 83 yards, running twice for a six-yard average and by making at least three kickoff tackles, one of which possibly was the game's biggest play. On this, Ron Smith fumbled at his own 22 and the Colts quickly made it 14–0.

"We traded Hawkins because he didn't fit our plans," Hecker explained without much emotion. "And I thought it was a tremendous trade. We'll get a future and a player to be named. Would I do it again?" he repeated a question. "I'd do it a thousand straight times."

The Falcons coach made it clear he had hardly been aware of the controversial ex–South Carolina star's contributions Sunday.

"I can't be watching Hawkins out there," he said as a smile broke across his face. "I've got enough problems of my own. Besides, I had enough problems watching him when we owned him."

When informed of his statements, the Hawk replied, "Print it!"

It had been fun seeing my old friends again. It wasn't really Norb's fault that the Falcons were failing. If anybody was at fault it was Rankin Smith, whom Lombardi had told that Hecker was not yet ready for a head coaching job.

Friday, two days before our game with Detroit, eight other card players and I were to stand trial on gambling charges. Along with my mouthpiece, Joe Porkorny, I was ready to stand charges. Joe Porkorny was a lawyer whom I had met at the Gridiron Club. He was a regular there. Enough said.

Joe had been a fullback at Maryland in the 1940s. He was portrayed perfectly by Jack Warden in the motion picture *And Justice For All*. He was big and gruff, with a great sense of humor. Since no one else had a lawyer, Joe agreed to represent all ten of us. The fee for Joe's services was set at three hundred dollars apiece. This money was to be paid to Joe in twenty-dollar installments whenever we ran into him.

We appeared punctually at 10:00 A.M. Jurisprudence was not as prompt. The wait was two hours. No one thought to bring a deck of cards. The press was there to squeeze the last bit of humor out of the arrest. "What are the odds on the case?" a writer asked me. I replied that I was not allowed to gamble.

A photographer asked me to step outside for a picture. I went to the phone and called the Colt general manager, Harry Hulmes. "Harry, this is the Hawk. The police are allowing me one phone call. What does my contract say about relations with the press? Isn't it carrying it a bit too far to be photographed here today? I see, then I don't have to cooperate with them? . . . Uh, huh. I can even throw something at the camera then? Good, I'll keep that in mind. While I'm at it, tell the coaches I'm being detained."

The photographer told me he would wait outside and get a picture of me coming out of the court like Jimmy Hoffa. The thought of that shot got my attention. I excused myself and went to check out the premises.

While I was gone Bert introduced Larry Lookout to the press. "Get a picture of this guy, he's your real story. Can you imagine a lookout man running the barbershop being jerked outside? He's finished in this town as a lookout man. Everyone has put him on waivers."

I came back and informed the photographer that there were three exits from the place and that the odds were two to one against him getting the shot, but I would not cover the bet.

At high noon we the accused were summoned into the courtroom before Magistrate F. Vernon Boozer. (Wouldn't you know that I'd get a judge with a name like that?) The judge asked, "How do you plead?" One by one, nine of us pleaded not guilty. Bert, the last of the accused, confused everyone by pleading guilty. Joe, the attorney, and the judge were all taken off guard, but Judge Boozer proceeded, ignoring Bert's plea.

The offense began the battle with the defense. The offense said police had "heard clicking" of chips and conversations pertaining to the game of poker. The defense suggested that since the police hadn't knocked at the barbershop door they might have been trespassing.

The offense said the police had in fact knocked but there had been no answer. Then they tried to force the door with a crowbar, but the lock wouldn't pop. After that they waited a half hour, entering when three alleged card players left. The door had not even been locked.

"What did you see when you entered the room?" Boozer asked the officer. "Nine men around the table," said the offense. "There were chips on the table and eight decks of cards."

"Were the cards distributed as if the men were playing?" he asked.

"No sir," the officer replied. "They were in stacks."

A brief argument ensued between the two officers as to the number of chips. One said there were 140, the other said 279. Boozer broke in and said, "Really, isn't this immaterial?"

"Was there money in evidence?" There was not. "Or a piece of paper with notations on it, indicating they might have been playing for money?" There was not.

Since the cards hadn't been distributed, there was no proof that a game was in progress. Since there was no sign of money, there was no proof that the chips had value. In short, there was no case.

Judge Boozer decreed that all charges be dropped. It was then that our high-powered attorney spoke his first and final words, "Thank you, Judge Boozer."

Nine of the accused refused to pay Joe. I finally finished paying him, in full, five years later, twenty dollars at a time.

As Bert was driving me to practice, I asked him why he had pleaded guilty. "If my friends in Philadelphia found out there was a poker game and I wasn't in it, I would lose face," was his reply.

Bert's own column the next day read:

INSIDE STORY ON THE INSIDE STRAIGHT CAPER

It is on rare occasions that a reporter has an opportunity to cover his own arrest and to not give a full accounting of the night's proceedings would serve to unjustly point the finger of insinuation at many of the principals.

The Loch Raven Pleasure and Inside Straight Club has gathered on many occasions over the past few years to discuss politics and, on occasion, deal some friendly poker.

There was no reason to believe that Halloween night was to be any different than any other of the nights spent with political insomniacs whose restless spirits sometimes led them to "Savage Sam's" Barbershop in Loch Raven Plaza. It was on this same night, however, that some other restless spirits decided that Halloween would be a good night to look in on matters at "Savage Sam's" Barbershop and to play their own version of trick or treatment.

Entrance to "Savage Sam's" Barbershop was a well thought-out piece of police work. They knocked on the door and it was immediately opened by Larry Lookout. He was yanked outside. Now where have you ever heard of a lookout getting yanked out of a card game? His reputation is ruined and you can be assured he is finished as a lookout.

Led by a Lieutenant and a Sergeant, Baltimore County's answer to Toody and Muldoon, they poured into the back room and blew their first line when they announced, "This is a card game."

Well, practically everybody knew it was a card game so no one paid much attention to these lumberjack-looking guys, armed with fire axes, crow bars, pneumatic drills and oversized mallets.

A quick personal perusal said they were just some guys from theatrical outfitters pulling a Halloween prank on the Loch Raven Pleasure and Inside Straight Club.

This opinion was soon dispelled when one of the arresting officers realized the folly of the opening statement and attempted to get some recognition by then announcing, "You're all under arrest."

One of the members made a last minute plea on behalf of the assembled citizenry when he suggested to the police that the chips were nothing more than success symbols and whoever at the end of the night has the most chips is considered by his peers as "the most."

You know, that's how that expression got started, "You're the most." This plea was to no avail.

Toody and Muldoon were not biting. Ten of the "most wanted" criminals in one night was too much to give up.

We were then asked to freeze for a team picture. Neither of the two Brownie cameras worked and to this day no one is sure if they ever got the group shot they were after.

So, off to the Towson bighouse went Savage Sam, No. 25, Black Bart, Silent, Harry Hairdo, Big Poison, Careless Carmen, Annuity John, and Legs Davis to be summarily photographed, fingerprinted and given a number.

It took 15 policemen four and a half hours typing one-fingered to book 10 men. The trip to the bailiff's in two police vans had to be stopped twice because half of the prisoners got lost on the way.

And, of course, upon finally arriving at the bailiff's office, it was closed.

The following Sunday found No. 25 in your football program catching a touchdown pass against the Packers and he thereby became the first player in the NFL to save two games in one week.

The stigma and attendant publicity that disproportionately identified No. 25 in your program and pro football with gambling can never be remedied.

The evidence was so insufficient that the judge could not even be sure there was a game in progress. The verdict of innocent in this case has little importance. The damage of identification has been done.

There is some small value, however, in knowing that this may be one of the few times the scales of justice may have tipped in favor of the guilty.

The next week we whipped Detroit, 41–7. Ray Perkins injured his knee in the game and would be lost for the rest of the season. I caught my fourth touchdown pass of the season, so things were still going well with me. I continued to play on, fast and loose.

After the Detroit game I wandered by the Gridiron Club about ten o'clock Sunday night to check on my friend, Joy Boy. There were just a couple of customers in the place, so we started playing shuffleboard. It developed into an unusually interesting game that went on for a long time until I noticed the sweeper, Tommy, cleaning up. "Tommy, what time is it?" I asked. He answered it was eleven in the morning. "What day is it?" I asked.

"Why, it is Tuesday," he said. Good God! I was late for practice. I raced to my car with a beer in my hand. When I reached the stadium it was 11:30 and the offense and defense had already split up and were watching films of the Detroit game.

When I stumbled into the offense's meeting rooms, the lights were off and the projector was on. As I entered the darkened room, I fell over a desk, causing a roar of laughter from my teammates. As the laughter continued, I picked myself up and settled into my seat beside Unitas. "Damn, you smell terrible," he remarked in a loud fashion. This brought more laughter from my teammates. Shula was not laughing. I stayed awake through the film and, as we were leaving the room, Shula announced that we were to dress out in full uniform. Ordinarily on Tuesday we went out in shorts and T-shirts and barely broke a sweat. Shula was angry, however, and I was the object of his disapproval. Throughout the practice he neither spoke to me nor looked my way.

After practice Shula stopped by my locker to have his say. "Hawk, I've put up with a lot of shit from you, but this time you've stepped over the line. If you ever embarrass me again like you did today, you're finished." I was looking into the eyes of the meanest Hungarian I had ever seen. There was little doubt that he meant it.

Someone once wrote: "Everybody has a skeleton in his closet, but when the skeletons outnumber the clothes, you've gone too far." Or as Dan Jenkins says, "To err is human, but when the eraser wears out ahead of the pencil, you've overdone it." It was time for me to curtail my off-field activities. Shula was so furious with me that he had completely forgotten to fine me.

I went to my apartment and slept until ten o'clock the next morning. I had played shuffleboard, non-stop, from ten o'clock Sunday night until eleven o'clock Tuesday morning. It may not have been a record, but it was a very competitive try.

We improved our record to 9–0–2 the following week in San Francisco. That day I received a crushed nose. I'd had my nose broken maybe a half-dozen times, but this was special. When we arrived back in Baltimore at 2:00 A.M., I checked into the Union Memorial Hospital for surgery. I was released on Tuesday.

Around 3:00 A.M. Wednesday morning, I woke up from my sleep with a gagging feeling. Something was in my throat. I went to the bathroom, opened my mouth and looked in the mirror. Sure enough, something white was hanging from the roof of my throat. I reached inside and pulled it out of my mouth. It was the gauze from the packing in my nose. There was no turning back. Nothing was left to do except keep on pulling. Pulling the surgical gauze out through my mouth hurt like hell, and I marveled at how much gauze they could stuff in one large nose. It was like pulling loose thread from the sleeve of a shirt; it just kept coming. It may be an exaggeration, but I would almost swear that fifteen feet of gauze came out through my mouth.

I was repeating the process at practice that day on my other nostril when Shula happened by. He almost threw up, but allowed that anyone who wanted to play that badly could play for him. "Hawk," he said, "you're starting again this week." Although Raymond Berry, the greatest receiver who ever played the game, was ready to play again, Shula allowed me to start against the Dallas Cowboys that Sunday.

We beat the Cowboys 23–17. It was my finest hour with the Colts. I caught eight passes for 124 yards, almost as many passes and more yardage than Don Meredith had managed for the entire Cowboy team. None of my catches were for touchdowns, but I set up what would prove to be Raymond Berry's last touchdown pass reception.

I was unconscious in the game, executing routes and catches taught to me by my mentor. I was playing out of my mind, and far above my capability. After one such catch, I came to the sideline to be greeted by Jimmy Orr. "Señor," he said, "you just ain't that good."

"Be quiet, Jimmy, don't wake me from this beautiful dream," I said. Without knowing it, I was having my last gasp before dying, and I didn't want to ever wake up. My chances for the Don Kellett award looked better and better.

Sometime during the Dallas game I suffered a depressed cheekbone fracture. Until Tom Brookshire mentioned it to me in a postgame interview on TV I wasn't even aware of it. When I looked in the mirror there was an indentation about the size of a golf ball under my left eye. Back I went to the Union Memorial Hospital for repairs. The Colts were now 10–0–2, but still just holding on to a one-game lead over the Rams, who were keeping pace.

Raymond Berry remained on the bench as we beat the Saints at home. Late in the third quarter of the New Orleans game I had caught a nothing little sideline pass and stepped peacefully out of bounds, when for no apparent reason New Orleans defensive back Dave Whitsell rapped me viciously in the nose with his forearm. Once again my nose was broken.

This didn't make any sense at all. Dave was a nice guy, but he was such a docile player that Weeb Ewbank had once levied a fifty-dollar fine on anyone who blocked him. Why suddenly had he become so violent? For three weeks in a row I had been victimized by cheap shots. The answer, I guess, is that people like myself with average talent know when someone is playing over his head, and they make every effort to wake him up and bring him back to reality.

Back again I went to the Union Memorial Hospital. It was getting to be monotonous; every Sunday I ended up in the hospital. I felt like a regular on "M.A.S.H." I even gave some thought to moving out of my apartment and into the damn hospital.

Once upon a time I was what you might describe as a fairly handsome man. After three straight weeks of pounding, however, my face was a mess. I looked like a panda bear. Both eyes were completely encircled with blackish-purple rings, the skin above and beneath the bruises was yellowish, and my nose, if you could call it that, was a squashed, crooked object. Between the hospital and the police station, the authorities now had more pictures of me than my mother did.

Thus far it had been a marvelous year for the Colts. With a record of 11–0–2, we had been through thirteen games without a loss. It was the first time a team had accomplished this since the Chicago Bears did it in 1934. We had done this despite the fact that we were an injured team. We had twelve players who had missed four or more games, and five of those players were All-Pros. This was truly a complete team.

Notwithstanding our heroics, however, the Rams trailed us by only one game in the Coastal Division, and they had held right in there with a 10–1–2 record.

On the fourteenth and final week of the regular season we were in Los Angeles for the showdown game. We needed only a win or a tie to clinch our division. If the Rams beat us they would represent the Coastal Division. Our overall records would be identical, but the rules were that in the event of a tie, the title would be decided by comparative scores between the two teams in their two games against each other.

On Tuesday Shula took me aside and told me that he was going to start Raymond Berry in the game against the Rams. Both of us knew that I had had one hell of a year, and Shoes wasn't sure how I was going to take being benched. He was relieved when I told him that I would not be upset about being replaced by a backup who had caught five hundred passes more than I had.

We left for the West Coast healthier, happier, and more determined than I could ever remember. There were 77,277 people at the coliseum to witness our do-or-die game with the Rams. We were flatter than piss on a plate. The Rams buried us 34–10. After the first quarter it was never a contest, as the Los Angeles fearsome foursome sacked John seven times.

Just that quickly a glorious season had ended. We were out of it. It was over. We lost one game, and didn't even make the playoffs. The circus was over and the monkey was dead.

The four-hour flight back to Baltimore was a quiet one. Nobody was mad; we were just shocked. What do you have to do to win a championship?

I was not prepared to go back to Atlanta. I stayed in Baltimore for a couple of days for the Don Kellett Award. It turned out that I didn't get that, either. Rosenbloom and the front office, knowing of no way to prevent the board from voting for me, cancelled the award and the Colts gave the $5,000 to charity. Not only that, but unwilling to forget the poker game, Shula had fined me $500.

The 1967 season, however, was not a total loss. I had led both the Colts and Falcons in fines in the same season.

37

I was back home in Atlanta watching the playoffs. Dallas, winner of the Capital Division with a 9–5 record, knocked off Cleveland for the Eastern Division crown. Green Bay, with a 9–4–1 record, had beaten the Rams for the Western Division title. A team we had beaten was to play another team we had beaten for the championship of the National Football League. In no way did this seem fair or equitable.

The game was played late in the afternoon in sub-zero temperature. The Cowboys were ahead, 17–14. With five minutes to play and sixty-eight yards to traverse, Bart Starr engineered a Green Bay drive to the Cowboys' one-yard line. On fourth down, with only thirteen seconds to play, Vince Lombardi disdained the field-goal attempt that would have tied the game and chose to gamble on Bart Starr's quarterback sneak for the win. Starr went into the end zone and the Packers won the game 21–17 and the right to represent the NFL in the championship game against the Oakland Raiders.

The Raiders had slaughtered the Houston Oilers 40–7 for the AFL championship that same day. Naturally, I had not bothered to watch.

As I watched the Dallas–Green Bay game I wondered what the Packers had that we didn't. Green Bay had played the entire season without either Paul Hornung or Jim Taylor, who had gone to New Orleans in the player-allocation draft. They had won the NFL championship with two running backs that nobody else wanted, Chuck Mercein and Ben Wilson.

It was not at all like Lombardi to gamble on a fourth-down touchdown and refuse an almost sure tying field goal. And why had he tried, of all plays, a quarterback sneak? These were questions to which I had no answers.

And who in the name of God were the Oakland Raiders? I had not even bothered to watch their game. I decided to go on down to Miami and watch this thing more and more people were referring to as the "Super Bowl." I didn't mind rooting for the Packers twice in nine years.

Just as it had the year before, the Super Bowl hype started early:

From news dispatches of January 4:

The Oakland Raiders, unlike most teams, will not have closed practices. There are no doors to close. The Raiders have been practicing on a field in the far corners of the campus of St. Andrew's Boys School in Boca Raton. There is only one access road leading to the practice field and the Raiders have stationed uniformed guards at the gate to bar everyone but authorized personnel. Security, needless to say, is stringent.

From the *New York Times*, January 5:

Al Davis, managing general partner of the Oakland Raiders, said today that "the great snow job" has begun. . . .

"If we play like we did against Houston, there is no reason why we can't beat the best," said Daryle Lamonica, Raider quarterback. . . .

"This team has a great deal of confidence," said John Rauch, the Raiders coach. The men on this team, I am sure, will respond to one more challenge, like taking on the very best team in all of football. . . .

"Imagine," said Al Davis, "The lil ol' Raiders on the same field with the Green Bay Packers. Imagine. . ."

"The Packers are favored by fourteen," said Jimmy the Greek Snyder from his Information Unlimited office in Las Vegas, Nevada. "It's a strong 14, at that. I don't just pick numbers out of the air. I analyze both teams and translate their strengths and weaknesses into the language of points. Their coach, Lombardi, is a big intangible and so is their record in the BIG games."

GREEN BAY, January 7 (AP):

About 250 fans assembled today at the wind-swept airport with temperatures ten degrees below zero to cheer the Green Bay Packers as they depart for Florida. The Packers left behind four inches of snow.

For reasons unknown to me, the game itself was starting to catch on. It was an obvious mismatch between the two teams, but people were coming from all over the country to see it in person. The attitude between the two teams was different from the previous years.

From news dispatches of January 8:

Al Davis, managing general partner of the Oakland Raiders, confirmed today that his team's pregame approach was one of formal flattery.

"They say I'm a wild man, an animal, a blood-thirsty savage," said Ben Davidson, 6'7", 265-pound end for the Raiders.

"I remember Ben when he was with the Packers," said Cherry Starr, sunning herself by the pool at the Gault Ocean Motel. "He was a very nice man and we all liked him. He didn't have a mustache then, but that doesn't matter, I guess."

"My father wore a mustache and I haven't been able to lick him yet," said Lombardi when asked about Davidson.

The rumors continued of the possible retirement of Vince Lombardi. Former players like Hornung were appearing. Former assistants were coming around as never before. Vince said that after the season was over he was going to take a long, hard look at himself. After his Friday appearance he told his team that Sunday might be the last time they would all be together.

The Super Bowl, in just its second year, was becoming a financial bonanza for the host city.

New York Times, January 12:

> The Carillon Hotel, one of the big ones on the ocean, is sold out at this time of year for the first time since it was built. Eastern Airlines said that 900 to 1,000 people flew to Miami Beach from New York, Cleveland, Detroit, Chicago and St. Louis on special package tours arranged by the airlines.
>
> Green Bay fans chartered ten planes carrying about 100 people each to Miami Beach.
>
> A capacity crowd of 75,546 would consume 40,000 Zum Zums, bratwurst and hot dogs.

FORT LAUDERDALE, Florida , January 13 (UPI):

> The Green Bay Packers yesterday added Dick Capp, a 23-year-old, 238-pound linebacker, to their roster. Capp, from Boston College, was released by the Boston Patriots of the AFL in the summer of 1966.

News dispatches, January 13:

> Of 36 pro football players vacationing in the Miami area on the eve of the Super Bowl game, 30 of them picked Green Bay to defeat the Raiders.
>
> Said Joe Namath, "Green Bay is just better all around. The Packers are one of football's great teams, probably the best ever."

It was enough to gag a maggot. What did Namath know about football? He had only been around for a couple of years, and knew nothing about the NFL. Where was he when we beat the Packers in November? This Packer team he was calling the best ever was probably the weakest Packer team since 1960. This upstart wouldn't know anything about the 1958–59 Colt team that *was* the best team ever. If he thought the Packers were good, the Raiders must really be a joke. I was certainly glad I could view this objectively!

Our seats were right behind the Packers' bench, about thirty rows up. No one in our group from Atlanta was pulling for the Raiders.

Green Bay won the toss and elected to receive. In the first quarter of the game, the Packers could manage only two field goals and led it 6–0. In the second quarter, Starr found Dowler down the middle for a sixty-two-yard score. It was now 13–0. With disbelieving eyes, I watched the Raiders cut that lead to 13–7 as Lamonica hit Bill Miller for a twenty-three-yard touchdown. The Raiders were making a game of it.

Just before the first half ended, Green Bay punted to Oakland's Rodger Bird. Bird fumbled the fair catch on his own forty-five-yard line. Dick Capp, activated the day before the game, fell on it for Green Bay. With just six seconds left, Don Chandler kicked his third field goal and Green Bay led 16–7 as the first half ended.

At halftime a group of older Packers got together in the locker room and dedicated the last thirty minutes of their energy to the "Old Man." Gregg, Jordan, Nitsche, Davis, Starr, Dowler, Kramer, Skoronski, Thurston, and McGee spread the word around to the rest of the players to settle down, be cool and calculating, so that they could take over the game.

Early in the third quarter, Starr had a third-and-one at the Green Bay forty-yard line. He faked the handoff to Wilson into the line and connected with Max McGee, who had replaced Dowler, for a thirty-five-yard gainer. Green Bay moved the ball to the two-yard line and Donnie Anderson scored to break open the game. Chandler's point after made it 23–7. Chandler added another three-pointer and Herb Adderley ran an interception back sixty yards for a touchdown for a 33–7 Green Bay lead. Late in the game, Oakland scored a meaningless touchdown and the final score of Super Bowl II read: Green Bay 33, Oakland 14.

After the game Oakland coach Johnny Rauch said the fumble of the punt just before the half ended was the turning point in the game. Others felt the turning point was Starr's third-and-one pass to McGee. The Colts had been burned so many times in the past in short yardage situations that I had to agree with the latter.

Lombardi's teams didn't gamble often, but their success ratio when they did could not be overlooked. Was it something Lombardi had learned under Red Blaik at West Point about the element of surprise? What factors had he considered when he picked up Chuck Mercein and Ben Wilson? What had he seen in Dick Capp to warrant activating him just twenty-four hours before the Super Bowl game?

I didn't know. I was certain only of the fact that somehow Lombardi always got his teams ready to play in the big games. Since his loss to the Eagles in the 1960 championship game the Green Bay Packers had never lost another playoff game. He had taken a last place team in '58 and turned them into world champions in '61 and '62, '65, '66 and '67. They were the only team in the history of professional football to win three consecutive championships.

Lombardi had proven he could not only win, but he could win in a hurry. He proved he could not only take his team to the top, he could keep them there. There was nothing left for Vince to prove. He resigned as head coach of the Packers that year.

Jerry Isenberg and Robert Lipsyte of the *New York Times* put Super Bowl II in its printed perspective.

Isenberg:

Somehow, the Green Bay Packers and the Oakland Raiders managed to get the Super Bowl played. The Green Bay Packers won it 33–14. The Green Bays also won it last year 35–10. The American league, therefore, over a span of two years, has cut the margin by six points. At their current rate of progress, the Americans should manage to get a tie somewhere around 1971.

Lipsyte:

It was an anti-climactic game in the sense that the millions spent to televise the game, the thousands to promote it, and the enormous emotion and work spent preparing for it, were not rewarded by either sustained drama or even moments of great excitement. Days before, an Oakland Raider said that playing the Packers would be like "playing our fathers." The boys of the Golden West were not quite ready yet.

38

It was hard to imagine that it had been ten years since Emlen Tunnell had told me that the first three years of pro ball would be the hardest. How vividly I could remember him saying that if I could make it through the first three years, I could play for ten. Well, 1967 would be my tenth year of professional football.

I had seen a lot of changes in those ten years. The owners, coaches, and players had almost all changed. George Halas had stepped down as coach of the Bears after having owned and coached the team since they were the Decatur Staleys in 1920. A new franchise had been added to the league, the Cincinnati Bengals. They would be coached and owned by Paul Brown. The number of teams and players in the NFL had more than doubled in those ten years. Phil Bengston had taken over for Vince Lombardi at Green Bay.

Without people like Jim Parker, Raymond Berry, and Lenny Moore, who had all retired, training camp was not the same. All three would soon be Hall-of-Famers. Together they were All-Pro selections sixteen times. The young Colts who replaced them were good players and fine people, but, well, they were different. From the 1958–59 championship teams only six players remained.

I, for one, was feeling old. The "characters" who once made training camp fun were gone. My legs were starting to hurt, and at night I would have to elevate them after each practice. The game of football had turned into work. Cameron Snyder and Larry Harris, two writers who had been covering the team, were the first to bring this to my attention. Both were close friends of mine, and both were in agreement that I should retire. They may have been right, but I felt I owed it to myself to take one last shot at the golden ring that had eluded me for so long.

I reported to training camp unsigned. General Manager Harry Hulmes had offered me a salary of $25,000 for the 1968 season. As a matter of principle, I refused the contract. It had taken me nine years to reach the salary of $24,000. In 1968 the average salary in the NFL was $26,000. I had had a really good year in 1967, and was only asking for the average salary. After ten years I felt like it was only fair.

When the Colts failed to budge on a $2,000 raise, I opted to play out my option, which meant that I would be taking a ten percent cut in pay over the previous year. It made no sense doing this, of course, but let's not forget that I was still a proud, stubborn hillbilly, and Appalachian natives are that way when it comes to principle. So instead of making $25,000 for the 1968 season, I was now playing for $21,600.

No Colt player had ever played out his option, and my refusal to sign did not set well with Rosenbloom. Apparently Carroll had not forgotten that I had declined to follow his instructions in regard to the poker game issue. His personal relationship with the Baltimore press had always been strained, and he may have been envious of mine. I had not noticed any changes in Carroll's regard for me, but then I would be the last ever to do that. He was a master at subterfuge.

In preseason games we beat the Oakland Raiders and the Miami Dolphins. The other league was not yet on par with the NFL. Both the Raiders' and the Dolphins' cornerbacks, however, used the bump-and-run coverage technique, which I couldn't beat. It signaled the demise of the slow white receiver in pro football. My days were numbered.

In our last preseason game with the Dallas Cowboys, John Unitas developed tendonitis in his right elbow. In the ten years I had played with John, he had never been without pain or injuries, but this was worse than it had ever been.

In August Don Shula had made a trade with the Giants for quarterback Earl Morrall. Earl had bounced around the league with four different teams since 1956, and somehow he had always managed to work himself into a backup role. A veteran of thirteen years, he had one thing going for him: experience.

So we started the '68 season with Earl as our quarterback. Nobody expected much of Earl, and the lingering hope of a return to form by Unitas was in the back of our minds. Each week our silent rallying cry was, "John will be well next week."

Bubba Smith was now ready to settle in at the defensive end spot, and Mike Curtis had fully recovered from knee surgery. Oh, had he ever! To replace Raymond Berry, Jimmy Orr had switched sides. Ray Perkins was playing behind Jimmy, and I had moved to the right side behind Willie Richardson to start the '68 season.

We got by our first two opponents with unimpressive wins, relying heavily on a strong defense. Morrall was less than sensational, but by the same token he wasn't hurting us, either.

In our third game we smothered the Steelers 41–7 as the Colts tied an NFL record by returning three interceptions for touchdowns. In that game we started believing in ourselves. After all, John would be back next week!

Next week Morrall threw touchdown passes of fifty, forty-five, and sixty-six yards and the defense allowed only one touchdown as we beat the Bears 28–7.

The following week we played the Browns. Down by seven points at the half, Shula turned to Unitas to start the third quarter. We were all looking forward to the patented Unitas rally, but John, far below par with the ailing elbow, was not up to the task. He threw three interceptions and completed only one of twelve passes as Cleveland handed us our first loss of the season, 30–20.

We put down the Rams the next week as Morrall passed for two touchdowns and ran for another in our 27–10 win. The Colt defense was awesome, sacking Ram quarterback Roman Gabriel five times. Mike Curtis, full of fury, was asserting himself as an All-Pro linebacker.

My wife had come up for the Rams game and was there in the stands when I went down with a torn gluteus maximus muscle. After the operation Ed McDonnell, the team surgeon, told her I would never play again and I would probably walk with a slight limp for the remainder of my life. He urged her not to tell me, but to let me find out for myself.

The Colts put me on injured waivers and I went back to our home in Atlanta to heal. This was the fifth time in ten years I had been placed on waivers. I was back home when the Colts shut out the Giants 26–0. It was the first time the Giants had been shut out in seventy-six games. The defense allowed Fran Tarkenton only ninety-eight passing yards.

I went back to Baltimore to have the wire taken out of my butt, then watched the Colts steal five passes in blanking the Cardinals 27–0. Since losing to the Browns, the Baltimore defense had surrendered only twenty points in four games. Our record was 9–1 and we were back on top of the Central Division.

It was a very determined team. With or without Unitas, they were making a run of it. Unitas's arm was not responding, but Morrall was doing everything we could ask of him and more.

On Monday after the Cardinals game I decided to stay in the area, because my thirty-day waiver period would be up in a week. I could taste blood with this team. They were doing everything a championship team needed to do. The doctor had told me the operation had been successful. He didn't think I *could* run on it, but then again he had never performed that particular operation, so he didn't know. Nobody had told me that I wasn't supposed to be able to run, and if nobody told me, how was I supposed to know? I had a few days to do nothing, so for whatever reason I went to New York.

While, along with most players of my day, I held New York City in contempt; nonetheless it fascinated me. The reason we were contemptuous was the incredible amount of publicity awarded to New York players. Second-team players were getting endorsements and commercials. Frank Gifford, Pat Summerall, and Al DeRogatis were being hired by the networks to do color commentating.

In that city of eight million, Billy Mathis was the only person I knew. Billy had played at Clemson and was now a fullback for the New York Jets. I had known him since college, so I figured I'd stay with him. Since the Giants were losing and the Jets were starting to get some attention, the shoe was on the other foot, so to speak. And I was curious about the quarterback with white shoes named Joe Willie Namath. Mathis was rooming with Tucker Fredrickson of the Giants in an apartment on Sixty-fifth and First. It was just around the corner from Mr. Laughs, which was the sports bar for pro athletes at that time.

I went out two nights with Mathis, Fredrickson, and Namath. It didn't take long to figure out who was the main man in the bars of New York. We hadn't left the first bar when I knew it was Fredrickson. Although all three players were handsome and single, Tucker was the favorite of the ladies. Even in Namath's own bar, "The Bachelors Three," I seated myself next to Tucker.

Tucker had been the No. 1 draft choice for the Giants in 1965. As a matter of fact, he was the first person picked in '65, ahead of Namath. Tucker had a quiet, confident manner, an impish smile, and a sweet little Huck Finn look that drew the attention of the ladies. He had a sensational first year with the Giants, but an injury to his knee had hampered him from that point on. Still, he was the player the city took to its heart.

Namath, on the other hand, was highly recognizable and more gawky in appearance. He wasn't at all the asshole I had expected. In fact, I liked him. He was confident all right, and I liked that, but he was a kid. He had been around for only four years. He would get his; then we would see how confident he was. Even though I had never seen him throw a football, I had already passed judgment on him. Without ever seeing Joe Namath play I was convinced that he was just another New York fabrication, all glitter and no gold, a Sonny Werblin creation who had become a New York fashion. This was show biz.

I left New York on the day I read in the papers that Jimmy Orr was hurt and the Colts were looking for a receiver. My waiver period was up on Sunday, so not knowing whether I could run or not I went to the equipment manager, got my uniform, and dressed out for practice. Shula was surprised to see me. "You can't play, can you?" he asked.

"I don't know," I answered, "but let's find out."

It was all right. I played on special teams in the Vikings game. Morrall completed thirteen of sixteen passes for 225 yards and two touchdowns in a 21–6 win. The next week our defense was awesome against the Falcons, with four interceptions, two fumble recoveries, and four sacks, chalking up the third shutout of the season, 44–0.

Our defense had gained so much confidence that they no longer talked of John's returning. Jimmy Orr and I did, however. Earl Morrall was playing like gangbusters, but there was still doubt in our minds. We were both afraid that Morrall would wake up. He was in that same zone of consciousness that I had been in the year before. After years of competent play Earl was now performing like a world champion.

We registered our twelveth win of the season on December 7 in frozen Green Bay. The Packers, with Lombardi now in the press box, could manage but one field goal. Without him the Pack was not the same team.

Our win over Green Bay had clinched our division championship. Although the Rams had kept pace throughout the season, their record of 9–2–1 left them a game and a half behind us. The last game in L.A. would be meaningless, so as a gesture of his appreciation, Carroll Rosenbloom had awarded us with a week on the coast with no curfew and no pressure.

The first thing I did when we arrived in Santa Barbara was to check the flight schedule for Las Vegas. There was none. There was no way you could get to Vegas from Santa Barbara. I saw Jimmy Orr strolling up to me. "Señor," he said, "You know where we ought to be, don't you?"

"Vegas," I answered, "but you can't get there from here."

"Yes, we can," he assured me. "I've already chartered two planes for tomorrow morning. There's room for six of us. Are you in?" The next day we were at the tables.

Monday was our day off, so we didn't have to get back until noon on Tuesday. It was only about an hour-and-a-half flight, so that posed no problem. We could gamble all night and that's what we did. About five o'clock in the morning, I went looking for Orr. I had set my credit limit at $2,000 and had already lost that and most of the cash I had brought with me. There was no way I could recover my losses with just the $240 I had remaining.

I found Orr at the dice tables and discovered he was losing, too. I asked how much money he had left. "About eight, I guess, " he replied.

I figured that to mean eight hundred dollars. We could now join forces. I figured that with our combined thousand dollars, maybe we could get our money back. "Lend me the difference," I said, "and take my two hundred and roll it. With one thousand you could get hot. I've seen you get hot before."

"I meant eight dollars," he replied. "That gives us two hundred forty-eight bucks to fight with."

About that time one of the ugliest red-headed women you would ever care to see walked up and asked Orr to buy her a drink. Since the drinks were free, Orr obliged. She was about fifty years old, with reddish-orange hair that grew in all directions. She had a large mole on her nose, was tackily dressed, and stood 5'2". I guessed her weight to be about 145 pounds. She was no bathing beauty.

I figured her to be a born loser, so I suggested to Jimmy that we let her roll the dice and bet against her. Jimmy said, "Naw, let's play the numbers." So we put one hundred dollars on the six and a hundred on the eight and she went to rolling the dice— *left-handed,* for Christ's sake! We let them roll.

I don't know how long she kept the dice without making her number, but it was the longest roll I'd ever witnessed. All I knew was that money was coming at me so fast that I couldn't keep it counted. After a while, we had $500 on every number on the board. I was collecting $650 every time this now-gorgeous lady rolled them. We were betting $500 on the hard eight and stuff like that. We were now playing with black $100 chips only.

Everyone in the place was watching her roll the dice. Jimmy was laughing and patting her on the back, and I was trying to figure out what kind of car we could buy her that would be good enough for her. There was no doubt in my mind that God had sent down this ugliest angel to watch over us.

One rack was filled with black chips, so I used the one beside me.

Money was coming in and Jimmy, cigar in mouth, was laughing.
We were well over ten-grand winners, just how much I couldn't
tell, it was coming in so fast. Then just as quick she threw a seven.
The bitch threw a seven!

Oh, well, I quickly recovered, nobody's perfect, not even God's
ugliest angel. The dice came to me and while my longest roll at dice
was five throws, we loaded up the numbers. Five hundred dollars
on all of them. The first throw was a six. The second was a seven-
craps. They raked the board. Damn, did they do that quickly! That
was a lot of money gone. We were back to our first rack of chips
again. Granted the money had come in fast, but it was going out
even faster!

Jimmy got the dice. Same procedure on the bets. Jimmy craps
on twelve. The table was raked again. The dice went back to the
red-headed person. I had a short conference with Orr. "James,
how do you feel about things now?" I asked. "Should we go strong
on her? We've got our money back."

"Señor," he said, "we didn't come out here to break even. Load
her up." So we played everything we had on her as she smiled
and rolled. She threw a deuce. Snake eyes, the worst loss you can
have. She wasn't from heaven, she was from hell! She even had
on a red dress, with orange hair, no less.

It was 9:45 A.M., and about that time Bobby Boyd, who had slept
all night, happened on us and suggested we leave. We were supposed to meet the pilots at 10:00 A.M. Bobby, always careful, left.
Jimmy and I stayed for one last drink. We toasted our stupidity.
I never again wanted to meet a short, fat, orange-headed, left-
handed woman with dice in her hands and a mole on her nose. We
borrowed twenty dollars from the pit boss and caught a cab to the
airport.

There were some problems with the airplane and we were an
hour late getting back. Santa Barbara was just ahead of us when
we informed the pilot that we would have to send him the money
for the trip. The pilot laughed. He understood; he had flown to
Las Vegas before. We were late to the meetings, and were fined by
Shula.

We beat the Rams for our thirteenth win of the season. Our defense had allowed only 144 points. They had tied a league record, set in 1963 by the Bears, for the fewest points allowed in a fourteen-game season. Shula was voted Coach of the Year for the third time in five years. Morrall led the NFL in passing and was voted the Most Valuable Player in the league. More importantly, Unitas had played the second half of our game with the Rams and had looked pretty good.

On December 22 we beat the Minnesota Vikings 24–14 for the Western Conference championship. Morrall threw two touchdown passes and Mike Curtis ran a fumble back sixty yards for a third score. Our defense held the Vikings to just eighty-five rushing yards. Except for the Cleveland Browns, no team had been able to move the ball on us throughout the entire season. We were to play the Browns in Cleveland the following week for the championship title of the NFL.

The temperature was below zero in Cleveland on December 29 when Tom Matte scored three touchdowns, and our defense handed the Browns their first shutout in 143 games. The 34–0 whipping served as revenge for an earlier season loss and the defeat by the Browns in 1964. So overwhelming was our defense that the Browns crossed midfield only twice in the game.

We were the champions of the National Football League for the first time since 1959, with a record of 15–1–0. We had won more games in a single season than any other team in the history of professional football. We also won the right to represent the National Football League in the Super Bowl game against the AFL's New York Jets in Miami, Florida.

We had run roughshod over the entire league and I saw no reason why it should stop now. I had come into this league in 1959 with a winner and a championship ring, and I was going out of this league with a winner and a championship watch.

39

Over 30,000 people turned out to greet us when we arrived at the Baltimore airport after the victory over Cleveland. They had waited patiently for nine years for this moment. Every Sunday since I had joined the Colts in 1959 they had filled Memorial Stadium. They had shared and suffered the same disappointment we had over those years of near misses in our attempt to bring the NFL Championship back to Baltimore. This night we had finally done it, and it was worth remembering.

It takes a win and a season like that to appreciate fully the game of professional football. It is not like Texas, Penn State, or Nebraska winning a national championship, where the celebration is basically confined to one particular state. In a win like ours, the entire country joined in our celebration. The upcoming Super Bowl would be viewed throughout the world.

That evening we gathered at the Golden Arm Restaurant to celebrate and savor the victory. Everybody loved everybody. Petty grievances and small differences were forgotten. This 15–1 team was being hailed by many as the greatest team ever assembled. Our defense seemed invincible. Cleveland was the fourth team that had failed to score a point against us.

Since I had returned to the team from Atlanta I hadn't gotten to know many of the younger players and their wives. Most of them didn't frequent my haunts. My favorites were Rick Volk and his wife Charlene. Rick was a twenty-three-year-old peachy-faced safety, in just his second year of pro ball. This fresh-faced young man looked more like the kid next door than a pro football player. Charlene, who was pretty, sweet, and charming, seemed like his younger sister.

Rick had come with the Colts at just the right time. He had broken into the starting lineup in his rookie season, and after two years as a starter he was unblemished. He had played on a team that had lost only two games in as many years. His career was all in front of him.

I was from the old school, and the Volks were unfamiliar with it. I was ten years older, and with thirty-two winters behind me I suppose I did look the part of the grizzled old veteran. They would stare at me in disbelief. My attitude and my life-style shocked them. They viewed me more or less as a dinosaur, or some other fossil from another age. I suppose that in a sense I was. The old school of players was becoming obsolete. Football was a young man's game.

Shula gave us a couple of days off, then we started preparing for the Jets on Wednesday. After two days of watching the Jets' defense on film I came to one conclusion. Super Bowl III should be a rout. We should be able to score fifty points against these people. I did not see one player in their defensive backfield who could make our team. As a matter of fact two of them, John Samples and Billy Baird, had already been cut by the Colts. The other two, Randy Beverly and Jim Hudson, had been released by other teams. All four defensive backs had come to Weeb Ewbank, our ex-coach and now the Jets' mentor, as free agents.

Six of the Jet players had already been released by the Colts. The linebackers were active, but too small to be taken seriously. The front four were small and unable to rush the passer. All in all, I thought that they were the poorest defensive unit I had seen in ten years of pro ball.

Happily I reported this to our defensive captain, Bobby Boyd. "Bobby, we can do anything we want to them," I said. "I honestly believe we can score fifty points against the Jets."

Bobby had a serious look on his face when he answered, "You may have to. The Jets have a damn good offense and Namath can throw the football with the best of them." It was unusual for Bobby to be so concerned. Usually he knew what he was talking about.

SANTA BARBARA, CALIFORNIA, January 2 (AP):

Jimmy (the "Greek") Snyder was admitted into the University of California at Santa Barbara Hospital today. Before he checked in, however, he listed the Baltimore Colts as an 18-point favorite to defeat the New York Jets in the Super Bowl.

New York, January 2 (NEA):

The New York Jets will beat the Colts in the Super Bowl. Some reasons are: The transiting Jupiter is sextile and the natal Mars and Pluto are trine in the midheaven and . . . well, there are eight other favorable points. Greek? No, astrology, pure and celestial. Snuff-sniffing, bearded professional astrologer Jonathan Booth drew up horoscopes for the Colts and the Jets to determine the winner of their game on January 12. Booth finds, in capsule form, that the Pisces Jets will have a great desire to win, while the Aquarius Colts will be plagued by over confidence. Booth, who has never seen a football game in his life, did not predict a final score.

The hype for what was now officially termed Super Bowl III was off and running. Watching the league sell this game was more enjoyable than the game itself. Late in the afternoon of January 3, the New York Jets were assembling in the VIP Lounge at Kennedy International Airport in Long Island. They would be flying to Fort Lauderdale at six o'clock to start training for Super Bowl III. The topic of conversation was Joe Namath. The Jet quarterback had surprised even his own teammates when he had committed the cardinal sin in sports just a few days earlier: evaluating an opponent in less than flattering terms for public consumption. He said Earl Morrall was not as good as many of the quarterbacks in the American Football League. He rated Daryle Lamonica, John Hadl, Bob Griese, and Babe Parelli, his own replacement, as clearly superior to Earl.

If there is a virtue that American sports fans usually demand from their prototyped athletes, it is humility. But Joe Namath was about as prototypical a football player as Muhammad Ali was a heavyweight boxing champion. Namath rose above the long-standing belief that public modesty was the appropriate repayment for the opportunity to succeed in sports. Why, Namath asked, can't an athlete admit publicly to drinking alcohol, smoking tobacco, making love to a beautiful woman, if, indeed, he does?

In Baltimore, Morrall was asked about Namath's evaluation of him by a reporter. "Joe's getting his newspaper space," Morrall said, "and that's what he's after, isn't it? He seems to thrive on being in the limelight. Any player on any team has opinions on other players, but players keep these opinions to themselves. At least that's the way it's been traditionally. Maybe Namath represents the new breed of athlete, the kind of athlete the coming generation wants. I hope not." The first volley had been fired and the war of words had officially commenced.

FORT LAUDERDALE, January 3:

> The New York Jets arrived here today to begin training for the Super Bowl. They will be using the same facilities the Green Bay Packers used last year, the Gault Ocean Mile Hotel for lodging and Fort Lauderdale Stadium for practice.

From news dispatches of January 3:

> The first two visitors the Jets had today at the Gault Ocean Mile Hotel were members of the Federal Bureau of Investigation. The FBI agents said they were making a routine investigation of Joe Namath's room. The room, number 534, was described by the hotel as the Governor's Suite. A year ago it was occupied by Vince Lombardi, coach of the Packers.
>
> Weeb Ewbank was sharing a room with his wife.

FORT LAUDERDALE, January 5:

A crowd of 250 people was on hand today to greet the Baltimore Colts who arrived by charter jet to begin training for the Super Bowl. The Colts will be quartered at the Statler Hilton Hotel and use the facilities of St. Andrew's Boys School in Boca Raton for practice sessions.

Don Shula, who had once played for Weeb Ewbank and later succeeded him, spoke briefly with the press. He was interrupted by a man who said, "Don, I've got a limousine waiting to take you to the hotel."

"No, thanks," said Shula, "I always ride with my players." Both Shula and Ewbank, so different but with so much in common, were handling their respective roles with courtesy and diplomacy.

Lou Michaels, Colt defensive end and placekicker, had agreed not to talk to his brother Walt, defensive coach of the Jets, until after the game. Baltimore defensive captain Lenny Lyles telephoned his old friend John Samples, defensive captain of the Jets, to inform him good-naturedly that "The Champions of the National Football League" had arrived. Mark Smolinski, captain of the Jets' special teams, was in the same church as Shula for mass, but sneaked out without having to speak to Shula. Shula had released Mark from the Colts in 1963.

I had run into Bill Mathis on Sunday and jokingly offered to bet him $500 and give him seventeen points. Billy refused the bet, saying he didn't gamble but if he did, he could get nineteen points in New York!

The only one who was popping off in public was Joe Namath. Like Fred "the Hammer" Williamson in Super Bowl I, Joe was doing all the talking. The first white anti-hero was on the horizon.

Dorothy and John Unitas paid a social visit to Lucy and Weeb Ewbank at the Gault Ocean Mile. They chatted for about an hour, but there was no talk of football. As John was leaving he ran into Namath. They shook hands and talked for a moment. Joe asked John how his arm was and John asked Joe about his knees. Neither of them received an answer!

Monday, January 6, was picture day for both teams. Football

players, many sports writers agree, are the most cooperative of all athletes in press relations. The Jets shattered that myth completely. Four of their best players—Namath, Hudson, Snell, and Boozer—were no-shows. At noon that day at the Statler Hilton, Shula was holding a press conference. When informed of Joe's no-show, he was astonished. "Namath what?" Shoes exploded. "He didn't show up for photo day? What the hell is Weeb doing?" Shula was shocked by Namath's disobedience. Players at that time simply did what they were told. When the questioning started, Shula regained his composure, "Yes, Namath has a quick release. Yes, his downfield vision is good. Yes, he has fast feet," he said. But, Shula concluded, "Namath hasn't been throwing against the defenses Earl has been throwing against."

When the questions shifted to Namath's criticism of Morrall, Shula was quick to defend Earl. After all, Morrall had had a great season. Playing with John Unitas ever-present in the background was difficult at best. John Unitas was the greatest quarterback who ever lived, and he had been the Colt leader for twelve years. "I don't know how Namath can rap Earl," Shula answered. "After all, Earl is No. 1 in the NFL. He's thrown all those touchdown passes. He's the Player of the Year. He's had a great season for us and we're proud of him. Anyone who doesn't give him the credit he deserves is wrong." Shula's voice rose and his neck thickened, "But I guess *Namath* can say what the hell he wants."

On Sunday night, Lou Michaels, our placekicker, and Dan Sullivan, a guard, had dinner in Jimmy Fazio's restaurant. After dinner they went to the bar. Lou spotted Namath and Jim Hudson. Lou left Sullivan and walked up to Namath. "You're doing a lot of talking, boy," Michaels said.

"There's a lot to talk about," said Joe. "We're going to kick the hell out of your team."

"Haven't you ever heard of the word modesty?" Michaels asked.

Namath didn't answer. He and Hudson went to their tables and ordered dinner. Before the food came Lou and Dan pulled up chairs and sat down with them. "You still here?" Namath asked Michaels.

"Damn right I'm still here," Lou said. "I want to hear everything you've got to say."

"I'm going to pick you apart," Namath replied.

"You're going to find it hard throwing out of a well," Lou said.

"My blockers will give me time," said Joe.

"I never heard John Unitas or Bobby Layne talk like that," remarked Lou.

"I believe that," said Joe.

"Even if we do get in trouble, we'll send in Unitas, the master," spoke Lou.

"I hope you do because that'll mean the game is too far gone," said Joe. Namath excused himself and walked over to a nearby table to speak to a friend. Hudson, meanwhile, attempted to calm Lou. "Don't pay any attention to what Joe says," said Hudson. "You've got to understand him."

Lou, of course, didn't. Michaels grumbled something about cocky kids and ordered another drink. Namath returned before the drink arrived. "Suppose we kick hell out of you," said Lou. "Just suppose we do that? Then what will you do?"

"I'll tell you what I'll do," said Namath, "I'll sit down right in the middle of the field and cry."

There were contradictory reports of what happened after that. One story had Michaels inviting Joe outside. Joe had accepted and was on his way out the door when Hudson and Sullivan restrained Michaels. Another version was that Lou had offered to bet Joe five hundred dollars on the outcome of the game. Joe allegedly had produced five crisp hundred-dollar bills while Lou fumbled around in his pockets for tens and twenties before finally going to his shoe for the balance!

Either way, when the check came Joe paid for it with hundred-dollar bills and told the waitress to keep the change. This impressed Lou, who turned to Sullivan and said, "I knew there was something I liked about that boy. He's really not a bad guy." The two Jet players then drove Michaels and Sullivan to the Statler Hilton and dropped them off.

By the next day stories of the Namath-Michaels confrontation were on the wires and appearing in newspapers across the country. Whichever account you want to believe, it was clearly a meeting of both sides of the generation gap. If Lou's intentions were to scold, intimidate, or embarrass Joe, it had worked in favor of the quarterback with the white shoes. He seemed more confident than ever.

On Wednesday evening at the Miami Spring Villa, Joe was to receive the Miami Touchdown Club's Outstanding Player of the Year Award. Namath accepted the award, then unprecedentedly capped a week of psychological warfare by declaring, "We are going to win on Sunday. I guarantee you." This sounded like a small, frightened boy whistling his way through a cemetery. I figured Joe was scared to death.

I don't know whose idea it was for Joe to put himself in the hot seat. It was something that a boy from Beaver Falls, Pa., would not think to do, something a former Alabama quarterback under Bear Bryant would not dare to do, and something that Weeb Ewbank wouldn't approve of him doing.

My own hunch is that the architect and mastermind of this plot was Sonny Werblin. It reeked of show business. While Sonny no longer owned the Jets, no one will ever get me to believe that the character Broadway Joe wasn't conceived and developed by someone with a long, strong show business background. From a $400,000 contract to white shoes, fur coats, Fu Manchu mustache, llama rugs, night club broads, and Johnnie Walker Red Scotch, Namath's image had Werblin written all over it. After all, they had nothing to lose. Nobody in his right mind gave the Jets a chance of winning. It would be interesting to see if a psych job would work. The only hitch in the plan was that this was not opening night, this was a football game, a world championship game.

News release, Miami:

> Will Unitas be used in the game? "John has too much dignity to be used just to run out the clock," Shula answered.

News release, Miami:

New York Giant quarterback Fran Tarkenton: "The way to beat Baltimore is to utilize backs as receivers." Matt Snell, Jets running back: "How would he know; he lost to them 26–8."

From news dispatches:

Billy Ray Smith, defensive tackle of the Colts, when asked for an opinion on Namath, said: "The man can throw the football, but he hasn't seen defenses like ours in his league. Our defenses are as complicated as some teams' offenses. I think reading our defenses will be a new experience for the man."

It was the first Super Bowl for both teams. It was the longest week I had ever experienced. The game had long since been a sellout, so the hype wasn't necessary. There was no place to get away from it, to be by myself. The only time we were alone as a team was at practice. We couldn't sit down for a meal without having to sign a couple of dozen autographs. I now understood what Unitas had gone through all those years. Radio and TV interviews seemed endless. I even found myself being interviewed by a Japanese reporter.

Our wives had come down on Wednesday, but there were no diversions from this game. We stayed in our rooms most of the time to avoid the hassle of autographs, pictures, and those endless interviews. The phones in the room never stopped ringing. It was well-wishing friends, most of them needing tickets to the game. Old friends, new friends, and people you scarcely knew—all wanted tickets. Thirty-four tickets were stolen from my suitcase in my room. Close friends and relatives had to be taken care of, so it was back to scrounging around looking for more tickets to replace the stolen ones.

By Friday we were half out of our minds. I didn't know how the Jets were handling all this pressure, but it was getting to us. We were tired of all this hoopla, and past being ready to play the game.

Earl and John amazed me. That was where the real heat was, and both of them were holding up like champions. Their relationship all year had been nothing but professional. Anybody would naturally suspect some form of resentment to develop, but if so it certainly didn't show. They helped each other at all times. It had to be particularly tough on John, who for the first time since 1957 was not the center of attention. The new kid, Namath, had stolen the spotlight and put it directly on himself.

When we boarded the buses on Sunday to go to the Orange Bowl, tempers were on edge. No one kidded or joked. An unearthly silence fell over the bus as all members of the team withdrew into themselves. We were getting off the bus in front of the Orange Bowl when Jimmy Orr remarked to me that he was uncommonly tired. Now that he mentioned it, so was I. I felt like I had just finished a game, yet I hadn't yet dressed for one. It didn't concern me that I felt tired; I didn't figure in the game one way or the other. But Jimmy was never tired. I had never known him to leave a game for a rest of even one play. Jimmy would be prominent in the game. He was a big-play player. In his eleven years, he had averaged six touchdowns a year and over twenty yards a catch. In addition to that, Jimmy was a lucky player, often the benefactor of missed coverages and missed tackles. We needed James Edward Orr.

40

The crowd started arriving around noon for the 3:05 P.M. kickoff. That morning before we had gotten there the Miami Beach Police Department's bomb squad had pulled up in its bomb disposal truck, after a telephone caller had said he had planted a bomb in the stadium. A search ensued, and nothing was found that resembled a bomb. Arriving at the game were 75,377 mere mortals and President-elect Richard Nixon, Vice-President–elect Spiro Agnew, Senator Edward Kennedy of Massachusetts and his father Joseph P. Kennedy, and astronauts Frank Borman, Bill Anders, and Jim Lovell. Bob Hope and Jackie Gleason were sitting on opposite sides of the field.

During warm-ups I sneaked a quick look at Joe Namath. It was the first time I had ever seen him throw a football. He had a nice shoulder motion. His footwork was excellent and his release and feet were quick. He could, in fact, throw the football. I was impressed enough to point it out to Orr. Apparently Jimmy had never seen him throw, either, and he was equally impressed.

All at once there was Weeb Ewbank walking around in front of me, looking scattered and confused just as I had always remembered him on game days. Weeb was on our side of the fifty-yard-line, retrieving errant footballs which had wandered onto our section of the field. I spoke to Weeb and he muttered something about people having no regard for money or footballs any more. Weeb was beautiful.

During warm-ups everyone was anxious and tense, but that was routine before any game. I was returned to the scrimmage line and threw the ball to Mike Curtis, who would then hand the ball to our center. Mike was staring straight at me, or I thought that he was, when I released the ball. He must have been in a daze, because he never saw the ball until it grazed his face mask. He jumped back, startled, and then went into a rage. He started screaming at me and snarling. I thought he was going to attack me in front of 75,000 people. He was like a bomb set to explode. I felt sorry for the Jets. Mike was ready to play!

Just before the opening kickoff Orr shuffled up to me and said, "Señor, don't let Earl wake up today. Just let him sleep for three more hours." I knew what he meant.

We lost the toss and the Jets received the opening kickoff. Namath quickly revealed the Jets' game plan as he went to work on our defensive right side. Matt Snell gained three and then nine yards off the left side of the line. Rick Volk met Snell head on and had to be helped from the field. The impact of tackling Snell had knocked him unconscious. The Jets' drive stalled and their punt was returned to the Baltimore twenty-seven.

Morrall marched the Colts to four consecutive first downs. It was just as I had seen in the films. The Jet defense posed no problem. The drive ended at the New York nineteen and Lou Michaels missed a twenty-seven-yard field goal. No matter, there would be others to come. We were in total control of the game; Morrall was playing just as he had all season. He was moving the team and avoiding mistakes. He had not awakened.

Namath managed only one first down on the second series and the Jets punted to Tim Brown, who returned it twenty-one yards to near midfield. Morrall failed to move the ball and a fifty-one-yard punt by David Lee was downed on the Jets' four-yard line. On third down, Namath passed to George Sauer, who fumbled, and we recovered on the Jets' twelve-yard line. Jerry Hill gained one as the first quarter ended. It had been a quick first quarter.

On the second play of the second quarter, Morrall's pass to Tom Mitchell was tipped and the ball careened off Tom's shoulder straight up in the air. Randy Beverly intercepted in the New York end zone for a touchback. Beverly was beaten so badly on the play that he was in a position to intercept.

This kind of thing was starting to hurt. As poor as the Jets were, we were going to have to get something on the board soon, or they might make it a game. The first two scoring opportunities had gone down the drain, and the momentum was starting to shift. Momentum is nothing more than a positive frame of mind, and the Jets' morale seemed to be picking up.

Once again Namath went to work on our right side. Snell ran left for one, seven, six, and twelve yards. Joe then connected twice with Sauer for fourteen and eleven yards. The Jets' game plan was now obvious; they were going to attack our defensive right side. They had decided to go after our veterans, Ordell Braase, Don Shinnick, and Lenny Lyles. All three of these men had played under Weeb at Baltimore. All three men were good football players, even though none was an especially good athlete. Apparently Weeb never believed he could beat our defense; he had decided instead to beat one-half of it, our right side.

After almost six minutes of a beautifully executed drive, Snell ran left for a two-yard touchdown. Unbelievable as it may seem, the Jets were ahead, 7–0. This was not what I had expected at all. Namath had forecast that he would pick us apart. I thought he meant by passing the football. Instead he was mixing it up, and doing a beautiful job of it. The undisciplined one was calling a disciplined, patient game. I was less confident now, but not worried.

Morrall moved us to the Jets' thirty-eight-yard line and on fourth down Michaels missed his second field goal. After a thirty-five-yard pass to Sauer, Namath moved his club to our thirty-four yard line where Jim Turner missed his first try at a field goal.

On the second play of our possession, Tom Matte ran right for fifty-eight yards before being caught by five Jet players. On second down at New York's fifteen-yard line, Morrall's pass to Richardson was intercepted by John Samples on the two-yard line. Sweet Jesus, what was going on here? We had moved the ball into scoring position four times, yet the scoreboard read New York 7, Baltimore 0.

The Jets took over on their two-yard line and when three running plays failed they were forced to punt out of their own end zone. With less than a minute remaining in the first half, it was a perfect time to go for a blocked punt. We were prepared for the attempted punt block, having practiced and rehearsed it for two weeks. I was the man designated to block the punt.

Now, anything that happens just before the end of a half is magnified in value. Going in at halftime on a high note is particularly important in a game like this. Any time a big play is made by the special teams, it is an added bonus. A blocked punt in this situation could turn the game around. There was only one problem: I had never in my life actually blocked a punt. In twenty years of organized football I had never experienced the feeling of blocking a kick. Nobody, however, knew it but me. Raymond Berry would have been ashamed of my lack of preparation.

I was lined up on the outside of the line of scrimmage. I timed it perfectly. The instant the ball was snapped I sprinted, untouched, toward the Jets' punter. I was there in plenty of time to block the kick. In fact, I was there too soon. For one brief moment I thought that I might be able to tackle the kicker before he got the punt away. I wasn't sure what the rule was in regard to that, but that brief, fleeting moment of hesitation and doubt caused me to screw it up. I froze for just a tick, then I decided not to gamble and threw up my arms in front of the kicker. The punt went *under* my outstretched arms, and as the flag went down I ran into the kicker. After ten years of professional football, I had made a rookie mistake. My chance had come, but I was not equal to it.

As it turned out, the Jets were guilty of illegal procedure, so it nullified my penalty. They punted again and we took the ball on a fair catch at the Jets' forty-two-yard line. We had the ball again with good field position and forty-three seconds left in the first half.

From the sidelines Shula called a "flea flicker." Morrall handed off to Matte who headed right, stopped, and threw back to Morrall. Orr had conned Beverly, the defender, to sleep and was standing all alone on the goal line, thirty-five yards behind the nearest defender, waving his right arm in the air. Everyone in the stadium saw Orr—everyone except Morrall, who threw the ball down the middle of the field towards Hill. Jim Hudson, the Jets' safety, intercepted the ball and brought it out to the twenty-yard line, where he slipped and fell as the first half ended.

Morrall's failure to spot Orr wide open on the goal line was devastating. Everything that could have gone wrong for us had done so. Failing to score on six occasions had depleted us of any semblance of confidence, which is the single most important element a pro player relies on. We started doubting ourselves, looking forward to our next mistake.

Earl Morrall was crushed. He could not explain to himself how he had failed to see Orr, the primary receiver, standing on the goal line pleading for the ball. Whether the disparaging remarks previously levied at Morrall by Namath came into the picture, I have no way of knowing, but some recollection of his past with four different teams must have flashed through his mind. Jimmy Orr's and my own worst fear had been realized: Earl Morrall had awakened.

In the one minute before halftime we had twice missed almost certain scores. Six times we'd had scoring opportunities, and we had missed cashing in on them. We were frustrated, confused, dejected, and disillusioned. The football gods were definitely against us.

We tried regrouping in the locker room, but it was frustrating. There were very few adjustments to make. The right side of our defense was giving up some yardage, but after all was said and done they had allowed only seven points. Our offense had moved the ball up and down the field almost at will. There was no one person to blame. It was a scattered group of mistakes, first by one person, then by another. The score could easily have been 34–7 in our favor, yet we were trailing by 7–0.

Just before we returned for the second half, Shula addressed the team. "We're making stupid mistakes; we're stopping ourselves. You've got them believing they are a better team than we are. Let's go out there in the second half and take charge of the game the way we know we can." We left the locker room with fire in our eyes. Letting the Jets stay in the game was ridiculous.

Namath had done none of the things he had bragged of doing. He had executed a well-conceived game plan made by Weeb and his staff. Still, he had handled himself well, and remained poised and patient throughout the first thirty minutes.

We were ready to play again and felt we had put all our mistakes behind us, when on the first play of the second half, Matte fumbled the football. This was the most untimely error of them all. The Jets' offense was now supercharged. It was a horrible time for them to start thinking they could win.

The Jets took over the ball on our thirty-three-yard line, and Namath went right back to work on our right side. They managed two first downs before having to settle for Turner's thirty-two-yard field goal. The score was now 10–0, New York.

At halftime Shula had told John that if Earl didn't move the team in the first possession of the second half, he was going to replace him. Since the first series was a fumble on the first play, Shula gave Earl another chance. Three plays netted us minus two yards, and John was warming up his tired, hurt arm.

Now, with 8:04 left in the third period and with his team leading by ten points, Namath went to work and took charge of the game. After viewing the Colt defense he called most of his plays at the line of scrimmage. When the drive finally stalled after nearly five minutes had run off the clock, Turner kicked a thirty-yard field goal. The score was now 13–0.

After the kickoff hit the goal post, Unitas entered the game for the first time. He had no strength in his arm, and was off-target and poorly timed-up with his receivers. After three plays we punted back to the Jets.

Snell ran left for three. Namath threw left to Sauer for eleven, and again to him for thirty-nine yards to our ten-yard line and a first down. The left side of our defense was getting the day off. Logan, Boyd, Curtis, and Bubba Smith were frustrated from lack of action. The Colts had the football for only seven plays in the third quarter. The Jets, on the other hand, had controlled the football for almost thirteen minutes. All the while Namath's confidence was growing. He was calling a near-perfect second half. The third quarter ended with the ball on our six-yard line.

The fourth quarter started with Joe calling three straight running plays to his left that gained four of the six yards necessary. They settled for a nine-yard field goal, Turner's third of the game, and a 16–0 lead.

With 13:10 remaining in the game, Unitas was our only hope. He had conquered similar odds in the past. With a battered arm and a fighting heart, John had two things going for him: fierce determination, and a will to win. His very presence in the lineup lifted the team. Hanging heads were now raised, and the hands that had rested on hips were now clapping encouragement to their leader. With John on the field the complexion of the game completely changed. He rekindled the fire that had slowly been dying with each fresh mistake and that had disappeared completely in the disastrous third quarter.

Mixing the run with his short passes, John managed three first downs and moved the Colts to the Jets' twenty-five-yard line. On the second down, John went to Orr in the end zone, but his arm was not as strong as his wishes. The weakly thrown ball was intercepted by Beverly, his second interception of the day in the New York end zone. The entire drive had used up only two minutes and four seconds off the clock.

Now it was Joe's turn. His mission was different. With a sixteen-point lead, he needed only to run time off the clock and improve his position on the field. Joe stayed patiently on the ground. On third-and-six, he sent Boozer off the left side for a gain of seven and a first down. Snell gained another ten yards against our weak right side. A personal foul moved the ball into our territory. Snell gained another seven yards and Boozer picked up two more. Our defense held on third down and the Jets missed a field-goal try from forty-two yards. Keeping the ball on the ground, Namath had used up four and one-half minutes off the clock.

With 6:34 on the clock, Unitas missed his first three passes but converted with Orr for the first down on the fourth. On third down, John hit John Mackey for the first down and a personal foul against the Jets moved the ball to the New York thirty-seven-yard line. Reaching down inside himself somewhere, John hit Richardson and Orr to move the ball inside the New York two. Jerry Hill took it over for the score and we were finally on the board; New York 16, Baltimore 7.

Unitas had moved the Colts eighty yards in just three minutes. It had not been a pretty drive; in fact, it was painful to watch. It lacked the artistry and precision of Unitas's drives of the past. But we had finally scored; the ice had been broken.

With 3:14 showing on the clock, Lou Michaels made a perfect onside kick and Tom Mitchell recovered for us on the New York forty-four. Unitas, the master of time and tenacity, was back on the field. He completed two passes to Richardson and a third one to Orr. The ball was now resting on the Jets' nineteen-yard line, with over two and one half minutes still left to play.

The Orange Bowl was buzzing. Was it possible for a proud old man like Unitas to reach down in that bag of tricks and come up with some miracles to bail this one out?

The Jets' bench must have thought so. The once-confident Namath was pacing. He had respect for this wily old veteran. Joe was up and down the sidelines yelling and pleading for the defense to stop Unitas. Two minutes and thirty-seven seconds could be a lifetime when Unitas was running the show.

It was second and five on the New York nineteen when reality made its ugly appearance. The tricks and miracles were all used up. Unitas threw three incompletions and walked slowly off the field to the bench. He hadn't come close on any of the throws. His ailing arm had overruled his head and his heart.

If somehow we could have mustered a score then, I think we would have won that game. But all the fight went out of us when John couldn't get those five yards on three plays. We all knew it was over for us.

There was still 2:21 showing on the clock when Joe Namath took the snap from center. There was still time for us to win it, but Joe had other ideas. After having played a left-handed game since the first series of downs, Joe suddenly went right. Snell ran off the right side for gains of one, six, four, and two. They were small but important gains that were running down the clock and producing first downs. Only fifteen seconds were left in the game when they punted to our thirty-four.

On the next to last play of the game, John threw an incompletion. He then completed a fifteen-yarder to Richardson as the clock ticked down. Five . . . four . . .three . . . two . . . one, and the gun sounded the end of Super Bowl III and my football career.

As we made our way to the dressing room the crowd flooded onto the field. On the way in, I glanced at the scoreboard to verify the results. There had been no mistake. It read New York 16, Baltimore 7.

There are hurts and pains that are too devastating to be remembered vividly. I cannot describe the humiliation I felt. We had just disgraced ourselves, the National Football League, and every player who had ever played or coached in the game. There was no way to hold our heads up.

Our locker room was like a morgue. There was nothing we could say to each other, because no one understood what had happened. It was impossible, yet it was true. We had lost to the Jets—the dogass Jets. Namath had guaranteed the victory, and he had made good his promise. The once beautiful Orange Bowl had turned into the little shop of horrors!

I should have known then that I would never play another football game.

After the game I was standing between Mike Curtis and Unitas in the bathroom, shaving. The place was as quiet as a tomb. Players were staring down at the floor, running their hands through their hair. In a low voice I was discussing one of the Jet coverages with John. Suddenly and savagely, I was interrupted by a ranting, raving Mike Curtis. "Shut up, you son of a bitch, shut up! You don't know what you're talking about."

I felt as though I had been completely recycled. I had come into this league with a linebacker screaming at me, and I was leaving it the same way. Through the mirror I saw Mike's bitter, twisted face, fangs showing, screaming at me. Now here I was, standing with only a jockstrap on my body and a safety razor in my hand, looking at this beast of a person who was screaming insults at me. I was easily overmatched by Mike, but I was still a man and I still had my pride, so I had to react in some fashion.

I completely ignored him. I simply refused to acknowledge that this was happening to me. I shut up and went right on shaving as if nothing had happened. We were in such shock I don't think John even realized that this had taken place. At a time like this, you don't listen, anyway. You only pretend to hear. You're too wrapped up in your own thoughts and feelings to hear other people. John's feelings were of hurt, Mike's were of anger, and mine were of utter bewilderment.

John finished shaving and left. I finished shaving and left. Mike probably lathered up and shaved again, hoping to cut himself.

When we got back to the hotel, I found a note Libby had left in the room: "When you sober up, come on home. I'm sorry. Love Libby." She had taken the first flight out for Atlanta. She knew how I would react.

As I was leaving the room Charlene, Rick Volk's wife, came running down the hall screaming for help. Rick, who had been knocked unconscious in the game, was on the bathroom floor vomiting. His body was quivering in convulsions and he was swallowing his tongue. Rick was close to dying.

Fortunately, Dr. Freeman, the team physician, was checking on another injured player down the hall. He used a ballpoint pen to free Rick's tongue, and summoned an ambulance to take him to the hospital. At the hospital Volk regained consciousness and was placed in intensive care. His first conscious words were, "Who won?"

Just two weeks earlier Charlene and Rick had not a worry in the world. Now they had experienced not one but two nightmares in the same day.

I went down to the hotel bar and found John. I don't remember much after that. We didn't go to the team party; I do know that.

Some time that evening I wandered by the Palm Bay Club. I remember meeting Bear Bryant for the first time that evening. I also remember shaking hands with Billy Mathis. He and Joe Namath had just returned from Sonny Werblin's house. There wasn't much to say.

The next few days were pretty much a blur. I finally returned to Atlanta, quite daunted.

There was a lot of time to think during the spring of 1969, and a great deal to think about. Now that I was a free agent, I could negotiate freely with any of the twenty-six teams in the NFL. None of them called, not even the Colts.

I was a football person first and foremost. A football person lives from one game to the next. I wasn't aware of it then, but that Super Bowl loss would stay with me the rest of my life.

What had happened to us in that game with the Jets? Had Joe Namath been successful in intimidating Michaels and Morrall? Had he done to us what Cassius Clay had done to Sonny Liston? If so, this was indeed a very strong-willed and powerful person, who would dominate the game for years to come.

That didn't happen to be the case. Joe Namath quarterbacked the Jets for eight more seasons without winning another championship. In the eleven years he quarterbacked the Jets, he led them to only three winning seasons.

The real credit for the Jets' winning of the Super Bowl belonged to Weeb Ewbank. In the 1950s this nervous, unassuming little man had taken a losing Colt team and transformed them into world champions in just five years. Then he had turned right around and in only six seasons did the same thing for the New York Jets. No other coach has produced world championships for two different teams or two different leagues. This honest, gentle, sincere man, who cried real tears, now had to be recognized as one of the game's greatest coaches.

It was impossible to explain how we could have lost to a team we should have beaten by thirty points or more. If we had played the Jets ten times, we would have won nine of them.

However, I knew that it wouldn't do to say that, as it reeked of sour grapes. I had to come up with an explanation I could live with. I kept trying, but it wasn't until I began writing this book that I finally solved the riddle.

I was captain of the special teams. I had nothing to do with the offense or the defense that day. I needed to be as objective as possible. Our kickoff team had allowed only 23 yards in returns. In addition to that, we had recovered an onside kick. We had run up kickoff return yardage of 105 yards. We had averaged 44.3 yards per punt, while the Jets had averaged 38.8. We had 34 yards in punt-return yardage, and had allowed the Jets no yardage whatsoever.

I had personally made the tackle on the opening kickoff and shared in another. So there it was: there was the answer I was looking for. We had killed the Jets on special teams. I had graded myself out for this day with a perfect 100 percent. I had played a great game, but my teammates had let me down: all of them! I could live with that.

After only twenty years, Super Bowl III was finally over.

41

I t seemed that the only thing you could rely on was change. George Preston Marshall, longtime owner of the Redskins, had died. Vince Lombardi had come out of his one-year retirement and had taken the job as head coach of the Redskins. Chuck Noll replaced Bill Austin in Pittsburgh. John Madden replaced Rauch at Oakland.

Bobby Boyd, Ordell Braase, and Dick Symanski announced their retirement from the Colts. This left only Unitas, Lyles, Shinnick, and myself as the remaining Colts from the 1958–59 championship team.

Over sixty million people had viewed the past Super Bowl game, and that meant money, lots of money, for the owners of the future. Commissioner Pete Rozelle was being heralded as the second coming of Christ. In my ten years I had seen the game of professional football change from a sport owned by sportsmen to a business run by businessmen. It was now entertainment, run by television. Pro football had become a very profitable, corporate sports business.

While Pete Rozelle had been trying his best to maintain unity among the twenty-six owners with his slogan of "think league," the element of greed was already setting in. I questioned Rozelle's judgment on approving owners. How could Rozelle expect men like Rankin Smith and John Mecome to compete with Carroll Rosenbloom and Al Davis?

The really smart guys like Modell and Rosenbloom were thinking ahead. In preparation for the up-and-coming merger that would take place in the 1970 season, three teams would have to move over to the AFL; that would give each league an uneven thirteen teams. On May 10, 1969, Pittsburgh, Cleveland, and Baltimore each accepted three million dollars for moving their franchises out of the National Conference and into the American Conference of the National Football League.

How they finally arrived at these three teams is anybody's guess. All I knew was that I hated the idea of joining the "other league." The Jets had just humiliated us, and now we were going to join them. What I resented most was the idea of having to put my name on the back of my jersey. I was confused and hurt. Joining the people who had just beaten us was not my way of waging war.

Throughout the month of June I deliberated my status. I had been offered several jobs and business opportunities both in Baltimore and Atlanta. They were silly little jobs, like selling building material or insurance. I could not imagine having to work a full twelve months each year.

I had also been offered jobs in radio and television. Now that didn't seem so bad. One of the radio jobs included doing color work on the Falcon football games. While it paid only $175 a week, they claimed it would be great exposure, whatever that meant.

If Pat Summerall and Frank Gifford could get along in that business, I was sure I could, too. Norm Van Brocklin was now coaching the Falcons, and he would be good for lots of laughs. I'd heard he was fun to drink with, and the trips would break the monotony of everyday life.

I hadn't been sleeping well, and the hives that I had been scratching were telling me something. Every time I was troubled I broke out in hives. The hives told me I needed a change. It had been that way for years. I thought it over for a week or so. I couldn't play football for the rest of my life, and I was tired of scratching my hives. I didn't want to coach, and the idea of leaving the game cold turkey was frightening. As soon as people realized how much I knew about the game from hearing me on the air I was sure to be offered the general manager's job with the Falcons.

I finally talked it over with Libby, and as usual she was obstinate. "The children and I want you to be happy," she said.

"Do whatever it takes and it will be fine with us." I hadn't been much of a father or husband, so being around home more often to straighten things out might be just the thing to do.

I called Rocky Thornton and Bobby Boyd and told them of my decision. I was going to give myself a press conference at the Golden Arm and announce my retirement. I knew the Colts wouldn't pay for it, but I still had a few dollars left from my loser's share of the Super Bowl. Bobby agreed to let me off for half-price. I told Rocky to notify a few of my writer friends, but that was all. The best way to spread news in Baltimore is to tell Rocky not to mention it to anyone.

I picked up the phone and called Shula. I finally reached him in Ocean City on vacation. "Shoes," I said, "I will be thirty-two years old tomorrow and I am coming to Baltimore to officially announce my retirement. I am quitting this game while I am still on the bottom."

"Thank God," said Shula, "You won't believe this, but I was just now trying to figure out how I could justify keeping you around another year. What time and where?"

"The Golden Arm, around noon," I said.

"I'll be there," he said. "And unlike you, I'll be on time and sober!"

I boarded a plane for Baltimore the next morning and arrived at the Golden Arm around eleven o'clock. In the spring of '68, John Unitas and Bobby Boyd opened this restaurant, which immediately, of course, became the Colts' hangout. This was the owners' first venture into the restaurant business, and all did not go smoothly at first.

Rocky Thornton was the bartender and sometime manager. Oddly enough, Rocky was the restaurant's biggest drawing card. While seats were available in the restaurant, the bar was always filled. A horrible bartender but a natural entertainer, Rocky was funnier and more inventive than most stand-up comedians.

Rocky had never been married. He lived with his mother, Dorcas, and his ninety-two-year-old grandmother, Elfie. He never got to know his father well; he had skipped town when Rocky was a child. When Rocky's father died he left Rocky a coffee cup, fifteen hundred dollars, and two pieces of advice: "Never live on Calvert Street, and never drink shaving lotion, because it will make you bring back things you never took."

Bobby Boyd had come with the Colts in 1960, and he had made the starting cornerback job in just his second year. Bobby was short, stocky, and slow; it would be safe to say that he was the slowest defensive back in the league for the nine years that he played. Despite his lack of size and speed, however, Bobby had been All-Pro five years in a row.

Bobby was smart. His cunning little mind was always alert for an advantage. He knew every team's check-offs and audibles. When I had played against him in Atlanta, he corrected me on a missed assignment. He said, "Whitey, you missed the check-off, you were supposed to have run a post pattern." When I returned to our huddle, I was informed of the same by our quarterback, Randy Johnson. How could I go about beating someone who already knew what I was going to do before I did it?

Rocky always said that the easiest person to steal from was a thief. This was not the case with Bobby Boyd. If there was an edge to be had, Bobby found it. He had been beating me at bridge, gin rummy, shuffleboard, and various other contests from his first year on. Bobby had my hole card.

He was the most competitive person I'd ever met. I didn't mind losing to Bobby, because it was so much fun watching him work. He was intense. He hated to lose. I have never yet met an athlete who didn't want to win, but when you find one who hates losing so badly that he won't accept it, you have Bobby Boyd. When all else failed, some say, he cheated. If confronted with this, Bobby would stare you straight in the eyes and say, "Are you calling me a liar?" To look into those chilly, silver-blue, oyster eyes was terrifying. I could see madness in those eyes. I was not alone in my observation. He had the eyes of a cold-blooded killer, who knew without question he was going to either have to kill or be killed. There was enough money bet to make it worth the try. So Bobby won all confrontations and close decisions.

When I arrived at the Golden Arm, sportswriters Cameron Snyder and Larry Harris were already at the bar charging drinks to my tab. "If we're going to cover something as insignificant as this, we've got to get loaded," said Cameron.

"I understand," I agreed. Harris and I went to a booth. Cameron stayed at the bar.

"I've already got my story," said Cameron. "This may be my last free drink until the next Super Bowl."

"Larry," I said, "I want this to be clear. I'm not retiring, I'm quitting. When you can't beat the dog-ass Jets, you don't deserve the dignity of retiring. From here on, let it be known that this is a quitting party."

"You've got it," said Larry as he took out a note pad and began to scribble. "What are your reasons?" he asked.

I had ten reasons, I told him, one for each season I played:

1. If Joe Namath doesn't play, neither will I.*
2. The Colts can join the American League, but I won't.
3. When Tom Matte goes to the Pro Bowl, it's time for a lot of people to quit.
4. Pete Rozelle frowns on unsavory characters, and I don't have a friend who is not one.
5. John Unitas has barred me from this restaurant after today.
6. I'm allergic to Astroturf.
7. I just heard that Charlie Eckman is going to do the color for the Colts this year, and I'd rather listen to the games on the radio than watch them from the bench.
8. Coach Bobby Boyd knows all my escape routes from hotels and training camp, since he invented them himself.
9. Every barbershop I've been in lately has gone back to cutting hair.

---

* **Namath had been** ordered by Commissioner Rozelle to divest himself of his involvement in a bar because several of his partners were gamblers. He had refused, saying that he would quit football first. Later he acquiesced.

10. My bar bills, lawyer fees, fines, gambling losses, and
    supplementing Rocky's income are greater than my
    salary, so I no longer find it economically feasible to
    play on. I hereby quit. Not retire, quit.

By this time friends of mine were drifting in. Steve Rosenbloom, Carroll's adopted son, whom Bert had nicknamed "Hymie
the Mink," came by. Dick Symanski, who had just retired and was
joining Upton Bell in the scouting department, was there. Gussie,
Bert, Fingers, Garrett-Garrett the Fishman, Shula, Upton and
Bobby, Crazy Willie, Phil Killen and many more. It was getting to
be about that time!

We settled into the back room of the restaurant. I was at the
head of the table, since I was paying the bill. I got their attention
and began.

"For all these years you have laughed at and ridiculed me in
every way possible. Today, I am quitting, not retiring from the
National Football League. My somewhat turbulent career did not
warrant the dignification of retirement. So I am quitting, effective now. For all these many years, you have had nothing good to
say about me, but today will be different. Everyone must take the
floor and say one good thing about me.

"We'll start with you, Shoes."

I gave Shula the floor. He stood up kind of sheepishly and said,
"You all know how I feel about the Hawk . . . ." Someone snickered,
and Shula said no more. The laughter grew when he sat down.
"You all know how I feel about the Hawk . . . ." Now, what in the
hell did he mean by that? And what was so funny? The laughter
continued.

Seizing the opportunity, Bert Bell, Jr., stood up and declared,
"I think the Colts should retire the Hawk's jersey. Ball clubs are
always retiring the stars' jerseys, but they never do anything for
a stiff." When no one seconded the motion Bert sat back down.

It was Bobby Boyd's turn to go next. "I'll say this about the
Hawk . . . he's different, but he came to play." I wasn't totally sure
of what he meant, but that wasn't too bad, not from Bobby.

Rocky stood up next and said, "I'll tell you what Bobby Layne told me one time. Bobby Layne said Whitey was a player." Rocky always knew the right thing to say.

Gussie stood up and said, "Hawk ain't a good gambler, but he's a good guy. Does anyone know who won the fifth race at Garden City?"

On and on it went, until everybody had their say. It was just the way this city handled everything: with humor.

Suddenly I realized that I cared about these people, deeply. A part of me would be gone forever. It would never be the same again.

I had never allowed myself to be serious around these people before, and I would not start now. I jumped to my feet and announced, "I can't go through with this, I'll miss you all too much. I'm unretiring right now. I'm back!"

At that Shula jumped up and threw his napkin down on the table and stalked out. I quickly retired again, and we went to the bar and the party began.

Through the afternoon and evening we went right on. For everyone who left, there was someone to replace him. Crazy Willie told the story about his aging Daddy, whom Willie had found in the bathroom the night before at 3:00 A.M. He had lathered the bathroom mirror and was shaving it. Phil Killen told us about the time John LaVeck had turned two wild monkeys loose in one of the nicer restaurants downtown. Bob Ferry talked about the time Mr. Diz, a racetrack tout, had organized and handicapped Italian mule and donkey races on the beaches of Anzio during the height of the World War II battle.

Joy Boy told the story about the time Frank, my shuffleboard partner, got broke around Christmas time and held up his branch bank. Everybody recognized Frank and pleaded with him not to do it. He was arrested coming out the front door.

Manuel told about the time a guy robbed the bank in Waverly in a cab. He was arrested at a stoplight five blocks away. He hadn't told the cabbie that he'd robbed the bank.

Finally, as the place was thinning out around midnight, Bobby Boyd walked up to me and said, "Whitey, you don't retire from this game but once. We ain't gambling tonight, we're drinking. We're drinking straight shots until somebody falls."

I only remember the first three shots.

42

asten your seat belts and observe the no-smoking sign when it appears. We should be landing in Atlanta in about fifteen minutes if all goes well. The temperature in Atlanta is ninety. For those of you who will be traveling on with us, we should be on the ground in about twenty minutes. For those of you who are changing planes, there will be an agent at the gate to assist you. For those of you who have just retired, I wish you good luck, you're sure as hell going to need it! It's going to be a hell of a lot harder than you think."

I had fallen asleep. The quitting party we'd had was too much for me. I must be getting old. But then again, I never slept well on the floor.

The drive through the city and the walk through the airport had taken something out of me, too. I was going to miss those people. It would be strange not to be playing ball in the fall. I'd been playing football every fall all my life.

The gradual changing of the temperature and the season in September meant the start of football for me. After all these years, January 1 meant nothing to me. My new year always started in September. I was glad I had been offered that job on the Falcon game. To retreat from the game completely would be difficult.

All right now, it's time to start over. The past is just that. You've been lucky to have put off growing up for ten years longer than most people. It's time now to join the real world. You've got to find something else that you can enjoy as much as football. If you throw yourself into whatever that is, with the same enthusiasm, you'll do just fine. You're special; just remember that. You can make up for those ten years in no time flat.

I looked out the window and saw Stone Mountain and the sprawling city beneath. It seemed to have grown since I had left it yesterday.

Excuse me, ma'am, but did I hear the captain say something about good luck, or retiring, or anything to that effect? No? Good, I was hoping it was my imagination.

I turned to the passenger beside me. "Do you live here or are you just visiting?" "It's a great town, isn't it?" "What do you do?" "Oh, really, I'm thinking about going into the radio business myself. WQXI asked me to do the color work on the Falcon broadcasts. They should do much better this year with the Dutchman coaching them.

"I used to play with the Falcons. No, I've never done any radio work before, but it shouldn't be any problem. I know the game inside out and I've played for some of the greatest coaches of all time. To be honest with you, I'm not making but $175 a week, but you know, what the hell, you've got to start somewhere. They told me the exposure would be great. What does that mean anyway? Oh, I see. Well, I'll tell you what I'm not going to do, I'm not going to lie to people. All players aren't great and some of the games stink. I'm going to tell it like it is. If a guy isn't doing his job, I'm going to let people know it. And I'll tell you another thing, there are some bad owners and coaches in this game, who have no business being in it. I don't mind telling who they are, either. What do you mean, be careful or I'll be out of a job? No wonder you hear all those announcers saying 'great this' and 'great that'. That's bullshit and you know it. I'm going to broadcast to the people. The fans are the ones you owe your allegiance to. Without them there is no game. What's that? Yes, I may be naive, but that's the way it's going to be with me. To hell with the sponsors and management. Good luck to you too, asshole."

I put my radio headset on while we circled for landing. I'd listened to him as long as I was going to. A civilian, what in the hell did he know about football, or broadcasting? This know-it-all beside me didn't even know who I was. Here he was with that smug look on his face, telling me what I should or should not say on the air. I could tell by his wrists and neck that he had never played the game.

This ego stuff was getting the best of me. What had *he* ever done to warrant an ego? These damn rich kids who were buying up football teams were starting to think they were somebody, too. Come to think of it, even the stewardess had a cocky manner about her, until I called her down. I suppose the pilot thinks he's pretty special himself. He probably thinks he's good because he's never cracked up an airplane. The truth of the matter was that none of them had ever performed before sixty million people like I had. I was entitled to my ego. I had earned it. I was something special. I wonder how the pilot would react if he knew that seventy-five thousand people were waiting to watch him land?

We were now about thirty feet off the runway, just before *touch-down*. What right did they have to use that term? O.K., buddy, you'd better be good, I'm watching you closely. You think you're so special. Show me.

It was a perfect landing. As we taxied to our gate, I snickered to myself. I guess the pilot feels pretty good about himself now. Hell, anybody can fly an airplane.

As I approached the front of the plane, I spotted the pilot. He was a tall, nice-looking man with a confident smile. As I approached him I said, "Nice landing."

He smiled back and replied, "I hope you enjoyed it."

He looked a little confused when I winked at him and said, "But I was the only one watching." I stepped off the airplane for the first time as a civilian. A fool was being unleashed on the city of Atlanta.